Thomas Hardy, Poet

Thomas Hardy, Poet
New Perspectives

Edited by ADRIAN GRAFE *and* LAURENCE ESTANOVE

McFarland & Company, Inc., Publishers
Jefferson, North Carolina

ALSO OF INTEREST
Lines of Resistance: Essays on British Poetry from Thomas Hardy to Linton Kwesi Johnson, Edited by Adrian Grafe and Jessica Stephens (McFarland, 2012)

Intimate Exposure: Essays on the Public-Private Divide in British Poetry Since 1950, Edited by Emily Taylor Merriman and Adrian Grafe (2010)

LIBRARY OF CONGRESS CATALOGUING-IN-PUBLICATION DATA

Thomas Hardy, poet : new perspectives / edited by Adrian Grafe and Laurence Estanove.
   p.   cm.
   Includes bibliographical references and index.

   ISBN 978-0-7864-9538-2 (softcover : acid free paper) ∞
   ISBN 978-1-4766-2057-2 (ebook)

   1. Hardy, Thomas, 1840–1928—Poetic works.   I. Grafe, Adrian, editor. II. Estanove, Laurence, 1979– editor.

PR4757.P58T55 2015
821'.8—dc23
                                            2015028059

BRITISH LIBRARY CATALOGUING DATA ARE AVAILABLE

© 2015 Adrian Grafe and Laurence Estanove. All rights reserved

No part of this book may be reproduced or transmitted in any form or by any means, electronic or mechanical, including photocopying or recording, or by any information storage and retrieval system, without permission in writing from the publisher.

Front cover image by Laurence Estanove

Printed in the United States of America

McFarland & Company, Inc., Publishers
  Box 611, Jefferson, North Carolina 28640
  www.mcfarlandpub.com

Table of Contents

Acknowledgments   vii

Introduction (ADRIAN GRAFE and LAURENCE ESTANOVE)   1

I—Landscape into Memory

"Thinking Like a Mountain"? Hardy's Poetic Vision of "Environment" (ADRIAN TAIT)   10

Reclaiming English Bones: Corporeal Commemoration in Hardy's War Poems (MELANIE EAST)   26

"Wild Wavering": Between Pastoral and Elegy (FARHI ÖZ)   44

II—Misalignments

Rhyming Events and the Pessimistic Muse (STEPHEN TARDIF)   60

The End Game: Thomas Hardy's Looking Glass (RICHARD D. BEARDS)   75

From Pessimism to Idealism: The Pressure of Paradox (LAURENCE ESTANOVE)   82

III—Specters of Doubt and Faith

Agnosticism and Freethinking: The Influence of Leslie Stephen (ILARIA MALLOZZI)   100

The Shadow of God in *Poems of the Past and the Present* (STÉPHANIE BERNARD)   116

Uncomfortably Numb: "In Tenebris" (ADRIAN GRAFE)   133

IV—Poetic Craft and Accidentals

Messy Feelings, Tidy Forms: "Poems of 1912–13" (EMILY TAYLOR MERRIMAN)	148
Challenging Time: Philological and Lexicographical Landscape (EMILIE LORIAUX)	163
Hardy's Crafting of Barnes (HEATHER HAWKINS)	179
Punctuating Voice and Space (CHARLES LOCK)	193
Epilogue: The Transcendence of Things Seen (MICHAEL EDWARDS)	207
About the Contributors	217
Index	219

Acknowledgments

The editors acknowledge the support of the University of Artois, especially Claudine Nédelec, head of the research center Textes et Cultures, and that of the French Association for Thomas Hardy Studies (FATHOM). The editors are more than grateful to Sir Michael Edwards, a member of the Académie Française, for generously contributing to the project. Profound gratitude is also expressed to Charles Lock.

This book is dedicated to Richard D. Beards, who died while it was being edited. He always participated most enthusiastically and warmly in Hardy projects. He will be much missed.

Introduction

ADRIAN GRAFE *and* LAURENCE ESTANOVE

Thomas Hardy "is a great poet, for reasons that are perfectly clear. He has three qualities which are seldom found together except in the greatest poets: abundance, variety, and complete competence."¹ Everything that Eliot claims here—for Tennyson, since he it is of whom Eliot is writing—is true for Hardy. Eliot did not notice or perhaps want to notice that if these three qualities—abundance, variety and competence—are indeed the marks of the greatest poets, Hardy had them. Eliot goes on, further on in the same piece, to have a dig at Hardy the poet: "to qualify the despair [of *In Memoriam*] with the adjective 'religious' is to elevate it above most of its derivatives. For *The City of Dreadful Night*, and *A Shropshire Lad*, and the poems of Thomas Hardy, are small work in comparison with *In Memoriam*: it is greater than they and comprehends them."² Eliot implies here that Hardy's poems are "derivatives" of Tennyson's, a notion that an extremely high number of Hardy's poems would not bear out. In *After Strange Gods*, Eliot makes two comments on Hardy the novelist. First he says: "The work of the late Thomas Hardy represents an interesting example of a powerful personality uncurbed by an institutional attachment or by submission to any objective beliefs; unhampered by any ideas, or even by what sometimes acts as a partial restraint upon inferior writers, the desire to please a large public."³ Eliot's wording is tricky here. When he says that Hardy was "unhampered by any ideas," does he mean that Hardy was unhampered by ideas because he had none? Or that he had ideas but was unhampered by them? (Probably the first.) And when he says Hardy was "unrestrained by the desire to please a large public," does he mean that Hardy desired to please a large public—as was true up to a point since novels were his bread and butter—but was unrestrained by this desire? Or that Hardy had no desire to please a large public and was therefore unrestrained? (Probably the second.) Be that

1

as it may, Eliot goes on: "He seems to me to have written as nearly for the sake of 'self-expression' as a man well can; and the self which he had to express does not strike me as a particularly wholesome or edifying matter of communication."[4] Hardy's personality is for Eliot uncurbed, unhampered, unrestrained, and he aims at self-expression. Eliot seems here to be applying his own criterion of poetic impersonality to Hardy, the extinction of the personality, rather than reading Hardy as an artist with his own frame of reference. As for Hardy himself, he did not record much in his notebooks about Eliot or modern poetry. Next to two stanzas of "Prufrock" copied from a journal article in 1917, all he wrote was: "T. S. Eliot—a poet of the vers libre school."[5]

This collection of specially written essays affords a new opportunity to take the measure of a body of poetry, the realization of the size, quality and achievement of which only fully began to enter the broader reading public's consciousness with Philip Larkin's *Required Writing* volume, published in 1983. The volume included a partial transcript of Larkin's 1968 radio talk on Hardy the poet, "A Man Who Noticed Things," along with his review article "Wanted: Good Hardy Critic," first published in the *Critical Quarterly* in 1966. In *Required Writing*, Larkin printed the pieces side by side in order to stress the attention he felt Hardy's poetry deserves, along with, some twenty-five pages earlier, his review of a new edition of Emma Hardy's *Some Recollections*. This review, as is only to be expected, attends also to Hardy's love poems to Emma and the vagaries of his poetic inspiration. All the details and events of their courtship impressed themselves on the poet's mind—Hardy and Emma married in 1874—and remained half-buried there till Emma's death in 1912 called them out. In fact, coming after the "succession of scientific shocks"[6] which marked the nineteenth century, Emma's death and the onset of World War I combined to give Hardy what Taylor describes as a "critical shock."[7] Such upheavals, whether they be broadly epistemological or deeply personal, while engendering a sense of disillusion, spurred Hardy on to the creation of the elegies and war poetry studied in several of the essays here.

Hardy's life and poetry straddle the centuries. His poetry is neither wholly Victorian nor wholly twentieth-century or modern(ist) but a blend of these things. His relationship with time merits attention. This is not intended to suggest that his poetic art is largely retrospective, "Afterwards,"[8] even if in the twenties, Hardy is "In the Seventies."[9] Nor is it meant to recall a figure like Little Father Time in *Jude*, or evoke a question like time and tense in his poetry, superbly discussed by Galia Benziman in a recent article,[10] or even the epigrammatic view expressed by Hardy that life is

> A senseless school, where we must give
> Our lives that we may learn to live!
> A dolt is he who memorizes
> Lessons that leave no time for prizes.
> ["A Young Man's Epigram on Existence"][11]

The not-so-little irony of existence is that it is at once unbearable and too short.

The point is, rather, that Hardy the poet straddles the centuries, as does the perception of his poetry by editors and anthologists. What poems are considered as representative of a poet's work seem to change over the years, and indeed that is probably natural. Larkin perceived him as a writer of twentieth-century poetry, according him twenty-seven poems in his *Oxford Book of Twentieth Century English Verse* (OUP, 1973), more, in fact, than anyone else if one goes by poem-count as opposed to page-count. Larkin's selection from Hardy comprises poems either written or published before the beginning of the twentieth century, these being "She, to Him" and "Thoughts of Phena." It also features poems such as "The Ruin'd Maid" which chimes with the spirit of the nineteenth century more than that of the twentieth.

What about Hardy within the context of Victorian verse? First of all, it is worth remembering that Queen Victoria reigned from 1837 till 1901. Arthur Quiller-Couch's *Oxford Book of Victorian Verse* (OUP, 1912, reprinted many times up to 1971) includes four of his poems. Christopher Ricks's *New Oxford Book of Victorian Verse* (OUP, 1987) has seventeen of Hardy's poems, all of which, incidentally, were written and published during Victoria's reign. Ricks argues that Hardy is both a great Victorian poet and a great twentieth-century one, as against Eliot who wrote in 1935: "Thomas Hardy, who for a few years had all the cry, appears now, what he always was, a minor poet."[12] Clearly such categories as major and minor are not always useful, and anyway tend to change with the times. It is a pity that Eliot did not discern in Hardy the great experimenter in meter and prosody that he was.

More recent anthologies than Ricks's equally place Hardy at such a pivotal point. For example, in Caroline Blyth's recent *Decadent Verse: An Anthology of Late-Victorian Poetry, 1872–1900* (Anthem Press, 2009), Hardy appears with a selection of no less than sixteen pieces at the very end of the volume. Incidentally, Blyth devotes several pages of her introduction to Hardy's "The Darkling Thrush," more than any other specific piece, and obviously gives it a place of importance as "arguably the last poem to be written in the Victorian period,"[13] elsewhere describing it as "the last poem of the nineteenth century, or the first of the twentieth, depending on where you are coming from, and whom you are with."[14] On the other hand, from a twentieth-century perspective, Hardy's poems appear at the onset of at least two recent anthologies,

Edna Longley's *The Bloodaxe Book of 20th Century Poetry* (Bloodaxe, 2000) and Simon Rae's *News That Stays News: The 20th Century in Poems* (Faber & Faber, 1999).

Perhaps, given such staunch advocates of Hardy in relatively recent years as Larkin, Motion and Ricks, it need not be the aim of a volume such as this to do evaluative criticism. Nevertheless, one of Pound's responses to Hardy's poetry (in a letter to Ford Madox Ford, 26 May 1921) was: "Hardy gets through despite his funny way of writing verse."[15] Surely this is rich coming from Pound; and if anything, Hardy "gets through" *because of*, rather than despite, his "funny way of writing verse." Pound goes on: "Have just had a poem from him, full of every sort of inversion verbal, but so DAMN straight in thought."[16] Pound requested that Hardy criticize his work. Hardy replied: "As I am old-fashioned, and think lucidity a virtue in poetry, as in prose, I am at a disadvantage in criticizing recent poets who apparently aim at obscurity. I do not mean that *you* do, but I gather that at least you do not care whether the many understand you or not."[17] As if he needed to, Hardy stakes his credentials out here as a democratic poet for whom understanding, if not communion, is at a premium. But understanding and communion come after the fact that Hardy well knew, that poetry is not only a response to language but first and foremost a way of life. Nevertheless, the understanding of poetry that Hardy stresses here is something that a volume of this kind can always further. Hardy himself gives us some leeway in this respect in his "Preface to Select Poems of William Barnes" and the "Apology" that opens his *Late Lyrics and Earlier*. The nature of a poem, for example whether a poem is lyrical or non-lyrical, to Hardy's mind changes from reader to reader, and even, at different times, for the same reader, "according to his mood and circumstance."[18] In the "Apology" he writes that "poetry ... must like all other things keep moving, becoming."[19] This view suggests a poetry involved with the perception of natural flux, exploring mutability and therefore inevitably raising the question of permanence, material or otherwise, and finally of what transcendence, if any, is available.

In such a context, it seems appropriate to begin this volume with Hardy's reading of various dimensions of nature. The first section works at revealing the intertwining and interdependence of the human and the natural, more especially memory and landscape, thus reflecting the poet's own articulation of the Romantic and Victorian conceptions of Nature (A. Tait). Landscapes also incorporate the marks of historical events as signs or lines to be read and interpreted. In his war poems, Hardy thus illustrates that process of historical inscription by exploring the "relationship between bones, landscape and English history," whereby the acts of "mourning and memorializing" take part in the construction of national identity (M. East). The inscription of bodies in landscapes—the literal process of incorporation—also raises the question of the elegiac quality of Hardy's verse. As for all other labels tentatively applied to him, the ranking of Hardy as an elegist is a very uncertain vision. The way his own approach to nature often includes considerations of death and mourning reveals a form of oscillation between the pastoral and the elegy (F. Öz).

Indeed, the nostalgic impulse in Hardy's verse is underpinned by the complex temporal patterns that shape it. Hardy projects onto the backdrop of an ideal congruence of circumstances—a backdrop of "rhyming events"—the actual "misalignments" of reality; yet, rather than an outright pessimistic stance, Hardy's poetry weaves an "aesthetic of sadness" (S. Tardif). This aesthetic is especially borne out in his mirror poems in which similar disjunctions literally—because optically—reflect existential and psychological fractures. The sense of "self-deception writ large" (R. Beards) apparent in Hardy's world view deserves to be renegotiated because it does not automatically imply a wholly pessimistic outlook: the poetic mind remains undeceived and alert to what Hardy perceives as the illusory nature of human aspirations (L. Estanove).

Such paradoxical adjustments to the "misalignments" of reality call for a new reading of Hardy as a poet of doubt. Leslie Stephen's influence on the poet's agnostic positions enabled Hardy to move beyond the dramatic impact of Darwinian epistemology on the poet, and to reach for a more open, grounded, and humanistic approach to poetry writing (I. Mallozzi). For Hardy, more than novel writing, poetry becomes the natural medium for the utterance of religious denial, longing, or revolt, since poetry and religion "modulate into each other" ("Apology," *Late Lyrics and Earlier*).[20] Hardy's poetry voices his acknowledgement of God even as it expresses the poet's religious doubts (S. Bernard). His specific use of Biblical intertexts, either ghostly woven into his own words or held out organically as transplanted epigraphs, connects the universal resonance of such texts with a personal sense of the sacred, since Hardy exploits them for the expression of his own poetic sensitivity at a fraught time in his life (A. Grafe).

Just as Hardy's pessimism and perspective on faith need constant reevaluating, so does the poet's reputedly awkward style. What Eliot saw as "careless style" is particularly efficient in shaping the poet's conflicting reactions to love and death.[21] The "Poems of 1912–13" famously reveal how artistic creation is revived by loss, but also how the poetic mind shapes remorse and nostalgia into verse, striving to order those emotions, by definition fleeting and chaotic: "The carefully crafted verses [...] were written to last" (E. Taylor Merriman).

Hardy's feeling for the English language and the poetic possibilities it offered him can be traced to his apprenticeship with William Barnes and concomitantly to his engagement with the philological and lexicological research of his day, as attested by his poetic tributes not only to Barnes but also to Liddell and Scott (E. Loriaux). As an editor of Barnes's work, Hardy played an essential part in the transmission of his elder's legacy, while attempting to override what he saw as "the negative effects of the regionalist label upon his own and Barnes's work" (H. Hawkins). If Hardy worked at writing both his models and himself into the English literary and linguistic canons, such permanent inscriptions nonetheless bear the marks of uncertainties, hesitant strokes and alterations revealing the idiosyncratic irregularities of an artful craftsman. Hardy's apparent "indifferen[ce] even to the prescripts of good writing"[22] are truly "moments of defiance enacted in the name of poetry" (C. Lock), where the slightest punctuation adjustment or accidental can carry the most passionate and powerful voicing.

The liberties of Hardy's poetic craftsmanship enable him to express the contradictions of experience and the fluctuations of affect. Such contradictions are ultimately reflected in the aporia of language: what oscillates is meaning itself, and the relation between words and experience. The "tremulousness of sensibility and of language" (M. Edwards) which Hardy's poems convey thus reveals a unique form of transcendence that is at once immediate, ungraspable and protean.[23]

This volume seeks to deepen the reader's understanding and enjoyment of Hardy's poetry, either by offering perspectives, such as ecocriticism, that chime with current critical concerns; re-evaluations of long-held views; and, partly by virtue of the mere size of Hardy's poetic output, readings of some poems which have not so far received a great deal of critical consideration. Conversely, the attention brought to bear here on some of Hardy's nature poems and elegies shows their abiding attraction for scholars and their ongoing ability to raise new questions. Hardy's view on the necessity that poetry should "keep moving [and] becoming" must be equally true of responses to poetry, and the contributions to this volume confirm the multifaceted dynamism of current responses to Hardy's poetry.

Notes

1. T. S. Eliot, "In Memoriam" in *Selected Essays* (London: Faber and Faber, 1972; first edition, 1932; third enlarged edition, 1951), 328. This is the first sentence in Eliot's article on "In Memoriam"; it is about Tennyson.

2. *Ibid.*, 336.

3. T. S. Eliot, *After Strange Gods: A Primer of Modern Heresy* (London: Faber & Faber, 1933), 54.

4. *Ibid.*
5. Lennart A. Björk (ed.), *The Literary Notebooks of Thomas Hardy* (Basingstoke: Macmillan, 1988), Volume II, 227.
6. See Adrian Tait's essay in this volume.
7. Dennis Taylor, *Hardy's Poetry, 1860–1928* (New York: Columbia University Press, 1981), 90.
8. Thomas Hardy, *The Complete Poems*, ed. James Gibson (Basingstoke: Palgrave, 2001; first edition, London: Macmillan, 1976), 553.
9. *Ibid.*, 459.
10. Galia Benziman, "The Self-Resisting: Hardy's Ambivalent Evocation of Romantic Childhood" in *Lines of Resistance: Essays on British Poetry from Thomas Hardy to Linton Kwesi Johnson*, eds. Adrian Grafe and Jessica Stephens (Jefferson, NC: McFarland, 2012), 15–28.
11. *Complete Poems, op. cit.*, 299.
12. Christopher Ricks (ed.), *New Oxford Book of Victorian Verse* (Oxford: Oxford University Press, 1987), xxx.
13. Caroline Blyth (ed.), *Decadent Verse: An Anthology of Late-Victorian Poetry, 1872–1900* (London: Anthem Press, 2009), 36.
14. *Ibid.*, 40.
15. Brita Lindberg-Seyersted (ed.), *Pound/Ford: The Story of a Literary Friendship* (New York: New Directions, 1982), 59.
16. *Ibid.*
17. Letter from Hardy to Pound, 18 March 1921. *Thomas Hardy: Selected Letters*, ed. Michael Millgate (Oxford: Clarendon Press, 1990), 357.
18. Thomas Hardy, *Selected Poems*, ed. Harry Thomas (London: Penguin Books, 1993), 194.
19. *The Complete Poems, op. cit.*, 561.
20. *Ibid.*
21. This is the continuation of the quotation from *After Strange Gods* given in the first paragraph of the present introduction: "[Hardy] was indifferent even to the prescripts of good writing: he wrote sometimes overpoweringly well, but always very carelessly; at times his style touches sublimity without ever having passed through the stage of being good" (T. S. Eliot, *op. cit.*, 54–55).
22. *Ibid.*
23. For a Heideggerian approach to the question of landscape of transcendence, see Roger Ebbatson, *Landscape and Literature, 1830–1914, Nature, Text, Aura* (Basingstoke: Palgrave Macmillan, 2013) and Jonathan Taylor's review in *TLS* (19 September 2014).

I

Landscape into Memory

"Thinking Like a Mountain"?
Hardy's Poetic Vision of "Environment"
Adrian Tait

The aim of this essay is to explore the way in which the early verse and verse drama of Thomas Hardy extends our understanding of what eco-critics have called a Victorian (as opposed to a Romantic) ecology. As such, it forms part of a wider eco-critical project whose premise may be simply stated: what the environmentalist posits as a crisis in the relationship between humankind and its environment, the environmental critic reads as a crisis of objectivity. The crisis lies in the fact that, as Latour remarks, the environmentalist is "absolutely incapable of defining the common good of a dehumanized nature"[1] to which one might add: because incapable of describing (or fully realizing) nature, which is as result dehumanized.

This is a reason why, in the twenty-first century, Hardy remains a compelling and visionary presence, and, in the words of a leading British eco-critic, "an obvious candidate for the eco-critical canon."[2] In verse (and verse drama) scattered throughout his writing career, he responds to and engages with the crisis of objectivity—of representation—that preoccupies the environmental critic. In doing so, he reaches out to a new, more complex, and more complete vision of a totality that would now be called "the environment."

My starting point is a short but striking poem which appeared in Hardy's first verse collection, *Wessex Poems* (1898). Entitled "Nature's Questioning,"[3] it engages with what was, even late in the Victorian period, a distressing possibility: that the natural world could not, after all, be searched for God or for evidence of Him. In the poem, "Field, flock and lonely tree" (l. 2) challenge the poet to explain the deeper meaning behind their existence:

> "Has some Vast Imbecility,
>   Mighty to build and blend,
>   But impotent to tend,
> Framed us in jest, and left us now to hazardry?
>
> "Or come we of an Automaton
>   Unconscious of our pains? ...
>   Or are we live remains
> Of Godhead dying downwards, brain and eye now gone?
>
> "Or is that some high Plan betides,
>   As yet not understood,
>   Of Evil stormed by Good,
> We the Forlorn Hope over which Achievement strides?" [l. 13–24]

Where Wordsworth might, perhaps, have mused aloud amidst the solitary splendor of lake and mountain, and made its echoes into answers, "Nature" here interrogates the narrator; and yet the narrator can only reply "No answerer I..." (l. 25).

That reluctance—that refusal—is a reminder that Hardy's views were shaped, not only by the controversy caused by *The Origin of Species* and *Essays and Reviews*, but by a wider and more general mood of skepticism that undermined both the comforting certainties of Christianity, and the compensatory if less clearly defined alternatives offered by Romanticism. If the narrator of "Nature's Questioning" offers silence by way of answer, it is not because he or she has shirked a sacred poetic responsibility to speak the truth, but because in truth there is nothing beyond silence; nothing beyond Matthew Arnold's "withdrawing roar" of retreating beliefs.[4] As the poem concludes, "Meanwhile the winds, and rains,/ And Earth's old glooms and pains/ Are still the same, and gladdest Life and Death neighbours nigh" (l. 26–28).

If "Nature's Questioning" is about a universe from which God or gods are absent, the corollary is that, beyond the simple cycle of life and death on which the poem's last line insists, there is no great purpose or meaning to what we might now call the natural or non-human world. There is only what, in the poem that precedes "Nature's Questioning," Hardy simply called "mechanic artistry" ("To a Motherless Child," l. 13).[5] Significantly, Hardy therefore rejects both the conventional spiritual or religious reading of the universe, and "Nature," the duly capitalized construction contemporaries placed upon the natural world.

Whilst Hardy rejects the nineteenth-century notion of "Nature," he is not the less fascinated by it. In another of the *Wessex Poems*, he returns to the same complex and contentious subject. The poem is called "In a Wood,"[6] and it is dated both 1887 and 1896. "[T]o dwellers in a wood," opens *Under the Greenwood Tree*, "almost every species of tree has its voice as well as its feature."⁷ In the poem, however, the voice of the trees is interpreted for us by a visitor, and his view of the wood is learned rather than lived.

Wooed by a Wordsworthian faith in a nature that "never did betray" the "heart that loved her" (l. 14), this "City-opprest" narrator seeks "sylvan peace" (l. 13) amidst the trees.⁸ Instead, he encounters a scene that is anything but "ordered, purposive, benign."⁹

> Sycamore shoulders oak,
> Bines the slim sapling yoke,
> Ivy-spun halters choke
>   Elms stout and tall.
>
> Touches from ash, O wych,
>   Sting you like scorn!
> You, too, brave hollies twitch
>   Sidelong from thorn. [l. 21–28]

Dismayed, the narrator realizes that there is no more peace to be found in this Darwinian "war of nature" than in the human society from which he has fled.¹⁰ Both worlds are ruled by conflict and competition and are, like the narrator, self-interested; trees are "to men akin— / Combatants all!" (l. 19–20).

Like "The Ivy-Wife," another of the poems in Hardy's first collection, "In a Wood" therefore consciously inverts the image of "nature" as stable and serene. Instead, it draws a parallel between natural and human environments, and portrays each as hostile and highly competitive.

Written towards the end of a period shaped by a succession of scientific shocks, Hardy's poem was not the first to point out the parallel. By then, it was acceptable, if not conventional, to side with Herbert Spencer in seeing biological struggle as a scientific endorsement of "industrial competition and imperial expansion": these were the natural and inevitable consequences of a universe re-imagined by science and a world re-shaped by free trade.¹¹ But as others were at pains to point out, the "survival of the fittest" assumes a moral dimension where there is none. T. H. Huxley went further. The practice of "that which is ethically best," he said in a lecture on "Evolution and Ethics" in 1893, "involves a course of conduct which, in all respects, is opposed to that which leads to success in the cosmic struggle for existence"; "let us understand, once for all, that the ethical progress of society depends, not on imitating the cosmic process, still less in running away from it, but in combating it."¹² Nature is neither cruel nor kind, but as Hardy observed, "an indifferent and unconscious force at the back of things 'that neither good nor evil knows.'"¹³

In other words, Hardy's own views differ from those of his (very Victorian) narrator. In the poem, the speaker imagines nature benign, and finds it hostile; the same speaker who thinks to find in nature a place of "sylvan peace" instead encounters a gladiatorial arena in which trees shoulder, sting and choke each other, "Cankering in black despair/ If overborne" (l. 31–32). But given Hardy's own insistence on nature's fundamental "indifference," it is clear that the narrator's second response is no less exaggerated and artificial than his first. The poem parodies both positions. In so doing, it acts not only as a challenge to contemporary literary tropes, but as a wider critique of the Victorian's deeply anthropocentric insistence that "Nature" act as some kind of extended metaphor for the human condition.

That response makes Hardy's position virtually unique amongst contemporaries: in stepping beyond the projection of human needs and wants onto the environment, and accepting "Nature as a process governed by Chance," he makes "a complete tabula rasa of Christian and Idealistic values."[14] In the world of "In a Wood," then, nature is no longer magical, but mechanical; stripped of the divine, it ceases to be a source of solace or spiritual strength.

Herein lies the promise—and the challenge—of a post–Darwinian world. Hardy's realization of a "Nature" demystified by modern science is a first step towards its substitution by our own sense of "environment," from which environmentalism—and environmental ethics—in turn derive. At the same time, the "disenchantment of the world" is nothing less than a mechanism for its destruction, as Adorno and Horkheimer pointed out in their seminal deconstruction of the "program of the Enlightenment."[15]

Remarkably, both arguments find a parallel in Hardy's verse, and both flow from his sense of a natural world stripped of the divine. If, in a Hardyan universe, God does not exist, then there is no special place for man—for the human—within that universe, and nothing to differentiate him from any other creature. As Hardy realized, Darwin had, in distancing or dismissing God, also dissolved the "traditional distinction between mankind and nature": and if the narrator of "In A Wood" instinctively recoils from the reality of the environment he encounters, it is, perhaps, because nothing now separates him from the natural world he is so accustomed to patronizing.[16] The distinction between self and place has collapsed. In the words of one of Hardy's last published poems, "Drinking Song,"[17] narrator and narrated are alike, after all:

> We are all one with creeping things
>   And Apes and men
>   Blood-brethren,
> And likewise reptile forms with stings [l. 49–52]

This is a pivotal shift in attitude—and in values—and it resonates throughout Hardy's poetry. Its impact is perhaps most obviously felt in Hardy's second verse collection, *Poems of the Past and the Present* (1902), which represents a cautious but distinct shift towards a perspective we might now describe as "ecocentric."[18] Here, Hardy reflects on his own recognition that (as he explained in a letter of 1909), the "discovery of the laws of evolution, which revealed that all organic creatures are of one family, shifted the centre of altruism from humanity to the whole conscious world collectively."[19] As he added a year later, in a letter to the Secretary of the Humanitarian League, "[f]ew people seem to perceive fully as yet that the most far-reaching consequence of the establishment of the common origin of all species is ethical."[20] The result is a sequence of seven poems. They include "The Caged Thrush Freed and Home Again," "Birds at Winter Nightfall," "The Puzzled Game-Birds," "Winter in Durnover Field," "The Last Chrysanthemum," "The Darkling Thrush,"[21] and, of course, "An August Midnight,"[22] with its assertion that "longlegs," moth, "dumbledore" and "sleepy fly" "know Earth-Secrets that know not I" (l. 12).

Significantly, these poems suggest that, even as Hardy wrestled with the unpalatable prospect of a universe empty of meaning and entirely indifferent to human hopes and fears, he still felt a profound fellow feeling with the non-human, natural world, and a deep-rooted desire to engage with it.

This fellow feeling in turn underlines what is at stake. As I have already suggested, Hardy was all too aware of the dangers inherent in what Adorno and Horkheimer described as a "fully enlightened earth," radiating "disaster triumphant."[23] That concern finds its parallel in "Heiress and Architect,"[24] a poem Hardy first drafted in 1867, and one of the five "oddly assorted" pieces that conclude *Wessex Poems*.[25]

In this remarkable but rarely reproduced poem, the hopes and aspirations of the eponymous Heiress are slowly and systematically picked apart by an "arch-designer" (l. 2), a "man of measuring eye" (l. 56) whose brutal and reductive reasoning collides with and crushes her hopes[26]:

> "Shape me," she said, "high halls with tracery
> And open ogive-work, that scent and hue
> Of buds, and travelling bees, may come in through,
> The note of birds, and singings of the sea,
>   For these are much to me."
>
>   "An idle whim!"
>   Broke forth from him
> Whom nought could warm to gallantries:
> "Cede all these buds and birds, the zephyr's call,
> And scents, and hues, and things that falter all,
> And choose as best the close and surly wall,
>   For winters freeze." [l. 13–24]

What freezes is, of course, "his cold clear voice, and cold clear view" (l. 8). "Women and nature have an age-old association," wrote Carolyn Merchant in a pioneering work of eco-feminism, *The Death of Nature* (1980), and because of it (she contended) both have been subjugated by patriarchal societies, never more effectively and efficiently than by the advanced industrialized countries shaped by scientific revolution.[27] With her willingness to transgress the boundaries that would separate the two, the Heiress seems to symbolize just this association of woman and nature. Conversely, the architect's relentless, insistent logic—a logic based on a "law of stable things" (l. 11) that nowhere exists in the natural world, and is very much a figment of the Enlightenment imagination—recalls what Ebbatson called "the universe of death" bequeathed by the mechanistic thinking of Locke's Newtonian psychology."[28] He seems to stand for "calculation, coldness, and death," and the "banefulness of his last words, which end the poem, suggests a note of malicious triumph: "For you will die."'[29] Zietlow considered the poem impenetrable, its meaning "ambivalent"; I would contend that this is a post-modern fable of startling and stark simplicity, for truly the Heiress is (as Zietlow also notes) "the inheritor of the means of life."[30]

Hardy's indictment of reason and rationality—his challenge to what Adorno and Horkheimer called the "triumph of the factual mentality"[31]—reflects his recognition of what inevitably follows from it. In "The Mother Mourns," also from *Poems of the Past and the Present*,[32] (Mother) Nature is overheard complaining that the brightest of her creations has learnt to find fault with her, that humankind:

> "No more sees my sun as a Sanct-shape,
>   My moon as the Night-queen,
>   My stars as august and sublime ones
>   That influences rain: [l. 45–48]

These things (and more) humankind now holds "in doubt and disdain" (l. 20). But there is a twist to the poem, as the Mother goes on to explain:

> [...] ... My species are dwindling,
>   My forests grow barren,
>   My popinjays fail from their tappings,
>   My larks from their strain.
>   "My leopardine beauties are rarer,
>   My tusky ones vanish,
>   My children have aped mine own slaughters
>   To quicken my wane. [l. 73–80]

The implication is unavoidable: since the natural world is no longer seen as sacred or special, humankind has no reason to exercise restraint, for the Mother has taught it none; and so "my tusky ones vanish." But humankind is itself just another species. There is no law of nature to guarantee its survival.

And with that thought in mind, it may be appropriate to turn to a poem in which, to use Aldo Leopold's famous phrase, Hardy appears to "think like a mountain" (1949).[33]

The poem is "Zermatt—To the Matterhorn,"[34] and it was written following a visit in 1897. In the sonnet, Hardy describes the first ascent of the Matterhorn, during the descent from which four of the seven climbers perished. Hardy later met one of the survivors, Edward Whymper, whose own popular and highly colored account of the fateful day is an account of a mountain "conquered" and possessed ("the Matterhorn was ours!").[35] First drafted some thirty-two years later, Hardy's poem celebrates the achievement in terms of which Whymper would have approved. It describes a supreme moment in human history, a "tragic feat of manly might" (l. 7) that alone rescues the Matterhorn from obscurity: it is as though, until that moment, the mountain's existence was of no consequence ("of history thou hadst none," l. 8).

But this is not the sum of a poem whose secondary, and perhaps deeper, meaning is suggested by Hardy's archaic but respectful form of address ("thou"). In the sestet, the focus shifts to the mountain itself.

> Yet ages ere men topped thee, late and soon
> Thou didst behold the planets lift and lower;
> Saw'st, maybe, Joshua's pausing sun and moon,
> And the betokening sky when Caesar's power
> Approached its bloody end: yea, even that Noon
> When darkness filled the earth till the ninth hour. [l. 9–14]

The poem's message may be simply, if inelegantly summarized: if the entire history of humankind can be fitted into the life of a single mountain, all its triumphs are trifling. As Leopold himself wrote, "behind these obvious and immediate hopes and fears there lies a deeper meaning, known only to the mountain itself."[36]

For the environmentalist, this quiet indictment of human hubris is undeniably powerful; but beyond this (admittedly telling) juxtaposition of deep or geological time with humankind's (brief) history, an obvious difficulty remains. As Clark notes, Leopold's "striking phrase" is also "strictly nonsensical."[37] "Thinking like a mountain" is a literal impossibility. If mountains offer any message, it is that we cannot impose our own interpretations upon them.

Intriguingly, that thought finds its echo in Hardy's first sighting of the Matterhorn. Arriving by night, he was able to see it only as "an absence of stars."[38] As *The Life* adds, "[h]e meant to make a poem of the strange feeling implanted by this black silhouette of the mountain on the pattern of the constellations; but never did so far as is known."[39]

Yet Hardy did write a poem which echoes this strange sense of a mountain present in spite of its absence, visible in spite of its invisibility. Entitled "The Schreckhorn (With Thoughts of Leslie Stephen),"[40] it was first published in 1906 in Frederic William Maitland's biography of Stephen, and it later appeared in Hardy's own verse collection, *Satires of Circumstance*, in 1914. Nevertheless, the poem itself is dated 1897. As the subtitle suggests, it is a sonnet tribute to Hardy's acquaintance, the renowned Alpinist and author of *The Playground of Europe*. Here, the mountain is read as "a guise of him" (l. 4), "spare and desolate" (l. 2). In fact, Hardy's description of the Schreckhorn's aloofness is at odds with the hyperbole of Stephen's own response to it—Stephen thought it "the grimmest fiend of the Oberland"[41]—but in both, the mountain is reduced to an aspect of the man. A single, powerful phrase escapes this interpretation. In the sestet, Hardy describes the mountain as a "silent adamantine shape" (l. 12). "Adamantine" may appear to refer back to a human quality (adamant as in stubborn and inflexible), but it originates in the name of a (supposed) mineral or rock, and in fact means "incapable of being broken, dissolved, or penetrated."[42]

The dictionary definition immediately recalls Whymper's language of possession and conquest, a language whose inherent sexual violence Hardy's own poem hints at ("...ere men topped thee"). Yet the exacting choice of "adamantine" once again lays bare the absurdity of these human impositions: the mountain will always remain inviolate. And there is a wider point to be made, about the impossibility of reading meaning into a self-contained natural world. As Heidegger was later to remark:

> A stone presses downward and manifests its heaviness. But while this heaviness exerts an opposing pressure upon us it denies any penetration into it. If we attempt such a penetration by breaking open the rock, it still does not display in its fragments anything inward that has been opened up. The stone has instantly withdrawn again into the same dull pressure and bulk of its fragments.[43]

The rock, like a mountain silhouetted against a night sky, "shows itself only when it remains undisclosed and unexplained":

> Earth thus shatters every attempt to penetrate it. It causes every merely calculating importunity upon it to turn into a destruction. This destruction may herald itself under the appearance of mastery and of progress in the form of the technical-scientific observation of nature, but this mastery nevertheless remains an impotence of will.[44]

There is, however, another and perhaps more meaningful way in which to engage with and understand Leopold's phrase. When Leopold wrote that "only the mountain has lived long enough to listen objectively to the howl of the wolf,"[45] he was referring to a specific problem: the wider but largely overlooked impact of America's state-by-state extermination of wolves. As Clark notes, Leopold was gesturing towards a more holistic, eco-centric view of the environment that recognizes the complex interdependencies which bind ecosystems together, but also make them vulnerable to the errant behavior of single species (like humans), and the consequent loss of keystone species (like wolves).[46] Arguably, this is exactly the kind of broader, ecological understanding that was not available at the time Hardy wrote these poems. On that basis, it is inappropriate to search his poetic output for the kind of eco-centric vision that Leopold has in mind.

And yet just such a vision can be found, contained within the unlikely form of *The Dynasts*. Published between 1903 and 1908, *The Dynasts* is, to quote its subtitle in full, "an epic-drama of the war with Napoleon in three parts, nineteen acts, and one hundred & thirty scenes."[47] It represents the fullest expression of Hardy's interest in the Napoleonic wars, a fascination that had already influenced novels like *The Trumpet-Major* (1880), short stories such as "The Melancholy Hussar" (1890), and poems, amongst them "Valenciennes" and "Leipzig," both of which appear in *Wessex Poems*.[48] It was also, in Hardy's own view, his *magnum opus*. For a brief period, this was the general consensus: writing in 1938, Rutland considered that there was "almost universal agreement" that *The Dynasts* was "the greatest of Hardy's writings, and the one which most clearly reveals the full stature of his creative genius."[49] Today, however, *The Dynasts* is amongst the least known and least discussed of Hardy's works.[50]

Yet Hardy's innovative verse-drama is remarkable not least for its sense that all life is linked, and linked by what he called the "Immanent Will." Hardy makes this clear at the very outset of *The Dynasts* when, in its "Fore Scene," "a new and penetrating light" exhibits "as one organism the anatomy of life and movement in all humanity and vitalized matter" (Fore Scene, 1).[51] The verse-drama's various spirits (a Shade of the Earth amongst them) see what its human players do not: the "fibrils, veins," "Will-tissues, nerves, and pulses of the Cause,/ That heave throughout the Earth's compositure" (Fore Scene, 1).[52] This is "the anatomy" of what Hardy called "the Immanent Will" whose "strange waves," "twining and serpentining round and through" "complicate with some, and balance all" (Fore Scene, 1).[53]

In both the verse collections from which I have so far quoted—*Wessex Poems* and *Poems of the Past and the Present*—Hardy engaged with the complex inheritance of a concept of "Nature" that a more skeptical and scientifically informed thinking had left behind. It reappears here, in *The Dynasts*, where Hardy talks about "Dame Nature," that "lay-shape" upon which humankind was once accustomed to "hang phenomena" (VI, I, 1),[54] encumbering it with ideas and expectations. In lieu, he offers "the Immanent, that urgeth all," and "rules what may or may not befall!" (V, II, 1).[55] Lacking "right or reason," its "terms inexorable" (VI, I, 1)[56] nonetheless dictate the shape and nature all of existence.

> At once, as earlier, a preternatural clearness possesses the atmosphere of the battle-field, in which the scene becomes anatomized and the living masses of humanity transparent. The controlling Immanent Will appears therein, as a brain-like network of currents and ejections, twitching, interpenetrating, entangling, and thrusting hither and thither the human forms [III, VI, 1].[57]

As Hynes and Pinion note, the concept of an Immanent Will or "First Cause" had already appeared under different names (such as a "Vast Imbecility" or an "Automaton") in both poems and novels.[58] In the most general terms, the concept owes something to Schopenhauer; more specifically, it adapts even as it radically modifies Von Hartmann, and his *Philosophy of the Unconscious*, first published in 1868.[59] The connections are, however, indistinct, and whilst Hardy's idea owes much to the late nineteenth-century intellectual milieu, the use he makes of it is quite his own.

Hardy's concept of an Immanent Will could, of course, be mistaken for another symbolic device in a highly stylized prose-poem. Hardy's spirit chorus is certainly imaginary, "contrivances of the fancy merely" (Preface).[60] The Immanent Will, however, is not, although Hardy's Spirits in part exist to draw attention to it. Nor does the Immanent Will form part of the "supernatural framework" Hardy always had in mind for *The Dynasts*.[61] It is, instead, what he called one of the "true realities of life, hitherto called abstractions."[62] And whilst Hardy undoubtedly set out to find some substitute for now spent "old theologies,"[63] the Immanent Will is no more a metaphysical concept than it is a metaphorical device. Through the concept of the Immanent Will, Hardy insists that the links that bind living things are real even if invisible to us. As he stated categorically in an explanatory letter of 1907, there is "no Will outside the Mass—that is, the Universe."[64] He remains "rigorously faithful to his monistic vision."[65]

It is nonetheless disconcerting to discover that Hardy's concept of a "First or Fundamental Energy" (Preface)[66] at work in the universe has its parallel in a hypothesis first postulated in the 1970s: that "the earth's living matter, air, oceans, and land surface form a complex system which can be seen as a single organism and which has the capacity to keep our planet a fit place for life."[67] It is, in short, analogous to James Lovelock's concept of "gaia."

This is not, of course, to suggest any kind of direct relationship between the two ideas. In origin, at least, they are very different. Hardy's philosophy might reasonably be described as a skeptic's substitute for that "local cult called Christianity," "Beyond whose span, uninfluenced, unconcerned,/ The systems of the suns go sweeping on" (VI, I, 1).[68] By contrast, Lovelock's "gaia" is a scientific premise built upon close observation of certain otherwise anomalous trends or tendencies apparent in the natural world: it is the case for biological (self-)regulation of climate. Yet "gaia" has itself come to be seen in less scrupulously scientific circles as its own form of religion. Insofar as both attempt to explain the universe and our role or relative (un)importance within it, E. O. Wilson's observation is relevant: "science is religion liberated and writ large."[69] Furthermore, one critic of Hardy suggests that "the Will includes the totality of all actions in the universe, including even what we think of as the physical, non-sentient world."[70]

The exact nature of the correspondence between Hardy's "Immanent Will" and Lovelock's "gaia" is, in the last analysis, less important than the fact that, through its insistence on the dynamic and active interrelatedness of all life, Hardy's vision anticipates (and suggests an answer to) a major problem for those who seek to construct an eco-centric or all-encompassing environmental ethic: establishing why the non-human world can be said to possess intrinsic value or inherent worth. Confronted with the fact of interdependence, the issue ceases to be important. If interconnected—if aware of the relational field in which we are situated—we will no more damage the environment than we would injure ourselves. This, truly, is "thinking like a mountain."

From an eco-critical perspective, therefore, Hardy's concept of the Immanent Will is central to his importance. Nevertheless, it remains an abstract and impersonal concept. Arguably, Hardy's greatest strength lies in his (apparently artless) ability to engage the reader with—and in so doing more fully realize—the living reality of "environment." "Winter in Durnover Field"[71] is a telling example. It forms part of the sequence in *Poems of the Past and the Present* to which I have already referred, and it takes the unusual form of a triolet, a French fixed verse-form dating from the thirteenth century. The triolet's peculiarity is that the first and second lines are repeated as the seventh and eighth, whilst the first line is also the fourth. In a poem whose single verse consists of only eight lines, this level of repetition creates a chorus-like intensity whose impact is only reinforced by the poem's limited rhyme scheme (ABAAABAB). Yet this interlocking pattern of rhyme and repetition could not be better suited to describing the scene of quiet desperation depicted here:

    Rook.—   Throughout the field I find no grain;
                  The cruel frost encrusts the cornland!

> *Starling.*—Aye: patient pecking now is vain
> Throughout the field, I find...
> *Rook.*— No grain!
> *Pigeon.*— Nor will be, comrade, till it rain,
> Or genial thawings loose the lorn land
> Throughout the field.
> *Rook.*— I find no grain:
> The cruel frost encrusts the cornland!

With lines split and shared between speakers—unlikely comrades united in adversity—the poem's artificiality of form does not consciously register; its spoken simplicity does. Terse and unsentimental, it dignifies and deepens a moment whose prosaic ordinariness would otherwise merit no mention at all. And this, perhaps, is the true value of Hardy's poetic vision of "environment": to quote Heidegger, it "tears human beings out of the habitual midst of their lives, so that they may be in a centre outside of themselves"[72]; it makes it possible not only to think, but to feel in terms that are exocentric.

At the outset, and perhaps quixotically, I defined environmental crisis in terms of an inability to describe—or fully realize—the "nature" to which Latour refers, which is as a result dehumanized. But the ability to think and feel outside the self—as Hardy does in remarkable but often overlooked poems like this one—is a defining characteristic of the human, and a standard by which we measure ourselves and each other. Perhaps the dehumanization of Latour's nature is not, after all, the result of our inability to describe or fully realize it. Perhaps it is only when, as in poems like "Winter in Durnover Field," we recall our essential humanity that it becomes possible to see—or rather, see beyond—"Nature" to the totality of which humankind is and will always remain a small and dependent part. As Parham remarks of the qualities that (re)define our sense of a Victorian ecology, it is a recognition "that 'human being' [...] ultimately resides in the nature and quality of humanity's relationship with other species and its surrounding physical environment."[73] Seen in these terms, the exocentric impulse in Hardy's poetic oeuvre is a compelling reason why, in a century dominated by environmental anxiety, his work remains both vital and relevant.

Notes

1. Bruno Latour, *Politics of Nature: How to Bring the Sciences into Democracy*, transl. Catherine Porter (Cambridge, MA: Harvard University Press, 2004), 21.
2. Richard Kerridge, "Ecological Hardy" in *Beyond Nature Writing: Expanding the Boundaries of Ecocriticism*, ed. Karla Armbruster and Kathleen R. Wallace (Charlottesville: University Press of Virginia, 2000, repr. 2001), 126.
3. Thomas Hardy, *The Complete Poems*, ed. James Gibson (Basingstoke: Palgrave, 2001), 66–67.

4. "Dover Beach" (1867), l. 25; Matthew Arnold, *The Poems of Matthew Arnold, 1840–1867* (London: Oxford University Press, 1913, repr. 1937), 402.
5. *The Complete Poems, op. cit.*, 65–66.
6. *Ibid.*, 64–65.
7. Thomas Hardy, *Under the Greenwood Tree*, ed. Simon Gatrell (Oxford: Oxford University Press, 1985, repr. 1992), 11.
8. F. B. Pinion, *A Commentary on the Poems of Thomas Hardy* (London: Macmillan, 1976), 22.
9. Bernard Richards, *English Poetry of the Victorian Period, 1830–90* (London: Pearson, 2001, first edition, 1988), 154.
10. Charles Darwin, *The Origin of Species by Means of Natural Selection*, ed. J. W. Burrow (Harmondsworth: Penguin, 1968, repr. 1984), 459.
11. Robin Gilmour, *The Victorian Period: The Intellectual and Cultural Context of English Literature, 1830–90* (Harlow: Longman, 1993), 133.
12. Cyril Bibby (ed.), *The Essence of T. H. Huxley* (London: Macmillan, 1967), 173.
13. Thomas Hardy, *The Life and Work of Thomas Hardy*, ed. Michael Millgate (Basingstoke: Macmillan, 1984, repr. 1985), 364.
14. Georg Roppen, *Evolution and Poetic Belief: A Study in Some Victorian and Modern Writers* (Oslo: Oslo University Press, 1956), 315.
15. Theodor W. Adorno and Max Horkheimer, *Dialectic of Enlightenment*, transl. John Cumming (London: Verso, 1997, repr. 2010), 3. *Dialectic of Enlightenment* was first published in 1944, and revised in 1947.
16. Gilmour, *op. cit.*, 84.
17. *The Complete Poems, op. cit.*, 905–908. Published in *Winter Words* (1928).
18. See Adrian Tait, "'The Mother Mourns': The Ecocentric Impulse in the Poetry of Thomas Hardy" in *Green Letters* 14 (2011): 57–71.
19. *The Life, op. cit.*, 373–374.
20. *Ibid.*, 376–377.
21. *The Complete Poems, op. cit.*, 147–150.
22. *Ibid.*, 146–147.
23. Adorno and Horkheimer, *op. cit.*, 3.
24. *The Complete Poems, op. cit.*, 75–76.
25. Trevor Johnson in Thomas Hardy, *Wessex Poems* (Ryburn: Keele University Press, 1995), 40.
26. See Pinion, *op. cit.*, 26.
27. Carolyn Merchant, *The Death of Nature: Women, Ecology, and the Scientific Revolution* (San Francisco: Harper & Row, 1990), xix. Merchant's aim was to "re-examine the formation of a world view and a science that, by reconceptualizing reality as a machine rather than a living organism, sanctioned the domination of both nature and women" (xxi).
28. Roger Ebbatson, *Lawrence and the Nature Tradition: A Theme in English Fiction, 1859–1914* (Sussex: Harvester Press, 1980), 5.
29. Paul Zietlow, *Moments of Vision* (Cambridge, MA: Harvard University Press, 1974), 14.
30. *Ibid.*, 14, 3.
31. Adorno and Horkheimer, *op. cit.*, 4.
32. *The Complete Poems, op. cit.*, 111–113.

33. Aldo Leopold, *A Sand County Almanac and Sketches Here and There* (New York: Oxford University Press, 1949, repr. 1968), 129.
34. *The Complete Poems, op. cit.*, 106. Published in *Poems of the Past and the Present* (1902), the poem bears the mention "June–July 1897."
35. Edward Whymper, *Scrambles Amongst the Alps* (London: Thomas Nelson, 1900, first edition, 1871), 382.
36. Leopold, *op. cit.*, 126.
37. Timothy Clark, *The Cambridge Introduction to Literature and the Environment* (Cambridge: Cambridge University Press, 2011), 77, 78.
38. *The Life, op. cit.*, 313.
39. *Ibid.*
40. *The Complete Poems, op. cit.*, 322.
41. Quoted in Trevor Johnson, *Thomas Hardy* (London: Evans, 1968, repr. 1971), 43.
42. *Oxford English Dictionary*, ed. John A. Simpson and Edmund S. C. Weiner (Oxford: Clarendon Press, 1989, first edition 1888–1928), 137.
43. Martin Heidegger, "The Origin of the Work of Art" in *Basic Writings*, ed. David Farrell Krell (London: Routledge, 2011), 110. Heidegger's lecture was originally delivered in 1935.
44. *Ibid.*, 110.
45. Leopold, *op. cit.*, 129.
46. Clark, *op. cit.*, 78.
47. Thomas Hardy, *The Dynasts* (London: Macmillan, 1978), title page.
48. See Richard Little Purdy, *Thomas Hardy: A Bibliographical Study* (London: The British Library, 2002), 31, 82, and *The Dynasts, op. cit.*, xi–xii.
49. W. R. Rutland, *Thomas Hardy: A Study of His Writings and Their Background* (Oxford: Basil Blackwell, 1938), 269.
50. See James Gibson, *Thomas Hardy: A Literary Life* (London: Macmillan, 1996), 149; Geoffrey Harvey, *The Complete Critical Guide to Thomas Hardy* (London: Routledge, 2003), 138.
51. *The Dynasts, op. cit.*, 27–28.
52. *Ibid.*, 28.
53. *Ibid.*
54. *Ibid.*, 62.
55. *Ibid.*, 87.
56. *Ibid.*, 62.
57. *Ibid.*, 172.
58. Samuel Hynes, *The Pattern of Hardy's Poetry* (Chapel Hill: University of North Carolina Press, 1961, repr. 1966), 158; Pinion, *op. cit.*, 176–8.
59. See Paul Turner, *The Life of Thomas Hardy* (Oxford: Blackwell, 1998, repr. 2001), 178, 189, 182–3, and Robert Schweik, "The Influence of Religion, Science, and Philosophy on Hardy's Writings" in *The Cambridge Companion to Thomas Hardy*, ed. by Dale Kramer (Cambridge: Cambridge University Press, 1999, repr. 2003), 68–70.
60. *The Dynasts, op. cit.*, 4.
61. *The Life, op. cit.*, 183.
62. *Ibid.*, 183.
63. *Ibid.*, 344.

64. Letter of 2 June 1907, in *The Collected Letters of Thomas Hardy, Volume Three: 1902-1908*, ed. Richard Little Purdy and Michael Millgate (Oxford: Clarendon Press, 1982), 255.
65. Hynes, *op. cit.*, 163.
66. *The Dynasts, op. cit.*, 5.
67. James Lovelock (1979) quoted in *The Green Reader*, ed. Andrew Dobson (London: André Deutsch, 1991), 265.
68. *The Dynasts, op. cit.*, 60.
69. Edward O. Wilson, *Consilience: The Unity of Knowledge* (New York: Alfred A. Knopf, 1998, repr. 2000), 6.
70. F. R. Southerington, *Hardy's Vision of Man* (London: Chatto & Windus, 1971), 160.
71. *The Complete Poems, op. cit.*, 148–149.
72. Martin Heidegger quoted in Clark, *op. cit.*, 58.
73. John Parham, "Editorial" in *Green Letters* 14 (2011): 5.

Works Cited

Adorno, Theodor W., and Max Horkheimer. *Dialectic of Enlightenment*. London: Verso, 1997, repr. 2010.
Arnold, Matthew. *The Poems of Matthew Arnold, 1840–1867*. London: Oxford University Press, 1913, repr. 1937.
Bibby, Cyril, ed. *The Essence of T. H. Huxley*. London: Macmillan, 1967.
Clark, Timothy. *The Cambridge Introduction to Literature and the Environment*. Cambridge: Cambridge University Press, 2011.
Darwin, Charles. *The Origin of Species by Means of Natural Selection*. Ed. J. W. Burrow. Harmondsworth: Penguin, 1968, repr. 1984.
Dobson, Andrew, ed. *The Green Reader*. London: André Deutsch, 1991.
Ebbatson, Roger. *Lawrence and the Nature Tradition: A Theme in English Fiction, 1859–1914*. Sussex: Harvester Press, 1980.
Gibson, James. *Thomas Hardy: A Literary Life*. London: Macmillan, 1996.
Gilmour, Robin. *The Victorian Period: The Intellectual and Cultural Context of English Literature, 1830–90*. Harlow: Longman, 1993.
Hardy, Thomas. *The Complete Poems*. Ed. James Gibson. Basingstoke: Palgrave, 2001.
_____. *The Dynasts*. London: Macmillan, 1978.
_____. *The Life and Work of Thomas Hardy*. Ed. Michael Millgate. Basingstoke: Macmillan, 1984, repr. 1985.
_____. *Under the Greenwood Tree*. Ed. Simon Gatrell. Oxford: Oxford University Press, 1985, repr. 1992.
_____. *Wessex Poems*. Ryburn: Keele University Press, 1995.
Harvey, Geoffrey. *The Complete Critical Guide to Thomas Hardy*. London: Routledge, 2003.
Heidegger, Martin. *Basic Writings*. Ed. David Farrell Krell. London: Routledge, 2011.
Hynes, Samuel. *The Pattern of Hardy's Poetry*. Chapel Hill: University of North Carolina Press, 1961, repr. 1966.
Johnson, Trevor. *Thomas Hardy*. London: Evans, 1968, repr. 1971.
Kerridge, Richard. "Ecological Hardy" in *Beyond Nature Writing: Expanding the Bound-*

aries of Ecocriticism. Ed. Karla Armbruster and Kathleen R. Wallace. Charlottesville: University Press of Virginia, 2000, repr. 2001, 126–142.

Latour, Bruno. *Politics of Nature: How to Bring the Sciences into Democracy*. Transl. Catherine Porter. Cambridge, MA: Harvard University Press, 2004.

Leopold, Aldo. *A Sand County Almanac and Sketches Here and There*. London: Oxford University Press, 1949, repr. 1968.

Merchant, Carolyn. *The Death of Nature: Women, Ecology, and the Scientific Revolution*. San Francisco: Harper & Row, 1990.

Parham, John. "Editorial," in *Green Letters* 14 (2011): 5–9.

Pinion, F. B. *A Commentary on the Poems of Thomas Hardy*. London: Macmillan, 1976.

Purdy, Richard Little, and Michael Millgate, eds. *The Collected Letters of Thomas Hardy, Volume Three: 1902–1908*. Oxford: Clarendon Press, 1982.

Purdy, Richard Little. *Thomas Hardy: A Bibliographical Study*. London: The British Library, 2002.

Richards, Bernard. *English Poetry of the Victorian Period, 1830–90*. London: Pearson, 2001.

Roppen, Georg. *Evolution and Poetic Belief: A Study in Some Victorian and Modern Writers*. Oslo: Oslo University Press, 1956.

Rutland, W. R. *Thomas Hardy: A Study of His Writings and Their Background*. Oxford: Basil Blackwell, 1938.

Schweik, Robert. "The Influence of Religion, Science, and Philosophy on Hardy's Writings," in *The Cambridge Companion to Thomas Hardy*. Ed. Dale Kramer. Cambridge: Cambridge University Press, 1999, repr. 2003, 54–72.

Simpson, John A., and Edmund S. C. Weiner, eds. *Oxford English Dictionary*. Oxford: Clarendon Press, 1989.

Southerington, F. R. *Hardy's Vision of Man*. London: Chatto & Windus, 1971.

Tait, Adrian. "'The Mother Mourns': The Ecocentric Impulse in the Poetry of Thomas Hardy," in *Green Letters* 14 (2011): 57–71.

Turner, Paul. *The Life of Thomas Hardy*. Oxford: Blackwell, 1998, repr. 2001.

Whymper, Edward. *Scrambles Amongst the Alps*. London: Thomas Nelson, 1900.

Wilson, Edward O. *Consilience: The Unity of Knowledge*. New York: Alfred A. Knopf, 1998, repr. 2000.

Zietlow, Paul. *Moments of Vision*. Cambridge, MA: Harvard University Press, 1974.

Reclaiming English Bones
Corporeal Commemoration in Hardy's War Poems
Melanie East

> [T]hese chronicles, even when they become musty with age, may be interesting not only to descendants of the family but to others who are not of their blood or name. It often has happened that an account of what befell particular individuals in unusual circumstances has conveyed a more vivid picture of those circumstances than a comprehensive view of them has been able to raise.[1]

Hardy wrote these lines just over a month before the end of the First World War in an introduction to *A Book of Remembrance*, the record of one Dorset family's wartime participation—a work that prizes the account of "particular individuals" over a "comprehensive view" of the Great War. For Hardy, an almost obsessive memorialist,[2] this brief piece provided another opportunity to shape the memory of the war for posterity by foregrounding the stories of particular individuals rather than contributing to a more generalized national memory—an opportunity Hardy never seems to have taken lightly. Later, he was given the similarly intimate task of designing and inscribing a memorial tablet for eleven fallen staff members of the Dorchester Post Office, which included their names and a fragment of his own poem, "Embarcation."[3] Besides simple commemorative projects like these, Hardy's poetic response to war was far more complex: he abhorred conflict, yet was drawn to write about it throughout his career as he attempted to capture the spirit of the personal memorial in tension with that of the group. Anyone who has studied Hardy's fiction and even his own autobiographical comments will be familiar with the author's insistence that he never presents a unified view of life or consistent philosophy, but rather, records "mere impressions."[4] Yet in the case of his war poetry, the political nature of the subject and his varied responses compel critics to search for more than these "mere impressions."

Conflict in Hardy's War Poetry

For most, the challenge is not in reading his Boer War poems, which reflect a pacifism we might expect of a novelist concerned with the tragedies of rabbits and birds, but in reading some of his poems of the Great War, which are informed by a surprisingly martial tenor, and which critics have generally dismissed. Even Paul Fussell's seminal study on how literary responses to the Great War shaped modern memory deals almost solely with Hardy's *Satires of Circumstance*, published before the war, and barely touches on his actual poetry about the war.[5] Similarly, Jahan Ramazani, one of Hardy's more generous critics, only includes "Drummer Hodge" when using war poetry to build his argument for Hardy as the first of modern elegists.[6] In all, Hardy's Great War poems are generally regarded as a blip in an otherwise respected body of war poetry comprised of the Boer War verses in *Poems of the Past and the Present* and *The Dynasts*. With the possible exception of a couple, Hardy's World War I verses fall under that category of war poems that has been Othered as patriotic and naïve in comparison to the more privileged position of Trench Poetry in shaping collective memory. Samuel Hynes has argued that Hardy's Great War poems were, amongst other things, "trite," "martial," "propagandistic," and embarrassing to admirers of his better lyrics.[7] Ultimately, he feels that Hardy "accepted the lies that war demanded, and imposed on his sense of the war's reality the romantic falsehood of wartime convention."[8] Yet Hynes has noted elsewhere that what was needed in the poetry emerging at the beginning of the war was a departure from the past that "rejected the old idealism, the exaltation and the escape of the spirit and all that."[9] Arguably, Hardy's war poems, even those of the Great War, do indeed reject idealism and even more specifically, an idealized "escape of the spirit." Hardy brought his own peculiar preoccupations and imaginative capital to the poems of both wars, and though they differ from the shocking, visceral responses of the soldiers that we have come to associate with an "authentic" war literature, many of them have their own unique power. Hardy's war poetry incorporates themes and concerns from the rest of his oeuvre, specifically, a fixation on bodies, graves, and the magical properties they infuse into a space through memory and associations. Thus, by shifting the focus to Hardy's anxieties about the breakdown of this relationship between body and space and its implications for English identity, readers may see a pattern in some of his odd inconsistencies that detracts from a view of his war poems as jingoistic and propagandistic in the most distasteful, narrow sense.

Revisiting Hardy and Englishness

Vital contributions to Hardy studies were made in the late 1980s and 1990s by Peter Widdowson and others who opened up more political, ideologically engaged conceptions of Hardy's work outside the de-historicized commonplace of Hardy as a pastoral writer.[10] Hardy's perceived contribution to Englishness has often been as memorialist of the rural, idyllic England of the past.[11] While Hardy certainly focused on a regional identity and history, Wessex was often used as a stand-in for an overarching, timeless English identity; however, the author of *A Laodicean* and *Jude the Obscure* clearly perceived that any viable, modern identity could not be grounded in the fictions of the past. Little has been done, though, in the area of historicizing his war poetry in terms of its resistance to a certain type of Englishness. One exception is James Whitehead's 2004 re-assessment of Hardy and national identity, which importantly argues that in certain of his "minor" novels and war poems, Hardy intentionally exploits a depiction of Englishness abroad to challenge the imperial attitudes in the construct of English identity. Whitehead emphasizes the importance of reading the Boer War poems in context by taking into account the way in which Hardy deviates from the celebration of empire common in the works of many of his contemporaries, such as Henry Newbolt and Kipling.[12] Whitehead further notes that in his frequent focus on the suffering of other countries in the Great War poems Hardy's "interest in England and Englishness remains subservient to a broader sense of international political responsibility," and that overall, his is a "positive poetic record."[13]

Whitehead's argument effectively re-positions Hardy's war poems away from the edges of his canon by proving them more commensurate with the tenor of the rest of his work. The focus, then, is on Hardy as an "internationalist," and much is made of Hardy's oft-quoted epistolary comment to Percy Ames that feelings of patriotism should be extended to the whole globe and that "*Foreignness*" should "attach only to other planets and inhabitants, if any."[14] While this statement accords with Hardy the evolutionary meliorist, the notion that he could be at home anywhere on the planet, and that *foreign* should be a concept limited only to extraterrestrials, does not exactly ring true if we note the frequency with which a particular, recurring speaker—a brooding, privileged witness who can visit the bodies and hear the voices of the dead overseas—is preoccupied with the specifically *British* dead. Several of the war poems reveal this persona's dismay at the loss of the physical presence of soldiers' bones, and the subsequent elision of particularity and heterogeneity in the construction of a national identity. Noting Hardy's attentiveness to bones and soil in his canon of war verse contributes, then, to Whitehead's conclusion that there is more to be done in the evaluation of Hardy's poetry and its role in shaping an English identity.[15]

Bones, Landscape and Memory

In Hardy's canon more broadly, the palimpsestic quality of the soil is an essential feature of Wessex scenery whereby traces of the past are literalized. Charnel bones are found in Egdon Heath, and in Casterbridge Roman soldiers are buried only a foot or two underground, reflecting Hardy's fixation on the relationship between bones, graves, and other physical markers of both local and national history. In a speech he wrote for the Society for the Protection of Ancient Buildings in 1906, Hardy draws a close link between the function of skeletal and architectural remains in his concept of memory. He ascribes a "spiritual attribute" to the work of preservation, which he insists is found in "human association." In the same speech, he laments the way in which bones are disinterred inside of churches to make room for structural changes and reinterred haphazardly, in one example alienating husband and wife from each other in an act of what he labels "facetious carelessness."[16] He sadly notes how often "plaintive records are lost to human notice" when headstones are shifted and jumbled together.[17] In Hardy's own life, such "human association" haunted many spaces, not the least of which was the church at St. Juliot where he had two plaques inscribed to commemorate the location of his first meeting with Emma. In fact, Hardy's inscription concludes: "as a record of his association with the church and neighbourhood."[18]

There are also several poems that imagine both chilling and comic descriptions of graves and their inhabitants such as "The Levelled Churchyard," "The Obliterate Tomb," "Transformations," and many others. In addition to these instances, his autobiography tells strange tales of bones. There are the "Romano-British urns and skeletons" discovered while excavating for the well at Max Gate,[19] and another story, an earlier one from the *Life*, relates a rather macabre episode while Hardy was working for Arthur Blomfield in London as an architect. In this instance, Hardy oversaw the relocation of remains in St. Pancras Churchyard where the railroad was scheduled to come through. The narrator describes him watching as human skeletons were exhumed from coffins, some of them crumbling apart when lifted.[20] Today in St. Pancras churchyard stands the Hardy Tree around which some of these graves were re-located. Appropriately, the tree has now grown into and over some of the headstones, so that the graves appear as organic extensions of the tree in a similar metamorphosis found in one of his well-known poems. "Transformations,"[21] from *Moments of Vision*, describes an almost identical scene and reveals the importance of the history of the soil to the speaker:

> Portion of this yew
> Is a man my grandsire knew,
> Bosomed here at its foot:
> This branch may be his wife,
> A ruddy human life
> Now turned to a green shoot.
>
> [...]
> And the fair girl long ago
> Whom I often tried to know
> May be entering this rose.
>
> So they are not underground,
> But as nerves and veins abound
> In the growths of upper air,
> [...].

In this poem, the dead are granted new life as they are organically subsumed into the vegetation. Here, the English landscape has become a literal historic record: the "nerves and veins" are part of the life of both the soil as well as the speaker, who remembers specific features of the dead. In a poem like "Transformations," Hardy imagines an almost mystical afterlife for dead bodies that is attentive to their particular associations: rather than neglecting individuality in favor of a homogenous historical identity, the persona retains a memory of the landscape comprised of the heterogeneous characteristics of the dead. In other words, this verse envisions the ideal bond between the dead, the landscape, and the living—an intimate relationship of memory and continuity that completely breaks down in the war poetry. Of course, such connections between bones, landscape, and identity can also be taken up in the discourses of authenticity and essentialism that drive ethno-nationalist projects; yet Hardy emphasizes particular memory in order to resist the generalized and often exclusionary construct of dominant memory.

This subtle sort of resistance is also at work in one of his best-known Great War poems, "In Time of 'The Breaking of Nations,'" which offers three vignettes of static rural life in ironic contrast to the violent tumult and chaos of war. The scenes of rural life are slow, silent, enduring, and despite, or even because of, their quotidian nature, they provide a sort of hopefulness in the face of chaos. The poem also ends with a contrast between two concurrent narratives and the assurance that the love story between the maid and her wight will live on as the annals of war are forgotten. Here, the particular stories of an individual community are privileged over the official "annals" that recount conflicts. Hardy's poem is neither pro- or anti-war, but rather, it shifts the focalization away from accounts of either glory or horror, and immortalizes the daily experience of the home front that is often neglected in narratives of war.

Lost Bones of the Boer War

If poems such as "Transformations" and "In Time of 'The Breaking of Nations'" enact the ideal connection between particular memory and space, then poems dealing with the divorce of dead soldiers from the English landscape highlight a physical loss to the historic record—a loss that is central to the persona's horror at war.

The clearest expression of a loss to English landscape is found in "Drummer Hodge,"[22]—perhaps the best known of all the Boer War poems. It was originally entitled "The Dead Drummer" when first published in *Literature* in November 1899, and the following note was added to the title upon publication: "One of the Drummers killed was a native of a village near Casterbridge."[23] On the one hand, dedicating this threnody to a particular Dorset son is representative of Hardy's desire to capture "human association"; yet the irony of the term *hodge* and the unsettling content of the poem are also indicative of the persona's dismay at the loss of this human association, both in the physical loss of bones, as well as in the loss of a particular soldier's identity and his place in a diverse national identity. Although it is useful to look at the way in which this poem resists the discourses of imperial war, as Whitehead has done, it is also important to look at how it registers a fracture in English identity that excludes the particularity of the farm laborer through the derisory epithet, Hodge. Hardy's 1883 essay "The Dorsetshire Labourer" is concerned with essentializing the particular identities of rural inhabitants and he rejects the pejorative nickname that creates what he calls a "uniform collection of concrete Hodges."[24] In this war poem, he emphasizes the dehumanization of the body lost to foreign soil by labeling him Hodge, and arguably even uses the term ironically to underscore not only his unknown identity to the Dutch, but quite possibly to the English officers as well, since the "They" at the opening of the poem are Othered from both the speaker and Hodge, and are (ironically) lumped into an homogenous group in the way Hodge has been. Thus, there are several levels of estrangement here: Hodge is not only alienated from English soil, but also from the fellow officers and those of Hardy's readership that employ the term at home. In other words, this poem departs from the romanticized narrative of English brothers-in-arms fighting for a collectively imagined homeland.

While the poem resists a depiction of unified Englishness overseas, it also reflects the speaker's anxiety over a national memory that misses these particular bones as part of the soil. The thrust of the poem is the persona's horror at Hodge's remote resting place. Poor Hodge is thrown into an unmarked South African grave "just as found," where instead of a tombstone, a "kopje-crest" marks his grave within a "veldt" (l. 2–3). This glaringly alien scenery is of vast importance to the persona. As seen earlier in "Transformations," the dead literally live on in the flora of the landscape, yet instead of mixing with Wessex soil, Hodge's vegetable reincarnation will be as "some Southern tree" (l. 16). The elegy's topos of "stellification," the subject's elevation into a new celestial body, is also present, but inverted where only "foreign constellations" (l. 5), "strange stars" (l. 12), and "strange-eyed constellations" (l. 17) stare down from the sky overhead. As Ramazani has noted, "Hardy teasingly recalls these transfigurations, but denies such an apotheosis to his dead soldier."[25] Thus, this is not simply a rejection of war and the patriotic jingoism used to support it—the poem demonstrates a concern for the loss of a body to foreign soil.

Rupert Brooke's well-known Great War poem, "The Soldier,"[26] employs the similar trope of the soldier's body lost overseas, but with a far different sentiment. Brooke's speaker pleads for his English readers to remember "That there's some corner of a foreign field/ That is forever England. There shall be / In that rich earth a richer dust concealed" (l. 2–4). These lines immortalize the fallen English soldier by appropriating a corner of foreign land. Tom Lawson points out that as British cemeteries overseas were officially transferred to the British government in World War I, they also captured the national imagination as sacred space enriched by English blood. The term *Holy Land* was even employed, alongside the language of empire, to mark the soil where English bodies lay.[27] Brooke echoes this rhetoric as he, like Hardy's earlier persona, sees a connection between bones and the landscape. In Hardy's poem though, rather than seeing a chance for England's gain, the persona only recognizes England's loss. Moreover, according to Brooke's speaker, the dead soldier retains a "pulse in the Eternal mind" (l. 10); yet, the only place in England's memory for Hardy's soldier is in the persona's poem, since as a Hodge, his particular memory is already effaced. Thus, in "Drummer Hodge" a part of England becomes a piece of the foreign, rather than a piece of the foreign becoming a part of England.

"A Christmas Ghost Story,"[28] another of the Boer War poems, opens with a speaker who shares similar concerns to the one in "Drummer Hodge," thus adding to the sense that there is a recurring persona preoccupied with the English dead. Though the pathos of this poem is significantly derived from the speech of the dead soldier, the persona's introductory lines affiliate this verse with the other war poems. From the very first line the speaker evokes images of an alien landscape, establishing the setting as "South of the Line, inland from far Durban" (l. 1), before moving on to directly address his auditors. In the second line he laments that in this distant land "A mouldering soldier lies—your countryman" (l. 2). This is a reminder that the dead bodies *belong* to the speaker and his English audience. The rhetorical pause indicated by the dash suggests that his audience needs this jarring reminder, as if the soldier has been forgotten. Samuel Hynes recounts a reaction to this poem in the *Daily Chronicle* that claimed the dead soldier was "a fine conception, but we fear that soldier is Mr. Hardy's soldier, and not one of the Dublin Fusiliers who cried amidst the storm of bullets at Tugela, 'Let us make a name for ourselves!'"[29] This response reveals how much Hardy departed from ruling versions of the English war dead. While the larger theme of the poem is a more universal yearning for world peace, the introduction to the poem again foregrounds the persona's preoccupation with lost bones and the danger of forgetting soldiers that do not fit the accepted type.

"The Souls of the Slain,"[30] another eerie poem of the Boer War, also dramatizes a conflict between particular memory and official rhetoric. In this poem, the persona's location is altered: instead of the bird's-eye-view over South Africa he held in the last two poems, he stands here on English ground, specifically the Portland Bill, which is characterized as "Many-caverned, bald, wrinkled of face" (l. 4)—a description suggestive of its age (as well as the persona's) and its unique geologic pockmarks, which, like human remains, are part of both English and local identity. As the persona broods alone in the dark night he witnesses a trail of "frameless souls" (l. 22) flying by him overhead on their return to England. The "sprites without mould" (l. 21) that he watches are not ghosts who appear with ghostly bodies, but on the contrary, they are souls shorn of the bodies that have clearly been left behind on the "earth's nether bord" (l. 27). This time the souls of the slain are on their way "homeward and hearthward" to "feast on their fame" and honor as soldiers (l. 35). Here, the essence of England is conjured in home and hearth, which these souls attempt to reclaim. However, many of them soon discover this reclamation is impossible, because their sacrifice is no longer important— some of them have even been forgotten altogether, and the story they were fed about the glories of war has proven false. Rather than remembering the soldiers for their bravery in war, which is the type of commemoration promised them in official, public, and even literary discourse, they are only remembered in their particularity. Mothers remember them as sons, and wives remember their "Deeds of home" (l. 63) and "Ancient words that were kindly expressed or unkindly" (l. 65). At the end, those lucky souls who were good fly home, while "those of bitter traditions" (l. 83) plunge into the forgotten regions of the sea. In a jarring simile, the speaker compares the rush of the souls who fly home to the Pentecost Wind, an allusion connoting both universality and particularity in the miracle that made the same Word recognizable in each person's own language simultaneously. Importantly though, *Wind* is paired with *thinned*, indicating the dying out of the holy wind so that the speaker himself is unable to hear or experience the transcendental message it brings. The memories of the individual soldiers are not accessible to him, as their physical bodies are missing from the rich, historical soil of the sort beneath his feet at the Bill. The Pentecost wind rushes away, and as a thinly veiled Hardy, the speaker is left with only sea-mutterings in its stead. In the end, the rhetoric of bravery and glory, of national pride and imperial bombast fails to stand up in "Souls of the Slain," and though some lucky few may be remembered at home, the associations of so many soldiers are lost in the metaphoric turbulence of the sea off of Portland Bill.

The Tension of Supporting and Resisting English Identity in the Great War Poems

While most of the Boer War poems are more easily assimilated into common perceptions of Hardy as a pacifist and, arguably, memorialist, some of his Great War poems are more difficult to identify as anything other than concessions to the popular tropes of the day. Yet identifying a similar preoccupation with a national identity built on various particular associations between bones and landscape provides a fresh perspective on continuities between both sequences of poems. Specifically, in "Before Marching and After," "Men Who March Away," and "A Call to National Service" the connection between England's land and identity is still present; however, in these poems where the persona has heard the rumblings of war just across the sea in "Channel Firing" (1914) the more imminent threat to English soil makes pacifism less of an option. The shift in the persona's perspective towards war parallels a shift in Hardy himself as reflected in a letter to F. A. Duneka written right after the outbreak of World War I. On September 28, 1914, he wrote: "You will know what a man of peace I am, & how ugly a thing war at its best is to me; but events proved to me with startling rapidity that there was no other course for us but to fight."[31] Hardy clearly felt convicted of England's justified entry into the war, since he added his name to an "Authors' Declaration" published in *The Times* only a short time after it began. Along with most of England's other literary luminaries, Hardy supported a declaration claiming war was unavoidable for Britain, who could not have refused without dishonor to defend Belgium and France.[32] In addition, these authors had been requested by the new Department of Information to issue public literary statements supporting England's entry into the conflict.[33]

Hardy's response to the government's call was to go home and write "Men Who March Away,"[34] which depicts a skeptical onlooker watching the departure of the troops. In a 1914 letter to Sidney Cockerell, Hardy indicated that he is the "friend with the musing eye."[35] Although the principal voice of the poem this time belongs to a soldier, the verse is addressed to a similar persona from the Boer war poems, whose doubt undercuts any sense of uncritical patriotism. In the face of such uncertainty, the soldier feels compelled to justify the reason for marching. Suitable to the repetitive stanzas and simple closed rhyme, the soldier also repeats the stock phrases of martial rhetoric that he has clearly consumed and must depend upon. The second last stanza, most obviously, repeats a sort of consolatory ideology that in both the Boer War poems and the rest of the Great War poems proves false: he assures himself that "Victory crowns the just" and more importantly, that "braggarts must/ Surely bite the dust" (l. 23–25). The insertion of "surely" after "must" suggests doubt, as if the extra word convinces him. We also see in the Boer War poems and in the Great War poems on the devastation in Belgium that it is *not* only braggarts who bite the dust. However, while the soldier's assurance that "victory crowns the just" may sound empty to the pessimistic observer, the soldier's claim that "England's need are we;/ Her distress would leave us rueing" (l. 18-19) would resonate with this onlooker if he is indeed the speaker of the past poems. Like the marching soldier, Hardy's persona would "rue" England's "distress." The persona of the earlier poems, so concerned with what was lost overseas, may be even more concerned with the direct threat to the English landscape—a threat more possible in World War I than in the Boer War.

Viewed by Whitehead as the "companion poem" to "Men Who March Away," "Before Marching and After"[36] is, like "Drummer Hodge," dedicated to the loss of a local native.[37] What differentiates the grave imagery in this poem, however, is its more hopeful tone. In contrast to the ironically generalized Hodge, the dead soldier subject of this poem is specifically named through his initials in the subtitle as Hardy's relation, Second Lieutenant F. W. George, who was killed in 1915.[38] In the poem, Hardy's persona reflects on the same connection between Englishness and landscape, yet unlike Hodge, Hardy's cousin is memorialized at home and in this way is reclaimed to the soil. As seen at the end of "Drummer Hodge," this poem begins with the visual backdrop of constellations and countryside:

> Orion swung southward aslant
> Where the starved Egdon pine-trees had thinned,
> The Pleiads aloft seemed to pant
> With the heather that twitched in the wind; [l. 1–4]

The imagery here invokes familiar Egdon and its lush heather and pine-trees, both of which offer a sense of home and identity completely opposite from the alien backdrop of "Drummer Hodge." Moreover, the soldier, still at home in Wessex, stands looking out at Orion and the Pleiads and even speaks to the "spring starlight" (l. 12). Hence, in this poem the constellations are a source of familiarity and comfort, and in a sense, perform the stellification characteristic of the traditional elegy. Hardy intentionally keeps his setting focused in Dorset, fixing his cousin in the home environment of the first two stanzas, and thereby memorializing him within a space that retains some semblance of cosmic order and meaning, despite the senselessness of death's "game." Though lacking any real idealization or apotheosis, the poem offers the sort of consolation for a relative (and his family members) that Hardy resists elsewhere. The dangerous "game" being played out on the Continent, and the simple fact that the body will never return home still haunt the background, but as a personal memorial for family, Hardy intentionally provides a degree of peace. In other words, this Great War poem enacts the reclamation of family bones metaphorically rather than physically, reflecting a similar preoccupation over bodies and local landscape for Hardy.

"A Call to National Service"[39] poses perhaps the biggest challenge to scholars attempting to make sense of Hardy's poetic response to war and account for what seems uncharacteristic in him. Rather than attempting an apologetics for a poem that was quite literally written to encourage enlistment, it is more productive to note the presence of some of the common threads that run through his war poetry. Read in the context of the Boer War poems and "Men Who March Away" this poem reveals the old concern for English soil and an acute sense that England is under threat, which necessitates action. A letter to Edmund Gosse in 1918 suggests an anxiety at the proximity of the war after rumors that submarines were spotted about the shore of Portland.[40] Whether or not Hardy feared a threat to English soil when he wrote "A Call to National Service," he revived the old anxieties of the persona as well as the soldier's claim that "England's need are we," and used these in the rhetoric of his call to arms. Whereas the persona previously focused his lament on the *loss* of English bodies, in "A Call to National Service" there is a focus on the threat to English *soil*. The speaker reminds his auditors that now is not the time to "leave our land/ Untended as a wild of weeds and sand" (l. 4–5). The wilderness imagery here indicates emptiness, the emptiness of a land without memorialized markers of its past and identity. The prospect of weeds also raises anxieties in the speaker who sees an organic connection between physical remains and the flora in "Transformations." Though a common martial trope, the call to defend land reflects the same preoccupation with preserving the English identity of the landscape. If Hardy felt compelled to join the war effort, it was not simply the case that war fired his imagination, but rather, his compulsion stemmed from a concern evident in the rest of his work.

Despite its late date, "A Call to National Service" was not Hardy's final response to war. Hardy submitted "And There Was a Great Calm" at the request of *The Times* for its special Armistice Day section of November 11, 1920, that was to commemorate the burial of the Unknown Warrior in Westminster Abbey. For a poet so often inspired by the resting place of bones, the widely anticipated ceremony readily provided material for one of his characteristic meditations on bodies and soil. Yet, *The Later Years* recounts the circumstances surrounding the request for the poem and that Hardy at first felt "disinclined, and all but refused, being generally unable to write to order. In the middle of the night, however, an idea seized him, and he was heard moving about the house looking things up. The poem was duly written and proved worthy of the occasion."[41] Though Hardy eventually consented to write the poem, his imagination does not appear to have been fired by the prospect of writing about the homecoming of English bones, despite the centrality of this theme to many of his verses. It is striking that the poem makes no reference to the repatriation of these remains: rather than fanning the strident nationalist fervor surrounding the day's events, he focuses on the end of war, and very conspicuously, on soldiers in general, rather than on English soldiers for this moment of great British unity.

Burying the Unknown Warrior was very much an appeal to a national imaginary that connected the triumphant (though broken and mourning) England with the Britain of the past through the title "Warrior," which was chosen over the other options of "Combatant," "Comrade," and "Fighting Man," and carries with it connotations of a past heroic age that inspired one newspaper even to label him the "Unknown Arthur."[42] Katherine Verdery has argued that in national events surrounding politicized dead bodies, "nationalisms are forms of ancestor cult, writ large enough to encompass localized kin-group affiliations. [...] [T]o rebury a dead person is not simply to reassess his place in history; it is to revise national genealogies, inserting the person as an ancestor more centrally into the lineage of honoured forebears."[43] Of course, being buried in the Abbey, an honored ancestor is what the Unknown became. On the one hand it was a tribute to the dead soldiers he represented to be elevated to the status of the nation's most prominent, for his epitaph was later revised to include the Biblical lines: "THEY BURIED HIM AMONG THE KINGS BECAUSE HE/ HAD DONE GOOD TOWARD GOD AND TOWARD/ HIS HOUSE"[44]; yet on the other hand, his bones served as a repository of consolatory platitudes and constructed Englishness.

At the repatriation ceremony Kipling's "Recessional"[45] was rolled out and included on the order of service in Westminster Abbey, and while its sober warning for the future of the empire and its call for humility were fitting for the service, his words were still being used to bolster a national image of humble England in mourning that referred to Britain's "Dominion over palm and pine" (l. 4), its "power" (l. 19), and "lesser breeds without the law" (l. 22). In other words, the burial of the Unknown Warrior provided another instance for uniting England and Empire and even connecting the Unknown to Victoria's glorious reign through the poem written for her Diamond Jubilee. For some critics, tombs like that of the Unknown Warrior are often sites of the "dominant memory" usually "of the community's leading social and political groups."[46] In *Imagined Communities* Benedict Anderson suggests that tombs of Unknown soldiers are the most "arresting emblems of the modern culture of nationalism" as they are "saturated with ghostly *national* imaginings."[47] As an emblem, the blankness of the Unknown's identity begged to be filled in, and so was quickly overwritten with a script of English humility and granted characteristics of an embodied, ideal British identity. A *Times* special correspondent in the Armistice Day edition even characterized the unknown soldier with a

> simple, wholesome face; rough he was and abrupt of speech [...]. And we knew him over there, in his billets, grousing, but wonderfully tender and helpful to the peasants whom he incommoded, to the little children and the patient, hard-worked French "mother" [...]. Bravery was his as a matter of course, as much a part of him as his humour, his tenderness, or his discontent.[48]

Thus, as memorials like this one proliferated, a homogenous identity was crystallized in the mythology of the Unknown Warrior, and a metonymic relationship was forged between the bones and the national character they represented. In 1923 the Unknown Warrior was even bestowed the title of Principal Knight and Supreme Head of the Order of Crusaders—a new patriotic organization—which was an honor the Unknown Warrior could hardly accept of his own volition.[49] This type of organization was similar to the Royal Society of St. George, a patriotic society for which Hardy declined a request to be vice-president a few months after the Unknown Warrior was buried.[50] In other words, though Hardy was deeply concerned with national history and cultural property, his war poetry generally omits the type of official, unified Englishness of the war and post-war years.

There were, of course, poets who were far more explicit in their resistance to national memorials of the war dead, such as Sassoon's angry response to the new Menin Gate. Completed only months before Hardy's death by Sir Reginald Blomfield, nephew of Hardy's early mentor, it was designed to commemorate the British cemetery in Belgium and was later derided by Sassoon in his poem "On Passing the New Menin Gate"[51] as a "sepulcher of crime" (l. 14) dedicated to those of the "nameless names" (l. 12). There is also the American example from a few years later in James Weldon Johnson's poem "St. Peter Relates an Incident of the Resurrection Day,"[52] wherein the American Unknown shocks everyone on Resurrection Day by being African American. While Hardy's poem is less obviously subversive, "And There Was A Great Calm" is not celebratory of the dead soldiers' sacrifice[53] and ends provocatively with an unanswered "Why?"

Hardy's war poems that do imagine the bodies of the dead, or that are concerned with soil and landscape do not resonate with the popular tropes of the day, and as Whitehead notes of his Boer War poems, they deserve to be measured by how they deviate from the work of his contemporaries. In a statement that would surely have appealed to Hardy, Katherine Verdery considers how the contested terrain of dead bodies and collective imagination might "enchant" and "enliven" the consideration of politics:

> [I]nstead of seeing nationalism, for instance, in the usual way—as a matter of territorial borders, state-making, "constructionism," or resource competition—I see it as part of kinship, spirits, ancestor worship, and the circulation of cultural treasures. Rather than speak of legitimacy, I speak of reordering the meaningful universe. I present the politics of corpses as being less about legitimating new governments (though it can be that, too) than about cosmologies and practices relating the living and the dead.[54]

In his own time, Hardy certainly saw the connection between bodies and nationhood in a similar way. Rather than contributing to a national political identity, Hardy's concern with bones is with a magical property that relates the living to the dead and to the past in the way "Transformations" imagines. The tension in Hardy's war poems then, is between resisting the popular rhetoric that shapes England's imagined community, and reminding his readers of the forgotten bodies of particular soldiers that were all part of a diffuse, heterogeneous identity ideally maintained through physical, present reminders of their absence.

Notes

1. Thomas Hardy, *Thomas Hardy's Public Voice: The Essays, Speeches, and Miscellaneous Prose,* ed. Michael Millgate (Oxford: Clarendon Press, 2001), 393.

2. See Michael Millgate's essay "Hardy as Memorialist" in *Thomas Hardy's Public Voice, op. cit.*, 475–482. Among other examples, Millgate notes that following Emma's death, Hardy became preoccupied with locating and preserving the various graves of her family members (478).

3. *Ibid.*, 481.

4. "General Preface to the Novels and Poems" for the 1912 Wessex Edition of Hardy's works in *Thomas Hardy's Personal Writings*, ed. Harold Orel (London: Macmillan, 1966, repr. 1967), 49.

5. See Paul Fussell, *The Great War and Modern Memory* (New York: Oxford University Press, 1975), 3–38 (chapter one, "A Satire of Circumstance").

6. Jahan Ramazani, *Poetry of Mourning: The Modern Elegy from Hardy to Heaney* (Chicago: University of Chicago Press, 1994).

7. Samuel Hynes, "Hardy and the Battle God," in *Thomas Hardy Reappraised: Essays in Honour of Michael Millgate*, ed. Keith Wilson (Toronto: University of Toronto Press, 2006), 256.

8. *Ibid.*, 254.

9. Samuel Hynes, *A War Imagined: The First World War and English Culture* (London: Bodley Head, Ltd., 1990), 30.

10. See in particular, Chapter One, "The Critical Constitution of 'Thomas Hardy'" in Peter Widdowson, *Hardy in History: A Study in Literary Sociology* (London: Routledge, 1989).

11. See Martin J. Wiener, *English Culture and Decline of the Industrial Spirit: 1850–1980* (Cambridge: Cambridge University Press, 1981, 2d. ed., 2004). Wiener explains how a mixture of "pastoral retreatism" and "nostalgic lament" in the face of rising industrialism led to a disproportionate emphasis on the rural aspect of Hardy's work, reducing it to a "one-dimensional" representation of a timeless England (52–53). See also Widdowson, "The Critical Constitution of 'Thomas Hardy,'" *op. cit.*

12. James Whitehead, "Hardy and Englishness," in *Palgrave Advances in Thomas Hardy Studies*, ed. Phillip Mallett (Basingstoke: Palgrave Macmillan, 2004), 210.

13. *Ibid.*, 223.

14. *The Collected Letters of Thomas Hardy*, eds. Richard Little Purdy and Michael Millgate, Vol. 5: 1920–1925 (Oxford: Clarendon Press, 1978), 202.

15. See Whitehead in Mallett (ed.), *op. cit.* Whitehead concludes: "A liberal at heart, politically engaged in a literary sense and yet avoiding active participation in politics, Hardy provides an extended analysis of Englishness that deserves wider critical notice" (226).

16. Thomas Hardy, "Memories of Church Restoration," in *Thomas Hardy, Conservation Architect: His Work for the Society for the Protection of Ancient Buildings, with a Variorum Edition of "Memories of Church Restoration"* (1906), ed. C J. P. Beatty (Dorchester: Dorset Natural History and Archaeological Society, 1995), 74.

17. *Ibid.*, 74.

18. Millgate in *Thomas Hardy's Public Voice, op. cit.*, 480.

19. Thomas Hardy, *The Life and Work of Thomas Hardy*, ed. Michael Millgate (London: The Macmillan Press, Ltd., 1984), 169.

20. *Ibid.*, 47.

21. *The Works of Thomas Hardy* (Hertfordshire: Wordsworth Editions, Ltd., 1994), 443.

22. *Ibid.*, 83.
23. Richard Little Purdy, *Thomas Hardy: A Bibliographic Study* (London: Oxford University Press, 1954), 109.
24. Thomas Hardy, "The Dorsetshire Labourer" (1883), The Dorset Page, http://www.thedorsetpage.com/genealogy/info/the_dorsetshire_labourer.htm, accessed 14 September 2012.
25. Ramazani, *op. cit.*, 42.
26. Rupert Brooke, "The Soldier" (1914) in *The Longman's Anthology of British Literature*, Vol. 2C, ed. David Damrosch (New York: Addison-Wesley Educational Publishers Inc., 1999), 2226.
27. Tom Lawson, "The Free-Masonry of Sorrow? National Identities and the Memorialization of the Great War in Britain, 1919-1931," in *History & Memory* 20.1 (2009): 109.
28. *The Works of Thomas Hardy, op. cit.*, 82.
29. Quoted in Hynes, "Hardy and the Battle God," *op. cit.*, 250.
30. *The Works of Thomas Hardy, op. cit.*, 84-87.
31. *The Collected Letters of Thomas Hardy, op. cit.*, 52.
32. Hynes, *A War Imagined, op. cit.*, 27.
33. *Ibid.*, 26.
34. *The Works of Thomas Hardy, op. cit.*, 506-507.
35. *The Collected Letters of Thomas Hardy, op. cit.*, 48.
36. *The Works of Thomas Hardy, op. cit.*, 512-513.
37. James Whitehead, "Thomas Hardy and the First World War Companion Poems: 'Men Who March Away' and 'Before Marching And After'" in *The Thomas Hardy Journal* 15.3 (1999): 85.
38. *Ibid.*, 85.
39. *The Works of Thomas Hardy, op. cit.*, 514.
40. *The Collected Letters of Thomas Hardy, op. cit.*, 249.
41. Florence Emily Hardy, *The Later Years of Thomas Hardy, 1892-1928* (New York: Macmillan, 1930), 214-215.
42. Stephen Goebel, *The Great War and Medieval Memory: War, Remembrance and Medievalism in Britain and Germany, 1914-1940* (Cambridge: Cambridge University Press, 2007), 34.
43. Katherine Verdery, *The Political Lives of Dead Bodies: Reburial and Postsocialist Change* (New York: Columbia University Press, 1999), 104-105.
44. K. S. Inglis, "Entombing Unknown Soldiers: From London and Paris to Baghdad," in *History & Memory* 5.2 (Fall-Winter 1993): 7-31.
45. Rudyard Kipling, "Recessional" (1897) in *The Longman's Anthology of British Literature, op. cit.*, 1811-1812.
46. Daniel J. Sherman, *The Construction of Memory in Interwar France* (Chicago: University of Chicago Press, 1999), 7.
47. Benedict Anderson, *Imagined Communities: Reflections on the Origin and Spread of Nationalism* (London: Verso, 2006), 9.
48. "The Unknown Warrior," in *The London Times* (11 November 1920), 15. *The Times Digital Archive*, 1785-1985, http://www.thetimes.co.uk/tto/archive/, accessed 15 September 2014.
49. Inglis, *op. cit.*, 19.

50. *Thomas Hardy's Public Voice, op. cit.*, 407.
51. Siegfried Sassoon, "On Passing the New Menin Gate" (1928), www.poemhunter.com/best-poems/siegfried-sassoon/on-passing-the-new-menin-gate/, accessed 1 Aug 2014.
52. James Weldon Johnson, "St. Peter Relates an Incident of the Resurrection Day" (1930) in *Complete Poems*, ed. Sondra Kathryn Wilson (New York: Penguin Books, 2000), 49–54.
53. Hynes, "Hardy and the Battle God," *op. cit.*, 258.
54. Verdery, *op. cit.*, 26.

Works Cited

Anderson, Benedict. *Imagined Communities: Reflections on the Origin and Spread of Nationalism*. London: Verso, 2006.

Beatty, Claudius J. P., ed. *Thomas Hardy, Conservation Architect: His Work for the Society for the Protection of Ancient Buildings, with a Variorum Edition of "Memories of Church Restoration"* (1906). Dorchester: Dorset Natural History and Archaeological Society, 1995.

Damrosch, David, ed. *The Longman's Anthology of British Literature*. New York: Addison-Wesley Educational Publishers, Inc, 1999.

Fussell, Paul. *The Great War and Modern Memory*. New York: Oxford University Press, 1975.

Goebel, Stephen. *The Great War and Medieval Memory: War, Remembrance and Medievalism in Britain and Germany, 1914–1940*. Cambridge: Cambridge University Press, 2007.

Hardy, Florence Emily. *The Later Years of Thomas Hardy, 1892–1928*. New York: Macmillan, 1930.

Hardy, Thomas. *The Collected Letters of Thomas Hardy*. Vol. 5. Eds. Richard Little Purdy and Michael Millgate. Oxford: Clarendon Press, 1978.

_____. "The Dorsetshire Labourer," in *The Dorset Page*, http://www.thedorsetpage.com/genealogy/info/the_dorsetshire_labourer.htm, 1883. Accessed 14 September 2012.

_____. *The Life and Work of Thomas Hardy*. Ed. Michael Millgate. London: Macmillan, 1984.

_____. *Thomas Hardy's Personal Writings*. Ed. Harold Orel. London: Macmillan, 1966; repr. 1967.

_____. *Thomas Hardy's Public Voice: The Essays, Speeches, and Miscellaneous Prose*. Ed. Michael Millgate. Oxford: Clarendon Press, 2001.

_____. *The Works of Thomas Hardy*. Hertfordshire: Wordsworth Editions, Ltd., 1994.

Hynes, Samuel. "Hardy and the Battle God," in *Thomas Hardy Reappraised: Essays in Honour of Michael Millgate*. Ed. Keith Wilson. Toronto: University of Toronto Press, 2006, 245–261.

_____. *A War Imagined: The First World War and English Culture*. London: Bodley Head, Ltd., 1990.

Inglis, K. S. "Entombing Unknown Soldiers: From London and Paris to Baghdad," in *History & Memory* 5.2 (Fall–Winter 1993): 7–31.

Johnson, James Weldon. *Complete Poems.* Ed. Sondra Kathryn Wilson. New York: Penguin Books, 2000.
Lawson, Tom. "The Free-Masonry of Sorrow?: National Identities and the Memorialization of the Great War in Britain, 1919–1931," in *History & Memory* 20.1 (2008): 89–120.
Mallett, Phillip, ed. *Palgrave Advances in Thomas Hardy Studies.* Basingstoke: Palgrave Macmillan, 2004.
Purdy, Richard Little. *Thomas Hardy: A Bibliographic Study.* London: Oxford University Press, 1954.
Ramazani, Jahan. *Poetry of Mourning: The Modern Elegy from Hardy to Heaney.* Chicago: University of Chicago Press, 1994.
Sassoon, Siegfried. "On Passing the New Menin Gate," www.poemhunter.com/best-poems/siegfried-sassoon/on-passing-the-new-menin-gate/, 1928. Accessed 1 Aug 2014.
Sherman, Daniel J. *The Construction of Memory in Interwar France.* Chicago: University of Chicago Press, 1999.
"The Unknown Warrior." *The London Times,* 11 November 1920, 15. *The Times Digital Archive,* 1785–1985. http://www.thetimes.co.uk/tto/archive/. Accessed 15 September 2014.
Verdery, Katherine. *The Political Lives of Dead Bodies: Reburial and Postsocialist Change.* New York: Columbia University Press, 1999.
Whitehead, James. "Thomas Hardy and the First World War Companion Poems: 'Men Who March Away' and 'Before Marching And After,'" in *The Thomas Hardy Journal* 15.3 (1999): 85–98.
Widdowson, Peter. *Hardy in History: A Study in Literary Sociology.* London: Routledge, 1989.
_____. *On Thomas Hardy: Late Essays and Earlier.* New York: St. Martin's Press, 1998.
Wiener, Martin J. *English Culture and Decline of the Industrial Spirit: 1850–1980.* Cambridge: Cambridge University Press, 1981, 2d ed., 2004.

"Wild Wavering"
Between Pastoral and Elegy
Fahri Öz

Thomas Hardy is a Victorian as well as a modernist poet showing the traits of both ages and acting as a figure of transition. The transitional status of Hardy is also evident in the way he treats the pastoral and the elegy, which rarely appear as distinct and independent genres in his poetry: his pastoral poems contain an elegiac strain, whilst his elegies are tinted with a pastoral haze.

Such cohabitation or wavering of the two genres is closely linked to his treatment of place. Hardy did not often move from one place to another but when he did, it suggested something decisive. He seemed intent on finding a place conducive to good health, creativity and happiness. In 1867 his sojourn in London was interrupted, upon which he went to Dorset: "Too much reading, too little sleep and exercise, the general insalubrity of the city and especially of the tidal sewer that was the Thames—all these factors contributed to a serious deterioration in Hardy's health, until he scarcely had strength in the mornings to hold the pencil and square."[1] The significance of place is also evident in quite an impressive number of his poems that dwell on either indoor or outdoor locales. Even the number of titles of poems with a conjunction or preposition of place might give an idea: 24 poems, for instance, begin with the preposition "in," 22 with "at" and 11 with "on," all referring to a location. He even wrote two poems with the same title, "On the Doorstep." Two poems have the word "place" in their titles ("Places" and "The Place on the Map"). Hardy's great interest in places can also lucidly be seen when those poems that deal with geographical locations (such as "At Castle Boterel," "The Bridge of Lodi," "On Martock Moor," etc.) are taken into consideration.

Though the closely related words "place" and "space" are used interchangeably, they denote different things: "*Space* indicates a sense of movement, of history, of becoming, while *place* is often thought to imply a static sense of location, of being, or of dwelling."² Place usually denotes a location endowed with security and value; space, on the other hand, suggests freedom and openness. While place implies where one can pause, space brings to mind movement. Also, one can differentiate between "an abstract realm of space and an experience and felt world of place."³ Place provides the individual with the ability to personalize a location, whereas space remains alien to such appropriation. Of the two terms, place has a more intimate and closer relation to the individual because it "says something not only about where you live or come from but who you are."⁴ Therefore, place has a crucial role in understanding human life, values and experiences. In the case of Hardy's verse, this quality of place charged with value judgments and identity leads the poet to shuttle between two states of being that correspond to the elegy and the pastoral. I shall be using place rather than space to discuss the pastoral and the elegy since it is more closely linked with the notions of experience and identity, and I thereby wish to demonstrate the role of place in the co-existence of these two genres in Hardy's poetry.

However, the generic issues unavoidably introduce certain hindrances and reservations. To begin with, it would be preposterous to treat Hardy as a pastoral poet, or one whose oeuvre is markedly pastoral. In fact, Hardy hardly ever portrays nature in purely pastoral terms; at best nature provides consolation only minimally, liminally and provisionally. Taking the pastoral as a form that effaces class differences, Empson states that "[t]he essential trick of the old pastoral, which was felt to imply a beautiful relation between rich and poor, was to make simple people express strong feelings (felt as the most universal subject, something fundamentally true about everybody) in learned and fashionable language (so that you wrote about the best subject in the best way)."⁵ The conventional or old pastoral that Empson talks about was already dead in Hardy's time. His antecedents being "master masons, with a set of journeymen masons under them,"⁶ Hardy was aware of class distinctions and their cultural markers, and never wrote about an Arcadia. But, of course, his poems teem with natural settings. However, as a result of a Darwinian view of life, the Wordsworthian conception of nature waned, claims Langbaum, who further remarks that "Hardy gives less emphasis in his poems than in his novels to nature's beauty."⁷ It should not lead one to think that nature or the pastoral has a diminished existence in his poetry; on the contrary, the pastoral exists but it does so only precariously soon to be turned upside down, as a past reflection which brings distress rather than bliss. Hardy's poems attest to the fact "that modern pastoral lyric is not a specifiable subgenre, but a modal variant of modern lyric in many ways of its forms."⁸

What is meant in this essay by the word pastoral is the use of nonhuman nature as a place where respite from the pressure of social rules and expectations turns out to be transitory and illusory, or, in the words of Gifford, "any literature that describes the country with an implicit or explicit contrast to the city."[9]

Likewise, Hardy's elegies do not stick to the rules and conventions of traditional elegy; they continue to live in new garments. His elegiac poems exhibit such diversity that it is difficult to call them elegies *per se*. The modern elegy, dismissing many a norm, has become "anti-consolatory, and anti-encomiastic, anti–Romantic and anti–Victorian, anti-conventional and sometimes anti-literary."[10] Therefore, the word elegy will be used here to refer to poems dwelling on loss and death of people or things. As the examples will show the elegiac mood emerges out of the pastoral which at first gives the impression of hope, renewal and happiness.

The elegiac mood arises in two ways: first, out of the loss of one's place, an uprooting of the individual from his or her authentic setting where he/she is born or bred; second, out of the realization that place has a memory of its own. Writing on the Boer War poem "Drummer Hodge," published in December 1899, Ramazani observes how Hardy reverses two generic motifs of elegy, namely, "the restoration of the dead to their home and their translation to the stars."[11] Equally interesting is the way the pastoral emerges as a dirge for the alienated dead subject who has been uprooted from his homeland. Drummer Hodge's final demesne is a place that is totally different from his birthplace. The Dutch words that are interspersed within the poem could provide a pastoral feel to the atmosphere if they appeared in a non-elegiac lyric; however, in this poem they only serve to heighten the impossibility of such exotic and enticing experience. Places also appear as locations with a kind of memory. In the poem "I Found Her Out There," an elegy written in December 1912 for Emma, Hardy similarly juxtaposes two different settings: the first one referring to her ocean-tossed hometown where she spent her childhood, and the second to her unattractive-looking burial place which Hardy seems to regret. The opposing places in this poem are indicative of the oscillation in Hardy's place poems. The first evokes a pastoral atmosphere in the past, whereas the second creates the present elegiac setting which contributes to the speaker's sense of guilt. The elegiac tone in Hardy is accompanied by a pungent sense of locus that arises out of his conception of place in dubious terms. His personae are drawn to natural settings where they lived happily, but they are soon drawn into contemplation, retrospection and gloom. The seemingly pastoral atmosphere in his poems is derailed by the persona himself or an interlocutor who directs the persona's attention to the past, and thus the past experience fails to secure consolation. The pastoral setting is still there but the feelings it arouses do not lead to any kind of contentment.

Hardy's place poems thus oscillate between the pastoral and the elegy, and the two genres hardly exist on their own or with their respective conventions. In such place poems as "Domicilium" (probably one of the earliest pieces by Hardy, written no later than 1860, printed in 1916), "Where the Picnic Was" (1912–13), and the often ignored "Under the Waterfall" (1914) the elegiac tone is muted or diluted; yet the existence of certain relics or traces helps uncover the mournful experience lurking behind the pastoral. This oscillation is activated by an implied listener, or the poet's inner voice which weakens the authenticity of the past experience and dependability of the speaker's evaluation.[12]

"Domicilium" (composed between 1857 and 1860) describes his birthplace at Lower Bockhampton, and is accompanied in Gibson's edition by the poet's own drawing. The poem, which Hardy himself calls "some Wordsworthian lines,"[13] records the changes his first home has gone through. It is quite telling that this early piece focuses on the poet's ancestral house, which demonstrates his interest in places within the nexus of past and present.

Domicilium

It faces west, and round the back and sides
High beeches, bending, hang a veil of boughs,
And sweep against the roof. Wild honeysucks
Climb on the walls, and seem to sprout a wish
(If we may fancy wish of trees and plants)
To overtop the apple trees hard by.

Red roses, lilacs, variegated box
Are there in plenty, and such hardy flowers
As flourish best untrained. Adjoining these
Are herbs and esculents; and farther still
A field; then cottages with trees, and last
The distant hills and sky.

Behind, the scene is wilder. Heath and furze
Are everything that seems to grow and thrive
Upon the uneven ground. A stunted thorn
Stands here and there, indeed; and from a pit
An oak uprises, Springing from a seed
Dropped by some bird a hundred years ago.

       In days bygone—
Long gone—my father's mother, who is now
Blest with the blest, would take me out to walk.
At such a time I once inquired of her
How looked the spot when first she settled here.
The answer I remember. "Fifty years

> Have passed since then, my child, and change has marked
> The face of all things. Yonder garden-plots
> And orchards were uncultivated slopes
> O'ergrown with bramble bushes, furze and thorn:
> That road a narrow path shut in by ferns,
> Which, almost trees, obscured the passers-by.
>
> Our house stood quite alone, and those tall firs
> And beeches were not planted. Snakes and efts
> Swarmed in the summer days, and nightly bats
> Would fly about our bedrooms. Heathcroppers
> Lived on the hills, and were our only friends;
> So wild it was when we first settled here."[14]

Highly descriptive and deictic, the poem records two persons' impressions of the house: the young Hardy's and his grandmother's. While the persona, whom we may associate with the young Hardy, provides a spatial description in a swooping cinematographic fashion, capturing the details around the house, his grandmother provides a temporal account of the place. In short, the poem is constructed on spatial and temporal axes. The persona's own description harbors almost no memories, no traces from the past; in the first stanza his gaze focuses first on the plants on the roof, the front garden and vegetation there, then quickly shifts further into the fields, other houses nearby "and last/ The distant hills and sky." In the second stanza the persona dwells upon the view behind the house where things grow profusely as if out of control. The grandmother's recollections, on the other hand, are densely interwoven with historical details, highlighting the inevitable victory of time over things. Her portraiture of the place pays more attention to particulars in terms of diurnal and seasonal changes: "Snakes and efts/ Swarmed in the summer days, and nightly bats/ Would fly about our bedrooms." The persona's perusal of the place does not have the coherence of the grandmother's description. This incoherence is obvious in the way the boy's gaze records things flittingly, further suggesting a kind of discomfort as if he would like to flee the place, go beyond "the distant hills and sky."

The poem does not refer to any human beings or signs of human activity except the house itself and the grandmother's cursory reference to an anonymous passer-by. The portrayals of the place by both the young boy and his grandmother abound in words that suggest wilderness: "wild" (used twice) and "wilder," "hard," "hardy," "untrained," "uneven," "uncultivated," "heathcroppers." The boy's description in the first and second stanzas alludes to horticultural items like "honeysucks," "roses," "lilacs," "herbs" and "esculents," which grow on their own and look very wild. Even the oak in the third stanza has sprouted "from a seed/ Dropped by some bird a hundred years ago," implying lack of human involvement. In the last two stanzas the grandmother's description gives a much more uncultivated scene infested with snakes and lizards, a desolate place with no company other than heathcroppers (a sheep or pony, living on open heath or down). This tension between the past and the present condition of the place demonstrates that the family homestead swings between the poles of safety and danger, dwelling and rootlessness, that the house possesses the qualities of both place and space.

Shifting between its much wilder unattended state in the past and relatively tamed, cultured one in the present, the poet's family house appears to be the setting for both pastoral and elegy. The poem is built on the persona's present observations and his grandmother's recollections of the domicilium. The grandmother "is now/ Blest with the blest." The elegiac tone, however, does not arise from her being dead, but from Hardy's realization that change is unavoidable: as his grandmother remarks in a quasi-erudite or philosophical manner "change has marked/ The face of all things." Hardy does not openly state here but he is different from the young boy who listened to the old woman. His uneasiness with the place mentioned above is balanced by his grandmother's story of the place which gives him a sense of belonging,[15] sharing a common history provided by the house and its environs. Thus, the house transcends being a mere dwelling to become the witness to the transformation of nature. Though the poem deserves to be called a pastoral due to its descriptive content, its retrospective aspect evokes and implies a sense of mourning for the irrevocable state of the homestead in the past and the changes it will suffer in the future. "Domicilium" moves in the last two stanzas from the spatial axis to the temporal one with the grandmother's speech, and it ends almost abruptly with her words. This is quite unusual for Hardy. Despite his liking for imperfections rather than perfected structures in artistic creation,[16] Hardy does not usually end his poems open-endedly. However, this poem ends without a sense of closure. The reason is that here the persona finds it difficult to provide a sense of ending; as a young boy Hardy is trying to digest the implications of what the grandmother has said.

"Domicilium" differs from Hardy's later poems focusing on places since it lacks overtly psychological and emotional depth. However, it foretells the poet's interest in place as the locus of contending human feelings that arise out of past experience and its present significance. In a sense it also heralds Hardy's fondness for introducing an interlocutor who accompanies the persona throughout his/her experience and the interpretation of that experience.

Unlike "Domicilium," "Where the Picnic Was" (composed in 1913, a year after Emma's death)[17] markedly sounds elegiac in that the speaker himself mentions the death of a woman. The poem introduces the speaker on a wintry day clambering a hill where he and three other people had a picnic on a summer day.

Where the Picnic Was

Where we made the fire,
In the summer time,
Of branch and briar
On the hill to the sea
I slowly climb
Through winter mire,
And scan and trace
The forsaken place
Quite readily.

Now a cold wind blows,
And the grass is gray,
But the spot still shows
As a burnt circle—aye,
And stick-ends, charred,
Still strew the sward
Whereon I stand,
Last relic of the band
Who came that day!

Yes, I am here
Just as last year,
And the sea breathes brine
From its strange straight line
Up hither, the same
As when we four came.
—But two have wandered far
From this grassy rise
Into urban roar
Where no picnics are,
And one—has shut her eyes
For evermore.

The speaker stresses the change of weather on his present visit to the place in winter; the remains of the picnic fire help him reconstruct the place and time of the picnic. The persona's upward climb on the hill suggests "a solitary version of what would otherwise be the procession of a funeral" and the heap of remaining burnt wood resembles a grave.[18] This elegiac tone is further bolstered by the fact that the speaker is accompanied by no one since two of the picnickers have moved to the city. Thus, by means of this spatial change the urban and the rural/natural settings are implicitly contrasted, which indicates the impossibility of a pastoral reunion. Hardy's treatment of the pastoral as a fleeting moment of respite from the grief of loss is in fact something that accounts for his reckoning with the Romantic tradition. The pastoral environment as a shelter from the turmoil of urban life and civilization or as a means of tackling the death of a dear one does not prove to be the case for him. His poem "In a Wood," for example, evinces the futility of searching for comfort in a sylvan setting. Whereas the Romantic Wordsworth in his "Nutting" finds an innocent, peaceful spirit in the woods, Hardy's persona playfully and mischievously finds enmity and discord amongst trees anthropomorphized as warriors stifling and destroying each other. Similarly in "Where the Picnic Was" nature cannot act as a source of comfort to the elegizing persona.

In addition to the spatial displacement, there is a tragic loss. The speaker suffers the death of a woman, someone especially dear to him. He is the only person who has come to see the spot like a criminal who haunts the crime scene, but this is in no way a consolation since he knows that he has been left alone. He also realizes that he has changed now and believes that he resembles the charred remnants of the fire: "Last relic of the band/ Who came that day!" Writing on the conventions of the elegy derived from rites and ceremonies, Sacks mentions "the elegist's need to draw attention, consolingly, to his own surviving powers."[19] Here, however, the elegiac voice is far from inserting his own powers since he himself is not very different from the remains of burnt wood in the picnic fire. This also attests to the lyric subject's desire to extenuate his sense of guilt. The persona's guilty conscience arises from turning a tragic experience into an opportunity for creativity, which Ramazani mentions among the traits of the modern elegy.[20] By depicting himself in terms of the burnt wood, the persona introduces himself as a debilitated subject, someone who has been physically if not linguistically emaciated.

At the end of the poem Hardy balances the elegiac and pastoral moods through the use of slant expressions. The speaker states bitter truths by means of euphemistic rather than direct statements when he refers to two of the picnickers who moved to the city and one who died. The euphemistic expressions mitigate the bitter feelings of death and separation that are already present in the poem. Contrasting the city and the country, Hardy describes the city as a place where people do *not* have picnics. The poem is in some way also an indirect critique of the urbanization and alienation that pastoral England has gone though. The death of the woman, likewise, is conveyed by means of a milder expression, in an attempt to diminish the gruesomeness of death. Thus, the poem encapsulates both individual and social problems. The first stanza clearly hints at the speaker's cheerless mood in the way he "slowly" climbs the "forsaken place" on the hill. The summer is gone and the landscape is barren as in Keats's "La Belle Dame sans Merci": "Now a cold wind blows/

And the grass is gray." Not only the speaker but also nature mourns, which brings to mind the idea of pathetic fallacy. Hardy creates similar images of desolation in his "Neutral Tones" (composed 1867), where neither the past nor the present can secure any comfort or joy: "Your face, and the God curst sun, and a tree,/ And a pond edged with grayish leaves." Langbaum, who interprets pathetic fallacy as an example of the new voice Hardy acquired through his revision of the Romantic poets, rightly observes that pathetic fallacy appears in Hardy as a combination of two views of nature, "nature's neutrality and malevolence."[21] Here nature is not outright unfriendly but obviously indifferent. The change in time and space once again squeezes the speaker of the poem into an impasse where neither pastoral nor elegy and the respective feelings they arouse can exist independently.

"Under the Waterfall"[22] was written fifty years or so after "Domicilium." It is based on an outing made by Hardy and Emma in 1870[23] and appears in *Satires of Circumstance* (published 1914). Beginning with a quasi–Proustian remembrance, it is one of Hardy's rare poems that borders on the pastoral *par excellence*.[24] The opening lines of "Under the Waterfall" attest to the fact that the female speaker is filled with an urge to tell her story like Coleridge's Ancient Mariner, who captivates people with his tale. The persona's reminiscences of the place and her confession-like narration are fuelled by an auditor. After the auditor's brief intrusion the persona talks about the picnic and what happened at the waterfall.

Under the Waterfall

"Whenever I plunge my arm, like this,
In a basin of water, I never miss
The sweet sharp sense of a fugitive day
Fetched back from the thickening shroud of gray.
    Hence the only prime
    And real love-rhyme
    That I know by heart,
    And that leaves no smart,
Is the purl of a little valley fall
About three spans wide and two spans tall
Over a table of solid rock
And into a scoop of the self-same block;
The purl of a runlet that never ceases
In stir of kingdoms, in wars, in peaces;
With a hollow, boiling voice it speaks
And has spoken since hills were turfless peaks."

"And why gives this the only prime
Idea to you of a real love-rhyme?
And why does plunging your arm in a bowl
Full of spring water, bring throbs to your soul?"

"Well, under the fall, in a crease of the stone,
Though where precisely none ever has known,
Jammed darkly, nothing to show how prized,
And by now with its smoothness opalised,
    Is a drinking-glass:
    For, down that pass,
    My love and I
    Walked under a sky
Of blue with a leaf-wove awning of green,
In the burn of August, to paint the scene,
And we placed our basket of fruit and wine
By the runlet's rim, where we sat to dine;
And when we had drunk from the glass together,
Arched by the oak-copse from the weather,
I held the vessel to rinse in the fall,
Where it slipped, and sank, and was past recall,
Though we stooped and plumbed the little abyss
With long bared arms. There the glass still is.
And, as said, if I thrust my arm below
Cold water in basin or bowl, a throe
From the past awakens a sense of that time,
And the glass we used, and the cascade's rhyme.
The basin seems the pool, and its edge
The hard smooth face of the brook-side ledge,
And the leafy pattern of china-ware
The hanging plants that were bathing there.

"By night, by day, when it shines or lours,
There lies intact that chalice of ours,
And its presence adds to the rhyme of love
Persistently sung by the fall above.
No lip has touched it since his and mine
In turn therefrom sipped lovers' wine."

In a way reminiscent of some personae in Robert Browning's dramatic monologues, the female speaker of "Under the Waterfall" launches her speech *in medias res*, and the use of the deictic "like this" shows that she has company. There is a listener in the poem but it is difficult to figure out whether the persona is talking to somebody in her presence or if it is her own inner voice that helps her continue talking. Whether the poem is a dialogue or a monologue is relevant especially since the persona reveals a secret, the testimony of a private experience: that there is a drinking glass hidden in the depths of the pool ("Though where precisely none ever has known"). By revealing the place of the glass which she values greatly, the persona becomes vulnerable since it is no more a secret. It sounds less convincing for the persona to disclose a secret, which suggests that the listener is no other than her own inner voice, and that she is talking on her own. However, the poem, in which details come out in fragments and in response to the listener's question, is also confessional in tone. In either case, "Under the Waterfall" is not simply a narrative; it reveals a lot about the speaker's struggle to make sense of an exquisitely beautiful summer day.

There is almost nothing explicit to support the existence of an elegiac tone in this poem. It is almost an Arcadian world free from care and toil. The tumbler that the lovers drink from falls but the mellifluous rhyming couplets suggest well-being and order. What is more, the poem provides an almost idyllic portrayal of the place: it is a hot summer day, the couple walk under "a sky/ Of blue with a leaf-wove awning of green," they have fruit and wine (the rhyming words "wine" and "dine" easily recalls the phrase "wine and dine"), they sit near the water, and drink from a chalice. Besides, even the natural elements are idealized and turned into poetic or cultural artifacts as in the case of the waterfall's rhyme and the leaves resembling chinaware designs. The chalice that drops from the persona's hands into the deep pool is still there and will remain there as the testimony of a beautiful day.

However, the changing versification and the use of eclectic or even unusual vocabulary in the poem suggest that the speaker cannot help feeling melancholy since that day can never be retrieved just like the glass that is lost in the water. This realization is evident in the way Hardy places the swift-moving quatrains in between the stanzas with comparatively slow rhythm. Most of the lines are written in iambic pentameters which are interrupted twice by dimeter stanzas:

> Hence the only prime
> And real love-rhyme
> That I know by heart,
> And that leaves no smart

The pentameter stanzas, however, are closer to natural speech rhythms and have a somber tone. The listener too poses her/his question in such relatively slow-moving pentameters.

In terms of unusual word choice, Hardy yokes together incompatible lexical clusters such as the sibilant line "sweet sharp sense of a fugitive day" when talking about the picnic; and to describe the sense of touch when the speaker plunges her arm in cold water, he uses the word "throe." The *OED* defines the word "throe" as follows: "A violent physical spasm or pang, esp. in the pain and struggle of childbirth or death. Also, a spasm of feeling; mental agony; anguish." It is quite striking that the speaker should use such an emotively strong word to refer to a pleasant past event. What is more, Hardy employs other words such as "smart" and "throb" that denote physical pain, unexpectedly so in such a romantic poem. These lexical choices likewise account for the speaker's oscillation between the sense of joy over a pleasant escapade and a sad realization that so exquisite an experience cannot be repeated.

The sad and elegiac mood is also apparent in the way the waterfall and the drinking glass are treated. The drinking glass, from which the two lovers "sipped lovers' wine" has a pivotal importance in the poem. However, this fanciful glass, or the romantically charged "chalice," is at the mercy of time. The speaker herself admits that it has "opalised"; the waterfall has already begun to turn it into a natural element. The process here is diametrically opposed to the one in "Domicilium," where the natural wild space (the heath) is transformed into a tamed domestic place. The glass in "Under the Waterfall" is a cultural artifact that finally returns to its former natural state. It goes back to where it originally came from. It loses its aesthetic form and function and metamorphoses back into sand, stone, mineral, water. The chalice is there, yet it cannot escape the ruination of the waterfall. What the poem does not openly state is more significant than what it directly expresses: the brook will continue to flow. Hardy introduces the drinking glass as permanent, not the waterfall. The glass, however, is a mute object, and with its submersion this muteness has been doubled; the waterfall, on the other hand, "speaks," "has spoken" and will continue to do so in the future. Yet the picnic and its accompanying feeling of happiness and romance are lost forever. The tangible existence of the drinking glass in the depths of the pool around which the poem revolves is also there to remind the persona of the dictum *tempus fugit*.[25] This explains the out-of-place use of such words as "throe," "throb," and "smart" in the poem. Thus the persona finds herself on the threshold of the elegy and the pastoral, oscillating between the two.

In the poems "Domicilium," "Where the Picnic Was," and "Under the Waterfall," place has therefore a vital role in understanding the way nature is viewed and experienced. Pastoral settings function as places providing comfort for only brief periods of time since the persona is soon besieged by the devastating past experiences. As Barbara Hardy writes, evoking the way Hardy pendulates between two approaches to natural setting in "At Castle Boterel," "[t]he poet is imagining the place as poets traditionally do, as symbolic and sympathetic, sacred to himself, but also moving beyond the personal to place it, with objectivity, in and before history. He creates two points of view, one self-centered and the other place-centered, and shuttles between the two."[26] Hardy's personae are rift between the subjective (personal) and objective (historical) treatment of place, which does not allow the existence of the pastoral and the elegy as independent genres.

Places, as mentioned earlier, are locations where personae experience things. This tension between personalized location (place) and the abstract location (space) leads Hardy's personae into a limbo where they waver between past happiness and present disillusionment. Lacking a purely pastoral quality, natural settings do not confer permanent consolation to the personae who still haunt and are haunted by such places. The personae in the poems studied here are eager to experience places as potentially pastoral locations, but are disillusioned since the pastoral prospects of these places have already been, or will be, devastated by time. Therefore, the pastoral in Hardy can be conceived only briefly and temporarily because his personae confront tragic experiences or bitter truths lurking behind natural settings.

Notes

1. Michael Millgate, *Thomas Hardy: A Biography* (Oxford: Oxford University Press, 1985), 101.
2. Cecilia Ahrfeldt, "Space and Infelicitous Place in the Poetry of Sylvia Plath," su.diva-portal.org/smash/get/diva2:443528/FULLTEXT01, accessed 8 July 2012, 4–5.
3. T. Cresswell, "Place," www.elsevierdirect.com/brochures/.../Place.pdf, accessed 5 Oct 2013.
4. Mike Crang, *Cultural Geography* (New York: Routledge, 1998), 103.
5. William Empson, *Some Versions of Pastoral* (London: Hogarth Press, 1986, first ed. 1935), 11.
6. Millgate, *op. cit.*, 5.
7. Robert Langbaum, *Thomas Hardy in Our Time* (London: Macmillan, 1995), 46.
8. Paul Alpers, *What Is Pastoral?* (Chicago: Chicago University Press, 1996), 300.
9. Terry Gifford, *Pastoral* (London: Routledge, 1999), 3.
10. Jahan Ramazani, *Poetry of Mourning: The Modern Elegy from Hardy to Heaney* (Chicago: University of Chicago Press 1994), 2.
11. *Ibid.*, 41.
12. Hardy's career as a novelist who for a long time hid his identity as a poet accounts for the ease with which he adopted in his lyrics novelistic techniques such as a listener (implied or otherwise) and dialogue. Hardy's affinity with Robert Browning and the dramatic monologue may again be linked in part to his novel writing. See Langbaum, *op. cit.*, 54 for this point.
13. Michael Millgate (ed.), *The Life and Work of Thomas Hardy* (London: Macmillan, 1984), 8.
14. Thomas Hardy, *The Complete Poems*, ed. James Gibson (Basingstoke: Palgrave, 2001; first edition, 1976), 3–4.
15. As Knoepflmacher states, the grandmother calls Hardy the young boy "my child" rather than "my grandchild," which implies a closer maternal and familial bond and affection between the two. U. C. Knoepflmacher, "Hardy Ruins: Female Spaces and Male Designs" in *PMLA* Vol. 105, No. 5 (Oct. 1990): pp. 1055–1070, http://www.jstor.org/stable/462734?origin=JSTOR-pdf, accessed 15 Aug 2011, 1057.
16. Hardy writes "Am more and more confirmed in an idea I have long held, as a matter of common sense, long before I thought of any old aphorism bearing on the subject: 'Ars

est celare artem.' The whole secret of a living style and the difference between it and a dead style, lies not in having too much style—being, in fact, a little careless, or rather seeming to be, here and there. It brings wonderful life into the writing [...] I think the art lies in making these [Nature's] defects the basis of hitherto unperceived beauty, by irradiating them with 'the light that was never was' on their surface, but is seen to be latent in them by the spiritual eye." James Gibson and Trevor Johnson, eds., *Thomas Hardy: Poems. A Selection of Critical Essays.* Casebook Series (London: Macmillan, 1987), 29–30.

17. *The Complete Poems, op. cit.*, 357–358.
18. Peter M. Sacks, *The English Elegy: Studies in the Genre from Spenser to Yeats* (London: Johns Hopkins University Press, 1987), 258.
19. *Ibid.*, 2.
20. Ramazani, *op. cit.*, 6.
21. Langbaum, *op. cit.*, 44–45.
22. *The Complete Poems, op. cit.*, 335–337.
23. Millgate (ed.), *op. cit.*, 74.
24. Hardy also deals with this picnic by the water in Pentargan Bay in the poem "After a Journey."
25. "On the Departure Platform" is another poem that exemplifies the fleeting nature of time; this time a male speaker confesses the irrevocability of any moment saying that "nought happens twice thus," abnegating any hope that the future will bring the same opportunities.
26. Barbara Hardy, *Thomas Hardy: Imagining Imagination in Hardy's Poetry and Fiction* (London: Athlone Press, 2000), 145.

Works Cited

Ahrfeldt, Cecilia. "Space and Infelicitous Place in the Poetry of Sylvia Plath." su.diva-portal.org/smash/get/diva2:443528/FULLTEXT01, 2012. Accessed 8 July 2012.
Alpers, Paul. *What Is Pastoral?* Chicago: Chicago University Press, 1996.
Crang, Mike. *Cultural Geography.* New York: Routledge, 1998.
Cresswell, T. "Place," http://booksite.elsevier.com/brochures/hugy/SampleContent/Place.pdf, 2009. Accessed 5 Oct 2013.
Gibson, James and Johnson, Trevor, eds. *Thomas Hardy: Poems. A Selection of Critical Essays.* Casebook Series. London: Macmillan, 1987.
Hardy, Barbara. *Thomas Hardy: Imagining Imagination in Hardy's Poetry and Fiction.* London: Athlone Press, 2000.
Hardy, Thomas. *The Complete Poems.* Ed. James Gibson. Hampshire: Palgrave, 2001.
_____. *The Life and Work of Thomas Hardy.* Ed. Michael Millgate. London: Macmillan, 1984.
Knoepflmacher, U. C. "Hardy Ruins: Female Spaces and Male Designs" in *PMLA* Vol. 105, No. 5 (October 1990): 1055–1070.
Langbaum, Robert. *Thomas Hardy in Our Time.* London: Macmillan, 1995.
Millgate, Michael. *Thomas Hardy: A Biography.* Oxford: Oxford University Press, 1985.
Millgate, Michael, ed. *The Life and Work of Thomas Hardy.* London: Macmillan, 1984.
Ramazani, Jahan. *Poetry of Mourning: The Modern Elegy from Hardy to Heaney.* Chicago: University of Chicago Press, 1994.

II

Misalignments

Rhyming Events and the Pessimistic Muse

Stephen Tardif

Many have tried in vain joyfully to utter the extremity of joy; here at last, in mourning, I see it expressed.—Friedrich Hölderlin[1]

In the second chapter of *Jude the Obscure*, the young protagonist, already crestfallen at his schoolmaster's departure, receives a further blow. Upon being punished for letting crows feed upon his employer's seed, he intuits a "flaw in the terrestrial scheme by which what was good for God's birds was bad for God's gardener," and the idea that "mercy towards one set of creatures was cruelty towards another sickened his sense of harmony"; "[e]vents," Jude realizes, "did not rhyme quite as he had thought."[2] This realization is presented, in the novel, as a precocious child's lugubrious lesson, one of many unfortunate but inescapable disappointments he must endure as he matures. Yet, the very chapter in which this realization occurs actually concludes with an event that does seem, somehow, to rhyme. After asking a man for the direction of the city to which his schoolmaster has departed, the child sees the "man [point] north-eastward, in the very direction where lay that field in which Jude had so disgraced himself. There was something unpleasant about the coincidence."[3] Thomas Hardy's last novel, then, is not devoid of patterned, coincidental repetitions in time; but all of its symmetries are sad.

The word "pessimism" first entered into the discussion of Hardy's work in reviews of his novels during the mid–1880s and it has remained a critical commonplace—albeit a contested one—ever since.[4] Hardy himself objected to this characterization of his art and, in the prefatory "Apology" to his *Late Lyrics*, he rebuffs such descriptions as "casual personal criticisms," a subject to be treated briefly before being "charitably left to decent silence."[5] His response to his critics, however, reveals a depth of thought and engagement which belies its brevity. The eponymous apology itself—offered "to good Panglossians" for poems which may present "disrespectful conceptions of this best of all possible worlds"[6]—is anchored in obvious allusions to both Leibniz and Voltaire; and the laconic definition of "evolutionary meliorism" which Hardy proposes—"the exploration of reality [...] with an eye to the *best consummation possible*"[7]—is modeled upon a formula invariably attached to Leibniz's version of philosophical optimism.

But when critics have described Hardy's art as pessimistic, they have not argued that the worst of all possible worlds is what is imagined therein. The term, instead, is used to convey the curious frequency with which characters in the Hardyan cosmos encounter discouraging failures and conspicuous disappointments; and, rather than being the caricatures of "casual and unreflecting"[8] readers, these estimations do, in fact, touch upon an essential aspect of Hardy's imagination—or, more specifically, the remit of its representational range. What is imagined in Hardy's fiction and poetry are not the worst worlds possible, but ones in which potential is deprived of possibility. Hardy's art—to borrow a phrase from Kafka—possesses "[p]lenty of hope—[...] no end of hope—only not for us."[9] It is not wrong, then, to employ the word "pessimism" in connection with Hardy's art—yet it can only be properly applied if understood without any pejorative or misanthropic connotations, since the hopeless inventions of Hardy's imagination imply nothing about his perception of the world. When discounting the accusations of pessimism in the "Apology" to the *Late Lyrics*, Hardy quotes from his earlier poem, "In Tenebris," as an explanation of the compositional method which his critics have misconstrued: "If way to the Better there be, it exacts a full look at the Worst."[10] Although the poet subsequently characterizes this "full look at the Worst" as an "exploration of reality" (*ibid.*), his verse is truer than its paraphrase: for it is not reality which is explored in the pessimistic permutations of Hardy's art, but alternative versions of it where the "way to the Better" has been blocked. Hardy's pessimism, then, takes a full look at a Worst that never was.

In her *Letter to a Priest*, Simone Weil writes that "men whose attention, faith and love are almost exclusively concentrated on the impersonal aspect of God can actually believe and declare themselves to be atheists, even though supernatural love inhabits their souls."[11] While Hardy's credentials as an agnostic remain beyond dispute, Weil's counterintuitive characterization of the atheist provides a useful parallel for approaching the putative pessimist. For, in his artistic contemplation of foregone possibilities, unrealized alternatives, and better byways which remain untaken, Hardy concentrates, not upon the impersonal aspect of God, but on the counterfactuals of progress along the path to the "best consummation possible." And the forfeit fulfillments imagined in his fiction and his verse are brought into a sort of liminal existence precisely through their *non*-fulfillment: they persist on the penumbra of possibility at the outlying edges of his imagined worlds, the dream of those within the dream.

This essay argues that peripheral contingencies of this kind can be conceptualized as "rhyming events," that curious idea which flickers briefly though Jude's mind at the outset of Hardy's last novel. The aesthetic logic that this notion implies helps to explain, not only Hardy's turn away from the novel as a literary form, but also the organization implicit in his subsequent poetic output. After an examination of the passage in *Jude the Obscure* wherein this concept appears—and a brief consideration of the issues which it raises—I offer a reading of "Under the Waterfall," a poem from Hardy's *Satires of Circumstance* that presents a paradigmatic pair of events which seem to rhyme.

God and Man in *Jude the Obscure*

In his famous essay, published two years after the Wessex editions of Hardy's novels appeared, Georg Lukács asserted that "[t]he novel is the epic of a world that has been abandoned by God."[12] Unlike the heroes of epic poetry who are guided through the world by divinities, the novelistic protagonist must find himself amidst the "God-forsakenness of the world," and the novel is always, therefore, "the story of the soul that goes to find itself."[13] It is through this very search, however, that the atheistic nature of the novelistic universe is revealed: "The abandonment of the world by God manifests itself in the incommensurability of the soul and work, of interiority and adventure."[14] A figural form of precisely this sort of search is enacted in the second chapter of *Jude the Obscure*, as the young Jude Fawley wanders home after his punishment:

> Jude went out, and, feeling more than ever his existence to be an undemanded one, he lay down upon his back on a heap of litter near the pig-sty. The fog had by this time become more translucent, and the position of the sun could be seen through it. He pulled his straw hat over his face, and peered through the interstices of the plaiting at the white brightness, vaguely reflecting. Growing up brought responsibilities, he found. Events did not rhyme quite as he had thought. Nature's logic was too horrid for him to care for. That mercy towards one set of creatures was cruelty towards another sickened his sense of harmony. As you got older, and felt yourself to be at the centre of your time, and not at a point in its circumference, as you had felt when you were little, you were seized with a sort of shuddering, he perceived. All around you there seemed to be something glaring, garish, rattling, and the noises and glares hit upon the little cell called your life, and shook it, and warped it.[15]

The theological allusions contained in this passage are striking and various. At the outset, Hardy plays on the notion that God's existence is "necessary": Jude's "undemanded" existence is implicitly compared with the "demanded" existence of the Deity, adduced in the famous proofs of Aristotle, Aquinas, and Anselm.[16] Jude's sense of his own contingency in the universe then leads him to imitate Job—to whom Jude's aunt has just compared herself[17]—by reclining on a "heap of litter."[18] While Job and Jude both suffer the affronts of injustice, Job pleads his suit to God Himself, whereas Jude must simply internalize injustice as the unwritten law of an impersonal universe, however much "Nature's logic" may sicken "his sense of harmony." But, there *is* no harmony in Jude's world. From Greek antiquity until the Renaissance, the concept of cosmic order was expressed through the metaphor of the *musica universalis*, the music or harmony of the spheres. Such a vision of the universe comes in for parody in this passage when, instead of the harmonious chiming of celestial spheres, Jude feels the shattering reverberations of disproportion, the shock produced by the friction between himself and his world.

Hardy's description of Jude as inscribed within the circle of his own existence is related to another pair of theological traditions about the self and God. According to St. Augustine's famous maxim, "God is nearer to me than I am to myself"; the Divine Other, on this view, resides at the self's true center.[19] But, in Hardy's novel, Jude feels thrust into the very position which, in Augustine's account, ought to be occupied by God. Hardy emphasizes this displacement through his use of the geometrical images of a circle and its circumference. His use of these images recalls a definition of God that can be traced back to Xenophanes, Parmenides, and Empedocles—but owes its most popular phrasing to the Medieval theologian, Alain de Lille—, which has it that God is a "sphere, whose center is everywhere and whose circumference is nowhere."[20] Pascal would famously modify this phrase, and replace God with nature[21]; but it is left to Hardy to add a further alteration to this *topos*, marooning a single man in the center of this infinite circle.

If this passage from *Jude* confirms Lukács' thesis about the atheistic nature of the novel, however, it does so, not because it constitutes a polemic against religion, but because it shares a similar frustration with the form of the novel itself. Hardy, in other words, uses the absence of God to stress the absence of order, and his later account of his repudiation of the novel emphasizes precisely this deficit of aesthetic organization. In recounting his turn from prose to poetry, Hardy recalls that the novel, for him, was "gradually losing artistic form, with a beginning, middle, and end, and becoming a spasmodic inventory of items, which has nothing to do with art."[22] To illustrate this artlessness *within* the novel, Hardy invokes and inverts a series of theological traditions to undermine the order and coherence which they seem to guarantee.

Empty Typologies

Against the backdrop of these repudiated prerequisites of order, Hardy proposes a principle of a different kind, a trope that offers itself, not as a metaphor of a higher harmony, but as one conscious of its own contrivance. Although the notion of rhyming events first appears in the novel under the aspect of absence—as a Providential symmetry which the world appears to lack—a different structure than the one which Jude imagines is evinced in the course of the novel itself.

In his classic study, *Fiction and Repetition*, J. Hillis Miller identifies the essential characteristics of Hardy's particular type of temporal organization. He first sets forward the "two alternative theories of repetition" found in Gilles Deleuze's *The Logic of Sense*: "The first exactly defines the world of copies or of representations; it establishes the world as icon. The second, against the first, defines the world of simulacra. It presents the world itself as phantasm."[23] Commenting on Deleuze's distinction, Miller elaborates on the first concept: "What Deleuze calls "Platonic" repetition is grounded in a solid archetypal model which is untouched by the effects of repetition"; from this perspective, "[t]he validity of the mimetic copy is established by its truth of correspondence to what it copies."[24] Miller then elaborates on the second type of repetition: "The other, Nietzschean mode of repetition posits a world based on difference. Each thing, this other theory would assume, is unique, intrinsically different from every other thing.... It seems that X repeats Y, but in fact it does not, or at least not in the firmly anchored way of the first sort of repetition."[25]

As different as these two models of repetition appear to be, however, Miller does not fix a firm distinction between them. In fact, after setting up these models, Miller complicates the very dichotomy he has established by inter-implicating these two modes in an intractable dialectic from which a "third," hybrid form of repetition emerges.[26] Drawing on Walter Benjamin's conception of the "opaque similarities" that exist between one's dreams and the reality from which they come, Miller observes:

> the opaque similarities of dream are baseless, or, if based at all, then based on the difference between the two things. They create in the gap of that difference a third thing, what Benjamin calls the image [*das Bild*]. The image is the meaning generated by the echoing of two dissimilar things in the second form of repetition. It is neither in the first nor in the second nor in some ground

which preceded both, but in between, in the empty space which the opaque similarity crosses."[27]

At this point in his exposition, Miller turns to Hardy's novel, *The Well-Beloved*, as an illustration of this "interaction of the two forms of repetition," because its protagonist "see[s] things in figures."[28] Miller further argues that this example is emblematic: "there is a strong inclination for people in Hardy's world to trace likes in unlikes. This is as true for the narrators of his novels as for the characters."[29]

This tracing of "likes in unlikes" resembles the typological mode of interpretation famously rearticulated by Erich Auerbach in his seminal essay, "*Figura*." After outlining the essential dimensions of this ancient reading practice, Auerbach distinguishes it from what Miller would call the Platonic notion of repetition by arguing against any "ground which precedes" the images linked in such configurations: "*figura* is something real and historical which announces something else that is also real and historical. The relation between the two events is revealed by an accord or similarity."[30] Hardy's *figura*, on the other hand, are silhouettes connected precisely through their dissimilarity; the past does not offer models for perceiving the present, so much as it limns the shape of unfulfilled expectations. Repetition, in Hardy, is constituted through difference, through empty typologies whose figures are linked only by loss.

Rhyming Events

Even though it is not difference but similarity which seems to be stressed in the temporal juxtaposition imagined in "Under the Waterfall," the two events which form the foci of the poem offer a clear illustration of Hardy's characteristic mode of repetition. In turning to an example of repetition in Hardy's verse, a distinction, delineated in Miller's essay, "History as Repetition in Hardy's Poetry," is relevant. Miller notes that, while the "formal structure of Hardy's fiction is generated by the juxtaposition of the retrospective view of the narrator," in his poetry

> these two perspectives are joined in a single mind. Many of the poems set side by side two times in the speaker's life, a past time when he was caught up in some human relationship, usually a love affair, and was centering his whole life on attaining the goal of his desire and a present time when he looks back on that episode in the perspective of its end in separation, betrayal, or death. This juxtaposition creates the characteristic formal structure of the lyric poems.[31]

The poem—a dramatic monologue given by a female speaker addressed to an anonymous companion—brings present and past into proximate contact through an unpremeditated reminiscence:

> Whenever I plunge my arm, like this,
> In a basin of water, I never miss
> The sweet sharp sense of a fugitive day
> Fetched back from its thickening shroud of gray.[32]

Although many critics have made sensitive comments on this poem, it has not attracted much sustained analysis—even though it serves as a kind of preface to the "Poems of 1912–13." The poets, however, have taken note: it is clearly evoked in W. H. Auden's "As I Walked out one Evening"—"'O plunge your hands in water,/ Plunge them in up to the wrist."[33] It is also echoed in Robert Frost's poem, "Directive," which concludes with the speaker's non-revelation of a hidden glass.[34]

The abrupt first lines of the poem, connect the speaker's present action with her past search for the glass, shared with her departed lover during their pastoral picnic, but which was then lost while being washed under the waterfall. The kind of "rhyme" that is constituted by these events seems self-evident; but, from the very outset of the poem, past and present evince a curious relationship. The opening lines make the appearance of the poem's lyric present coeval with the remembered event that the speaker's action recalls. Indeed, it is almost as if *the past calls forth the present*, since the sound of the waterfall is, for the speaker, the "only *prime*/ And real love-rhyme" that remains in her memory "by heart" (l. 5–7, my emphasis). The prominent use of the word "prime" not only establishes the ordinal priority of this happy memory in the speaker's mind, but it also elevates the past into a central position over the lyric present, making the speaker's action appear as a mere shadow of the original which it spontaneously and somatically brings to mind.[35]

The perceived connection between these two moments is so strong that the present actually begins to resemble the past. The structuring power of the past is stressed near the end of the poem when the relation between the speaker's actual and remembered actions becomes so uncanny that the poem's present setting begins to blend with her memory:

> The basin seems the pool, and its edge
> The hard smooth face of the brook-side ledge,
> And the leafy pattern of china-ware
> The hanging plants that were bathing there. [l. 43–46]

This final transmutation of the speaker's current, quotidian surroundings into the very scene of the lovers' past picnic gives the initial depiction of the waterfall at the beginning of the poem greater significance: the waterfall is said to be "[a]bout three spans wide and two spans tall" and it runs "[o]ver a table of solid rock" (l. 10–11)—a description of nature which is already decidedly domestic. Thus, by the end of the poem, it seems that the present not only resembles the past, but that the past actually realigns the present; the shaping force which each moment mutually exerts on the other complicates the very relationship between the supposed original and the apparent repetition.

But the illusory elision of time past and present which is enacted through the speaker's transformative descriptions only underscores the loss which links them both: the action of searching for a lost item, the lovers' shared glass. Even as the past is powerfully called back by the speaker's immersion of her arm—prompting her subsequent submersion in memory—, the recovery of time is made hollow by the unsuccessful act of recovery itself: the lost glass is "past recall," and the only thing which can really be "[f]etched back" is pain (l. 36, 4).

Anesthetic Representation

"Under the Waterfall" seems, therefore, to be a characteristically "pessimistic" Hardy poem: its speaker can be reminded of a happy afternoon, yet the past, her lover, and even the minimal remainder of an artifact—their shared glass—are lost. The glass, on this reading, is a kind of emblem, not simply of the speaker's departed paramour, but of the past itself, of the unrecoverable absence which subsists within the moment returned by her memory; and the two events of the poem "rhyme" only insofar as they echo this absolute loss. However, it is precisely by eluding both restoration and representation that the glass symbolizes something *more* than loss. The same claim that Cleanth Brooks made in *The Well Wrought Urn* for the vessel in Donne's "Canonization" could, in fact, be made for Hardy's glass as well: "it is the poem itself"—yet one displaying a very different "paradox of the imagination."[36] Beyond the reach of both the speaker's hands and the poet's depiction, the glass becomes a symbol for loss as such; through its very invisibility, it turns into the sensory lack around which the poem structures itself.[37]

From the outset of the poem, aesthetic data is stratified. In the first verse paragraph, after the plunging of her arm elicits a "sweet sharp sense" (l. 3), the speaker considers different sensory data—aural and visual—in turn. Between her first description of the hearth-like picnic's location (l. 10–13), discussed above, sound is the dominant sense, depicted at the beginning and end of her inaugural reminiscence; and the twice-mentioned "purl" of the waterfall (l. 9, 13) becomes, at the end of this verse paragraph, an endless, anthropomorphized "voice" (l. 15). It is this voice, moreover, which is repeated in the rhyme that the speaker's present action recalls, the sound which "never ceases/ In stir of kingdoms, in wars, in peaces" (l. 13–14). Contrasted with the speaker's fungible scene-setting description—"paint[ed]" with the palette of her present surroundings (l. 30)—is this, the unfailing sound of the waterfall's rhyme.

But the poem's central object, however, is outside the ambit of even this sense's scope; indeed, it is beyond the realm of aesthetic perception itself. In the speaker's second verse paragraph, at the apex of the recollection solicited by her interlocutor, the lost human artifact appears without appearing, its perduring presence announced in the arresting half-line sentence: "There the glass still is" (l. 37). This "opalized" but invisible object (l. 24), removed from the world of human use, has become incorporated into the timeless world of nature, untroubled by the "stir of kingdoms" and their conflicts. And the significance of the glass's integration into this world is revealed by the speaker in the poem's penultimate couplet, wherein she asserts that its "presence adds to the rhyme of love/ Persistently sung by the fall above" (l. 49–50). Yet, if it adds to the waterfall's rhyme, it does so in unseen silence. Indeed, what should crown "Under the Waterfall" is a description of what remains *under the waterfall* but the glass itself is never imagined in any kind of detail, attaining only the most minimal mode of presence. There is no poetic compensation for its absence: its only presentation in the poem is precisely as a kind of lacuna. The paradox at the heart of the poem is this missing *ekphrasis*: instead of the vanity of an image without presence, Hardy's poem offers the obverse, giving the reader a presence without an image; thus, the poem's locative title, pointing towards what the lyric itself declines to present.

"Under the Waterfall," then, achieves two apparently opposed ends, both succeeding and failing to represent a departed past. The poem gives memory an imaginative habitus in the vivid aesthetic data which the speaker describes; but, at the same time, it limns the limit of the poet's power through the lost glass's absent silhouette. But it is precisely in the articulation of this limit that the true power of the poem resides. For, instead of the stale satisfaction of a fictional fulfillment, Hardy offers more to his reader in this very image of loss.

The final couplet of the speaker's monologue emphasizes the last use of the lost glass: "No lip has touched it since his and mine/ In turns therefrom sipped lovers' wine" (l. 51–52). The lost glass is now kept at a saving distance outside of both the world's reach and the human scale of time itself; the lovers' picnic thereby becomes a kind of "past that was never present."[38] This does not imply that the past event which the speaker recalls did not occur, especially since the origin of the pastoral repast imagined in this poem can ultimately be traced to a specific moment in Emma and Thomas Hardy's courtship.[39] Furthermore, through the very loss of the poem's central artifact, the lovers' afternoon is likewise lifted out of the entanglement of linear time and into an enduring memory. The glass, then, is a placeholder for an unrepresentable center which the poem's rhyming events can echo but can neither repeat nor reproduce; and the poem itself becomes witness to this invisible symbol's endless song.

In a characteristically lapidary and ludic vignette, Jorge Luis Borges proffers a proof of God's existence by asserting that there is an indefinite, inconceivable integer which, nevertheless, defines the exact number of birds seen in his imagination's reverie.[40] This impossible number is not unlike the lost glass in "Under the Waterfall": the unimagined object that radiates its power throughout the poem precisely through its undifferentiated indefiniteness.

Counterfactual Feeling

Hardy's minimal depiction of the lost glass in this poem—with a presence inversely proportional to its description—would seem to be the antithesis of the Aestheticism propounded by Pater and Wilde in their celebration of sensation and their assertions regarding the autonomy of art.[41] Yet, the anesthetic poetic exemplified in "Under the Waterfall" admits a surprising parallel with this movement.[42] In "The Critic as Artist," Wilde's spokesman, Gilbert, remarks that "[a]fter playing Chopin, I feel as if I had been weeping over sins that I had never committed, and mourning over tragedies that were not my own."[43] Hardy's "pessimistic" art produces this same counterfactual effect; if his anesthetic representation declines to give imaginative directives, it does not thwart feeling.

Indeed, what remains in the absence of aesthetic stimulus is, precisely, pain. "Under the Waterfall" opens with an oxymoronic "sweet sharp sense" (l. 3), and the questions posed by the speaker's interlocutor are punctuated by an inquiry about the thing which can "bring throbs to [her] soul?" (l. 20). And, after identifying the location of the glass, the speaker recapitulates the sequence of the poem with her summary:

> And, as said, if I thrust my arm below
> Cold water in basin or bowl, a throe
> From the past awakens a sense of that time,
> And the glass we used, and the cascade's rhyme. [l. 39–42]

In this compendious reprise, pain is identified as the generative force of the speaker's address: it provokes her feeling for the past, the absent glass, and the waterfall's rhyme—that rhyme which has itself become interwoven into the fabric and form of her monologue's couplets.

This pain, however, is filtered through fiction: it is an invented pathos at a distance from any lyric "I." While an irreducible separation between speaker and poet is implicit in even the most sincere lyric utterance, Hardy exploits this structure to contemplate the affect of the poem from a distance.[44] Pain for the speaker, in fact, is knowledge for the poet; and, through her endurance of the pangs of recollection, Hardy finds not only the chiming symmetry of rhyming time, but a kind of consolation as well. It is telling that, when Hardy addresses the charge of pessimism in his "Apology" to his *Late Lyrics*, he initially appeals to the great poem of self-consolation, Wordsworth's "Ode: Intimations of Immortality," as a poetic precedent for the "grave, positive, [and] stark, delineations" which his collection contains.[45] But, despite his approving citation, a crucial difference persists between the compensatory consolations which these poets achieve: Wordsworth reconciles loss and gain in the first person; Hardy, however, inherits lessons from lives he never lived.

Beneath the rectos of reality, Hardy reads the palimpsestic versos of the imagination, and, through his poetic pessimism, he feels the pain of possibilities which only intersect with reality though his own art. In this pain, there is more than simply the "[s]trength in what remains behind"[46]: there is joy—the same joy which Hölderlin found in Sophocles' sorrow, the same feeling which Fichte found subsisting in suffering: "We at least feel ourselves and possess ourselves in the feeling of pain, and this alone already gives us an inexpressible happiness."[47] Hardy overcomes the vanity of the aesthetic in this bittersweet feeling of self; and, through his fashioning of events which rhyme, he forges an art beyond both what the senses can perceive and what time can taint.

Acknowledgments

For her helpful feedback on an earlier version of this essay, I would like to thank Elaine Scarry; warm thanks are also owed to Heather Brink-Roby, Nicole Miller, Daniel Benjamin Williams, and Annie Wyman.

Notes

1. This is one of the "Five Epigrams," entitled "Sophocles," *Selected Verse*, trans. Michael Hamburger (Baltimore: Penguin, 1961), 35.
2. Thomas Hardy, *Jude the Obscure*, ed. Patricia Ingham (Oxford: Oxford University Press, 2002), 12.
3. *Ibid.*, 13.
4. Reginald Gordon Cox, *Thomas Hardy: The Critical Heritage* (London: Routledge, 1979), xxi, 146. Early critical treatments in this vein include Lascelles Abercrombie, *Thomas Hardy: A Critical Study* (New York: Russell and Russell, 1912) and Alfred Noyes, "The Poetry of Thomas Hardy," *North American Review* 194:1 (1911): 96–105. The

concept of pessimism has not been a frequent point of focus for critics in recent years, but see Laurence Estanove's essay in this volume for a reconsideration of the subject.

5. *Thomas Hardy's Personal Writings: Prefaces, Literary Opinions, Reminiscences*, ed. Harold Orel (London: Macmillan, 1967), 53, 52.

6. *Ibid.*, 54.

7. *Ibid.*, 52; my emphasis.

8. *Ibid.*, 53.

9. Quoted in Max Brod, *Franz Kafka: A Biography*, trans. G. H. Roberts et al. (New York: Da Capo, 1995), 75.

10. *Thomas Hardy's Personal Writings, op. cit.*, 52.

11. Simone Weil, *Letter to a Priest*, trans. A. F. Wills (London: Routledge, 2002), 35–36.

12. Georg Lukács, *The Theory of the Novel*, trans. Anna Bostock (Cambridge: MIT Press, 1971), 88.

13. *Ibid.*, 90, 89.

14. *Ibid.*, 97.

15. *Jude the Obscure, op. cit.*, 12.

16. Hardy's use of an inverted theological concept to describe a finite creature is comparable to Gerard Manley Hopkins's catalogue of the natural world in the seventh line of his curtal sonnet, "Pied Beauty." According to Joaquin Kuhn, this line is a perfect inversion of the four attributes of God in Aristotelian metaphysics: God is infinite, eternal, necessary, and true, whereas nature is "counter, original, spare, [and] strange," "The Completeness of 'Pied Beauty,'" *SEL* 18:4 (1978): 685ff.

17. *Jude the Obscure, op. cit.*, 11.

18. See *Job* 2:8, *The Holy Bible Latin Vulgate* (Baltimore: John Murphy, 1899; repr. Rockford: Tan Books, 1971), 553.

19. The phrase is from St. Augustine's *Confessions*, Book III, Chapter 6, Section 11: "You were more intimately present to me than my innermost being, and higher than the highest peak of my spirit," *Confessions*, trans. Maria Boulding, O.S.B. (New York: Vintage, 1998), 44–45. The more popular version of this phrase which I have given—and which seems to incorporate a later phrase from the *Confessions*: "but what can be nearer to me than I am to myself," 212—appears to come from one of Meister Eckhart's sermons, "The Nearness of the Kingdom," which compresses both of Augustine's insights: "God is nearer to me than I am to myself; my existence depends on the nearness and presence of God," *Meister Eckhart, German Sermons & Treatises*, ed. and trans. M. O'C. Walshe, vol. I (London: Watkins, 1979), 110. For a bracing discussion of Augustine's phrase, see Jean-Luc Marion, *In the Self's Place: The Approach of Saint Augustine*, trans. Jeffrey L. Kosky (Stanford: Stanford University Press, 2012), 31, 97–98, 159, 260, and 284; Marion's entire argument, however, is relevant.

20. See Karsten Harries, "The Infinite Sphere: Comments on the History of a Metaphor," *Journal of the History of Philosophy* 13:1 (1975): 5–15. The history of this metaphor is also the subject of one of Jorge Luis Borges's essays entitled, "The Fearful Sphere of Pascal," *Labyrinths: Selected Stories and Other Writings*, trans. James E. Irby (New York: New Directions, 1964), 189–192.

21. Pascal's alteration is not a subversive substitution, however, as the immediate context of the phrase makes clear: "Let man then contemplate the whole of nature in her full and lofty majesty…. Nature is an infinite sphere whose centre is everywhere and

circumference nowhere. In short it is the greatest perceptible mark of God's omnipotence that our imagination should lose itself in that thought," *Pensées*, trans. A. J. Krailsheimer (New York: Penguin, 1995), 60.

22. *The Life and Work of Thomas Hardy*, ed. Michael Millgate (London: Macmillan, 1984), 309.

23. Deleuze quoted in J. Hillis Miller, *Fiction and Repetition* (Cambridge: Harvard University Press, 1982), 6.

24. *Ibid.*

25. *Ibid.* As an illustration of this second type of repetition, Miller offers, as an example, the moment in *The Mayor of Casterbridge* when Henchard thinks that he has returned to the place where he sold his wife and daughter, the "primal scene" of his tragedy; but, "as the narrator tells us, with Hardy's characteristic insouciant ironic cruelty, he has not correctly identified the place" (*ibid.*).

26. After noting that the second mode of repetition is dependent on the first, Miller observes: "Each form of repetition calls up the other, by an inevitable compulsion. The second is not the negation or opposite of the first, but its 'counterpart,' in a strange relation whereby the second is the subversive ghost of the first, always already present within it as a possibility which hollows it out" (*ibid.*, 9).

27. *Ibid.*; braces in original.

28. *Ibid.*, 12.

29. *Ibid.*, 13.

30. Erich Auerbach, "*Figura*," *Scenes from the Drama of European Literature: Six Essays* (Minneapolis: University of Minnesota Press, 1982), 29; the essay in question was translated by Ralph Manheim.

31. J. Hillis Miller, "History as Repetition in Hardy's Poetry" in *Tropes, Parables, Performatives: Essays on Twentieth-Century Literature* (Durham: Duke University Press, 1991), 116.

32. "Under the Waterfall," *The Complete Poetical Works of Thomas Hardy*, ed. Samuel Hynes, vol. II (Oxford: Clarendon, 1984), 45–46, l. 1–4.

33. W. H. Auden, *Collected Poems*, ed. Edward Mendelson, 3d. edition (New York: Modern Library, 2007), 135, l. 37–38.

34. I am grateful to Tim Kendall for pointing out this last allusion to me. See also John Fuller, *W. H. Auden: A Commentary* (London: Faber and Faber, 1998), 271.

35. Dennis Taylor notes the parallel between this poem and the famous remembrance-precipitating action of the narrator in the first volume of Proust's novel which, coincidentally, was published in the same year that Hardy's poem was likely composed: 1913; see *Hardy's Poetry, 1860–1928* (London: Macmillan, 1981), 182n. 43.

36. Cleanth Brooks, *The Well Wrought Urn* (New York: Harcourt, 1947), 21.

37. See Slavoj Žižek's account of the Lacanian Real: "whenever we have a symbolic structure it is structured around a certain void," *The Sublime Object of Ideology* (London: Verso, 1989), 72; see also 185.

38. Leonard Lawler argues that this phrase—a commonplace of continental philosophers such as Derrida, Deleuze, and Levinas—"probably in fact derives from [Bergson's] *Matter and Memory*," *The Challenge of Bergsonism: Phenomenology, Ontology, Ethics* (New York: Continuum International Group, 2003), 54. See also Jacques Derrida, *Voice and Phenomenon: Introduction to the Problem of the Sign in Husserl's Phenomenology*, trans. Leonard Lawlor (Evanston: Northwestern University Press, 2010), 54ff.

39. See Claire Tomalin, *Thomas Hardy: A Time-Torn Man* (New York: Viking, 2006), 384.

40. Jorge Luis Borges, "*Argumentum Ornithologicum*," *Aleph and Other Stories*, trans. Andrew Hurley (New York: Penguin, 2004), 148.

41. See, for example, Pater's "Conclusion" to *The Renaissance: Studies in Art and Poetry: The 1893 Text*, ed. Donald L. Hill (Berkeley: University of California Press, 1980), 186–190 and Wilde's "The Decay of Lying" in *The Artist as Critic*, ed. Richard Ellmann (Chicago: University of Chicago Press, 1982), 290–320.

42. Interestingly, Hardy—who is remembered more for his realist novels than his poetry—actually echoes Wilde's polemical rejection of realism in a notebook entry dated "August 5," 1890 wherein he writes: "Art is a disproportioning ... of realities, to show more clearly the features that matter in those realities.... Hence 'realism' is not Art," *The Life, op. cit.*, 239.

43. Wilde, *The Artist as Critic*, 343. For an illuminating discussion of this aspect of Hardy's poetry, see James Richardson's chapter, "Necessity and Possibility" in *Thomas Hardy: The Poetry of Necessity* (Chicago: University of Chicago Press, 1977), 1–30. See also Susan M. Miller's essay, "Thomas Hardy and the Impersonal Lyric," *Journal of Modern Literature* 30:3 (2007): 95–115. The exploration of experience beyond the scope of the first person in the content of Hardy's poetry is, perhaps, related to the wide range of its forms: the encyclopedic experimentation with different verse forms in Hardy's large poetic corpus is a kind of formal analogue to the wide range of experiences represented therein.

44. It is worth recalling Bakhtin's pithy crystallization of this aporetic structure: "It is just as impossible to forge an identity between myself, my own 'I,' and that 'I' that is the subject of my stories as it is to lift myself up by my own hair," *The Dialogic Imagination: Four Essays*, ed. Michael Holquist, trans. Caryl Emerson and Michael Holquist (Austin: University of Texas Press, 1981), 256. See also Hardy's poem "He Follows Himself," *The Complete Poetical Works of Thomas Hardy*, vol. II, 422.

45. *Thomas Hardy's Personal Writings, op. cit.*, 51.

46. William Wordsworth, "Intimations of Immortality from Recollections of Early Childhood," *Poems, in Two Volumes, and Other Poems, 1800–1807*, ed. Jared Curtis (Ithaca, NY: Cornell University Press, 1983), 276, l. 183.

47. J. G. Fichte quoted in Michel Henry, *The Essence of Manifestation*, trans. Girard Etzkorn (The Hague: Martinus Nijhoff, 1973), 670; see "The Way Towards the Blessed Life; or, the Doctrine of Religion," *The Popular Works of Johann Gottlieb Fichte*, trans. W. Smith, vol. II (London: Chapman, 1849), 133–134.

Works Cited

Auerbach, Erich. *Scenes from the Drama of European Literature: Six Essays*. Minneapolis: University of Minnesota Press, 1982.

Augustine. *Confessions*. Trans. Maria Boulding, O.S.B. New York: Vintage, 1998.

Auden, Wystan Hugh. *Collected Poems*. Ed. Edward Mendelson. 3d ed. New York: Modern Library, 2007.

Bakhtin, Mikhail Mikhailovich. *The Dialogic Imagination: Four Essays*. Ed. Michael Holquist. Trans. Caryl Emerson and Michael Holquist. Austin: University of Texas Press, 1981.

Borges, Jorges Luis. *Aleph and Other Stories*. Trans. Andrew Hurley. New York: Penguin, 2004.
Brod, Max. *Franz Kafka: A Biography*. Trans. G. H. Roberts et al. New York: Da Capo, 1995.
Brooks, Cleanth. *The Well Wrought Urn: Studies in the Structure of Poetry*. New York: Harcourt, 1947.
Cox, Reginald Gordon. *Thomas Hardy: The Critical Heritage*. London: Routledge, 1979.
Eckhart von Hochheim O.P. *Meister Eckhart, German Sermons & Treatises*. Ed. and trans. M. O'C. Walshe. Vol. I. London: Watkins, 1979.
Hardy, Thomas. *The Complete Poetical Works of Thomas Hardy*. Ed. Samuel Hynes. Vol. II. Oxford: Clarendon, 1984.
_____. *Jude the Obscure*. Ed. Patricia Ingham. Oxford: Oxford University Press, 2002.
_____. *The Life and Work of Thomas Hardy*. Ed. Michael Millgate. London: Macmillan, 1984.
_____. *Thomas Hardy's Personal Writings: Prefaces, Literary Opinions, Reminiscences*. Ed. Harold Orel. London: Macmillan, 1967.
Henry, Michel. *The Essence of Manifestation*. Trans. Girard Etzkorn. The Hague: Martinus Nijhoff, 1973.
Hölderlin, Friedrich. *Selected Verse*. Trans. Michael Hamburger. Baltimore: Penguin, 1961.
The Holy Bible Translated from the Latin Vulgate. Rockford: Tan Books, 1899; repr. 1971.
Kuhn, Joaquin. "The Completeness of 'Pied Beauty,'" *SEL* 18:4 (1978): 677–692.
Lawler, Leonard. *The Challenge of Bergsonism: Phenomenology, Ontology, Ethics*. New York: Continuum, 2003.
Lukács, Georg. *The Theory of the Novel*. Trans. Anna Bostock. Cambridge: MIT Press, 1971.
Miller, J. Hillis. *Fiction and Repetition*. Cambridge: Harvard University Press, 1982.
_____. "History as Repetition in Hardy's Poetry," *Tropes, Parables, Performatives: Essays on Twentieth-Century Literature*. Durham: Duke University Press, 1991.
Pascal, Blaise. *Pensées*. Trans. A. J. Krailsheimer. New York: Penguin, 1995.
Weil, Simone. *Letter to a Priest*. Trans. A. F. Wills. London: Routledge, 2002.
Wilde, Oscar. *The Artist as Critic*. Ed. Richard Ellmann. Chicago: University of Chicago Press, 1982.
Wordsworth, William. *Poems, in Two Volumes, and Other Poems, 1800–1807*. Ed. Jared Curtis. Ithaca, NY: Cornell University Press, 1983.
Žižek, Slavoj. *The Sublime Object of Ideology*. London: Verso, 1989.

The End Game
Thomas Hardy's Looking Glass
Richard D. Beards

In Oscar Wilde's *Picture of Dorian Gray*, the eponymous hero at one of his Aunt Agatha's parties observes a radical member of parliament and says, "like all people who try to exhaust his subject, he exhausted his listeners"[1] (in this instance, readers). With this note of caution in mind, I will consider five of Thomas Hardy's poems which employ the mirror or looking-glass image. These poems reveal noteworthy aspects of Hardy's sensibility, particularly his way of expressing perennial human dilemmas by using the looking glass as both tenor and vehicle.

The first of these poems, "At the Dinner Table" (*Late Lyrics and Earlier*, 1922),[2] is a monologue in which the speaker, a widow, reveals a nasty trick her late husband played on her fifty years before when he substituted a warped and distorting looking glass for the usual mirror on their dining room sideboard. She recalls that while sitting at dinner "in my prime, I well-nigh fainted with affright" when she sees herself in the mirror as "a haggard crone." Although her husband sees the effect and duly apologizes, resenting the brutality of his prank, she says she "spoke not all eve to him."

In the poem's present tense, a half century later, she sits in the same chair and sees the very same wrinkled image she had seen "In jest these fifty years before." The word "score"—she sees in her reflection "each wrinkle and score"—could be read as connoting twenty-year-time periods in addition to being understood as a "a crack, a device, a cut, notch, scratch, a mark with a line or lines" (*OED*). Thus, the husband's cruel jest meshes with the realities of aging, the early image of her prime self in the distorting mirror proleptic of the physical self she will become. This poem conveys Hardy's view of the inevitability of aging and simultaneously reveals an empty, "at odds" marriage. The cruel trick and the widow's momentary shock fifty years earlier is played against the larger, universal pattern of her husband's death and her own relentless decline. The mirror, the metaphorical vehicle, facilitates two grim Hardyan perspectives—the failure of domestic relations and the insults of the aging process. The word "jest" in the final line refers to the husband's mirror trick but also to Nature's subtle machinations over time. Although we know youth and beauty are impermanent, that we are decaying even as we admire these attributes, we avoid admitting the brutality of our evanescence until we are forced to do so by a looking glass which trumps denial with truth.

"I Look Into My Glass,"[3] the final poem in *Wessex Poems* (1898), written in four-line trimeter stanzas, with the third line of each stanza being four feet, typifies the Anglican hymn form familiar to Hardy from his childhood. The poem's speaker makes the painful discovery that the individual—specifically his spirit and body—does not age uniformly. While his physical self declines (the mirror he is peering into reveals his "wasting skin"), his heart does not "shrink" correspondingly. The twelve-line poem is shaped by the paradox that "our fragile frame at eve" can hold a heart capable of the "throbbing of noontide." Had his heart shrunk, the narrator muses, he could easily have been reconciled to "the hearts grown cold to me" as he awaits his "endless rest." "Endless rest" certainly does not suggest the "endless bliss" of the Anglican hymnal nor the comforts of heaven; in addition, a linguistically agile reader might also tease out "rest-less" from the "endless rest" combination. At any rate, Hardy is unequivocally limning the province of death and the grave. His obsession with the disconnect between the body and the spirit in regard to aging, his dismay at being emotionally whole and mentally whole while muscle, bone and flesh attenuate surfaces in other works as well.

In Book II, chapter 12 of *The Well-Beloved*, Jocelyn Pierston, after glimpsing himself in a mirror, asks "when was it to end—this curse of his heart not aging while his frame moved naturally onward?" The text continues to elaborate:

> The recognition startled him. The person he appeared to be was too far chronologically in advance of the person he felt himself to be. Pierston did not care to regard the figure confronting him so mockingly. Its voice seemed to say "there's tragedy hanging onto this!" But the question of age being pertinent he could not give the spectre up [...]. While his soul was what it was, why should he have been encumbered with that withering carcase [...]?[4]

Hardy pursues this theme in his journal: "I look in the glass. Am conscious of the humiliating sorriness of my earthly tabernacle, and of the sad fact that the best parents could do not do better for me.... Why should a man's mind have been thrown into such close, sad, sensational, inexplicable relations with such a precarious object as his own body."[5] One is here reminded of Freud's comment that he felt "profound displeasure" after catching a glimpse of his aging self in a train window.[6]

"I Look into My Glass" has been compared to George Herbert's "The Elixir," a well-known Anglican hymn in which the Christian soul's eye can, "if he pleaseth through it pass ["it" here is his glass] / And then the Heav'n espie."[7] As useful as Herbert's same stanza form poem might be for contrasting the believer's stance with Hardy's, Herbert probably refers to a window glass here (as in *I Corinthians*' "Through a Glass, Darkly") rather than to a mirror. Hardy's poem attributes to Time a will to "make [him] grieve" because passing time increases the gulf between his "fragile frame" and "noontide heart." The speaker awaiting his "endless rest" has little or no advantage. His "shaking fragile frame at eve" denies him repose, bliss, or even a small degree of peace.

In the title poem of *Moments of Vision*,[8] the speaker wonders at the source of a mirror's "magic" which gives, in addition to a reflection of our physical self, an image or adumbration of the "transparency" of our conscience: the magic "throws our mind back on us, and our heart,/ Until we start." The four-stanza poem is organized around four questions: Who holds the mirror? Who "lifts that mirror" and throws our mind back on us"? Why does the mirror give us "tincts" of ourselves we never otherwise see? And finally and most importantly, once the mirror has captured our "whole life foul or fair" where does it "glass it" (the last line, "Glassing it—where?" reveals Hardy's neo-logistic creativity)? The suggestion is that the mirror gives us a vision of our deep self and its dimensions but leaves unanswered the final question: "to what larger end or purpose?" The "Who/Who/Why/Where" sequence encrypts Hardy's perspective: there is no Greater consciousness and no larger purpose or meaning to our personal struggles. The view recurs increasingly in nineteenth and twentieth-century poetry and prose.

I think here of Robert Frost's poem "Neither Out Far Nor In Deep" in which he places people on the seashore, looking out to sea and comments in the last stanza that though they can neither "look out far" nor "look in deep," that is no obstacle "To any watch they keep."[9] Like Hardy, Frost recognizes limits to our knowledge of what lies, if anything, beyond. Both view their worlds as challenged by the shifting epistemologies of their time. Both fret about the individual's life in a universe devoid of wider, deeper meaning. This is not a case of the anxiety of influence but of two brooding loners considering how to establish purposeful direction, a larger meaning in the world in which they labor. While Frost concentrates on the watchers—those seeking what is there that keeps humans looking for a god-like controlling power, a meaningful script in the "out there," Hardy takes up the mirror image to make a rational post–Darwinian argument. His mirror poems are meditations on man's condition. The individual who gazes into the mirror is thrown back on his own resources and weaknesses and liabilities. In the prose "Apology" which prefaces *Late Lyrics and Earlier* (1922), Hardy's pessimism—which he emphatically and consistently denied—has less to do with the psychology of those who need a divine maker or director than with the spirit of his age. Who wouldn't have "obstinate questionings" and "blank misgivings" if they looked thoughtfully and skeptically at the evidence for God's existence? Hardy suggests that if one looks methodically "stage by stage" at human history, the best "consummation" possible is "evolutionary meliorism."[10] What he phrases as "the disordered years of our prematurely afflicted century" is a persistent subtext in his novels and poems. Those who question Hardy's skepticism—and many did, and do—are in the "Apology['s]" words "Panglossians." "The best of all possible worlds" mantra is self-deception writ large.

In "The Cheval-Glass,"[11] the poem's speaker explains to a friendly inquiring visitor why, in his cell-like bachelor's room, he keeps an oversized, cumbersome Cheval-Glass. The visitor assumes his monkish host hardly needs a full-length mirror, given its size and its owner's negligible vanity: "You never preen or plume/ Or look in a week at your full-length figure— / Picture of bachelor gloom." The question of "why" the glass is posed by the visitor in the first of the poem's eight stanzas. Its owner uses the following seven stanzas to explain his attachment to the mirror. In his innocence and "thoughtless of all heart-harm," the narrator formed a crush on a parson's daughter, "a creature of nameless charm." She eventually came to a tragic end, seduced by a man from a distant town, ill-used, driven to insanity and then to death. Her grieving father dies soon after, and at the auction of the family's belongings the narrator buys the Cheval-Glass which he had been told was "long in her use."

He had no more direct contact with, or experience of, the young woman than Dante did of Beatrice—he gazed at her as he walked past her parsonage home. That's it. The "relationship" he obsesses about is limned in the final three stanzas and suggests that this "picture of bachelor gloom" emanates from a fantasy, and a prurient one at that. In stanza six he confides that at dawn, and presumably from his bed, he imagines "her pale-face from there [in his newly purchased mirror]/ Brushing her hair's bright bands." He is a stranger to the intimacy of such a bedroom scene. Although "The Cheval-Glass" might correctly be called a dialogue, rhetorically Hardy is tapping into monologue territory. The reader is far more knowing than the naïve narrator. In the final stanza the narrator claims he bought the Cheval-Glass "for its revelations" and then "brought it oversea." He says he will never separate from it; ultimately he plans to have it broken up and buried "where my grave is to be." This is fetishism writ large.

As in his poems "Drummer Hodge"[12] and "The Son's Portrait,"[13] in which a mother buries a photo of her son that had been discarded by his estranged wife, burial implies continuance, respect and quasi-religious awe of the buried object. The Cheval-Glass is a sacred object to the narrator: it speaks for his sad life. The woman at the center of his consciousness is dead, never was his companion, and only ever was—and continues to be—an image, a fantasy. Her enigmatic smile when he summons her from the glass "ponderingly" and her hair brushing are the ratcheted-up fantasies of a lonely bachelor, substitutions for a real-life engagement with a woman.

What's interesting in this poem is neither the fetishized mirror nor the tragedy of the parson's daughter. We are drawn to the mind and imagination of the speaker, a bachelor too timid to engage in actual sexual relations who substitutes a fantasy partner by gazing in a mirror. Ironically, what "The Cheval-Glass" reveals is the person who never looks into it. As in "I Look into My Glass" and "Moments of Vision," mirrors allow for deep scrutiny, presenting not just the surface of the gazer but the "tincts" of the deep self. The bachelor of "The Cheval-Glass" creates his reality out of a fantasy: the woman who centers his life is dead and never was his companion. One is reminded of Hardy's comments about his own unnaturally slow maturation. "I was a child 'till I was 16; a youth 'till 25; a young man 'till I was 40 or 50."[14] While "The Cheval-Glass" is not necessarily autobiographical, the innocent voice of the narrator does suggest Hardy's long, slow and very possibly in-grown maturation.

Finally, "The Pedigree"[15] uses a mirror metaphor. Its speaker recognizes as he studies his pedigree that his ancestors have anticipated his physical attributes ("mien, and build, and brow") as well as "every heave and coil and move I made/ Within my brain, and in my mood and speech...." The pedigree chart is a "glass" in which he sees his every thought and reflection. As he glumly concludes, "I am merest mimicker and counterfeit!—." Unable to see himself as unique (*I am I,/ And what I do I do alone,*"), the speaker is forced to acknowledge he is the clone of his family's history, a flesh and blood "pedigree." The "Mage's mirror" which he projected onto the plain glass window square disappears in the process of his discovery, returning the window pane to its original "plain glass" through which he sees the "stained moon and [cloud] drift." The narrator initially equates the Mage's mirror with magic, with unpredictability and pure potential, but his vision of an open and pure future is abruptly cancelled by the realization that one merely performs repetitive acts. "The primest fugleman [...] [is] fogged in far antiqueness" (a "fugleman" being a trained soldier posted as a model before a line of soldiers practicing military exercises). The fugleman connotes the mechanical, lockstep nature of the speaker's repetition of his ancestor's thought and movements. The mirror-pedigree metaphor, certainly original to Thomas Hardy, concentrates the idea of "mirroring" as exact imitation, exact duplication. And to the narrator of the poem, this totally deterministic pattern devastates any notion of volition, choice, or individuality.

While the speaker pours over his pedigree in his study or bedroom, the world beyond the window is worn out, lacking in force, sickly: the moon is "in its old age"; "mute and cold it globed/ Like a drifting dolphin's eye seen in a lapping wave." Nature's exhaustion and moon's "green-rheumed eye" suggest a grim correspondence between the trapped and bound individual and a cold and dying—and perhaps collusive—natural world.

Looked at oppositely, one wishes Hardy had been both brave and vain enough to stare at himself in the mirror. The mirror poems suggest the extraordinary literary transition into themes of self-conscious longing, remorse, and reconsiderings that make Hardy a pivotal figure in the shift from nineteenth-century values and literary themes to those of the twentieth century. Thus Hardy, through the deceptively simple image of the mirror, crosses borders that become ground zero for a great deal of twentieth-century poetry and prose.

"At the Dinner Table," "I Look into my Glass," "Moments of Vision," "The Cheval-Glass," and "The Pedigree" fuse metaphor and meaning to present the ravages of time on the individual in a dour universe, a time-space in which aging, decay and demise are the only game, the end game. The futility of reaching out to others or searching for any greater life force than atomistic volition dooms the players. When Hardy submitted *Moments of Vision and Miscellaneous Poems* for publication, he did not expect much notice, for these poems "mortify the human sense of importance [showing] that human beings are of no matter or appreciable value in this nonchalant universe."[16] The final line of "Moments of Vision" makes this abundantly clear—"Glassing it—where?" And of course we have no answer.

Notes

1. Oscar Wilde, *The Picture of Dorian Gray*, ed. Peter Ackroyd (Harmondsworth: Penguin Classics, 1985), 45.
2. Thomas Hardy, *The Complete Poems*, ed. James Gibson (Basingstoke: Palgrave, 2001), 654–655.
3. *Ibid.*, 81.
4. Thomas Hardy, *The Well-Beloved* (Ware, Hertfordshire: Wordsworth Editions, 2000), 128.
5. Florence Emily Hardy, *The Later Years of Thomas Hardy* (London: Macmillan, 1930), 13–14.

6. Sigmund Freud as quoted in Mark Pendergrast, "Introduction" to *The Book of the Mirror: A History of the Human Love Affair with Reflection*, ed. Miranda Anderson (Newcastle, England: Cambridge Scholars Publishing, 2007), 5.

7. See Trevor Johnson, *A Critical Introduction to the Poems of Thomas Hardy* (London: Macmillan, 1991), 60–62.

8. *The Complete Poems, op. cit.*, 427.

9. Robert Frost, "Neither Out Far Nor In Deep" in *The Penguin Book of American Verse*, ed. Geoffrey Moore (Harmondsworth: Penguin Books, 1979; first edition 1977), 253.

10. *The Complete Poems, op. cit.*, 557.

11. *Ibid.*, 360–361.

12. *Ibid.*, 90–91.

13. *Ibid.*, 862.

14. Florence Emily Hardy, *op. cit.*, 14.

15. *Ibid.*, 460–461.

16. Florence Emily Hardy, *op. cit.*, 179.

Works Cited

Hardy, Florence Emily. *The Later Years of Thomas Hardy*. London: Macmillan and Company, 1930.

Hardy, Thomas. *The Complete Poems*. Ed. James Gibson. Basingstoke: Palgrave, 2001.

_____. *Selected Poems*. Ed. Andrew Motion. London: Everyman, 1994.

_____. *The Well-Beloved*. Ware, Hertfordshire: Wordsworth Editions, 2000.

Johnson, Trevor. *A Critical Introduction to the Poems of Thomas Hardy*. London: Macmillan, 1991.

Moore, Geoffrey, ed. *The Penguin Book of American Verse*. Harmondsworth: Penguin, 1977.

Pendergrast, Mark. "Introduction," *The Book of the Mirror: A History of the Human Love Affair with Reflection*. Ed. Miranda Anderson. Newcastle, England: Cambridge Scholars Publishing, 2007.

Wilde, Oscar. *The Picture of Dorian Gray*. Ed. Peter Ackroyd. Harmondsworth: Penguin Classics, 1985.

From Pessimism to Idealism
The Pressure of Paradox
Laurence Estanove

Pessimism is the most common label to have been ascribed to Thomas Hardy's work. It was so for his novels, and it was also the case when he started publishing poetry just before the turn of the 20th century. The reviews (even the positive ones) thus saw his collections of verse as "frequently inspired by a somewhat grim mortuary imagination"[1]; reviews of *Poems of the Past and the Present* from 1902 similarly explained that "[t]he best poems in it are brooding, obscure, tremulous, half-inarticulate meditations over man, nature and destiny,"[2] and that Hardy "has a morbid taste for the ghastly and the gruesome."[3] In 1918, the poet and critic Edmund Gosse, who was also incidentally a close friend of Hardy's, published an enthusiastic critical panorama of the latter's lyrical verse. Even there, we find a similar perception of that work, specifically of Hardy's fourth collection *Satires of Circumstance* (1914) whose poems Gosse saw as "hard and cruel shafts of searchlight."[4] Gosse further insisted that pessimism was indeed "the Hardy doctrine":

> But, of course, Mr. Hardy is a pessimist, just as Browning is an optimist, just as white is not black, and day is not night. Our juggling with words in paradox is too often apt to disguise a want of decision in thought. Let us admit that Mr. Hardy's conception of the fatal forces which beleaguer human life is a "pessimistic" one, or else words have no meaning. [...] His pessimism is involuntary, forced from him by his experience and his constitution.[5]

Such a labeling was therefore not necessarily a derogatory one. Yet Hardy was particularly sensitive to that vision of his work, and he relentlessly explained throughout his career that he was *not* a pessimist. In a notebook entry dated 25 January 1899, Hardy seems to consider that pessimism is the natural stance of poetry, that pessimism and poetry, or at least "great" poetry, are indeed inseparable. Typically, he illustrates his point by quoting the Scriptures, the Bible being to him the richest source of poetry in the whole of literature:

> Pessimism. Was there ever any great poetry which was not pessimistic? ...
> "All creation groaneth," &c.
> "Man that is born of woman," &c.
> "Man dieth & wasteth away," &c.
> "I go hence like the shadow that departeth" &c. (& other Psalms)[6]
> Is that pessimism, & if not, why not? The answer would probably be because a remedy is offered. Well, the remedy tarries long.[7]

One can easily detect here some key aspects of Hardy's writing: his instinctive need for self-justification in the face of criticism (the entry follows the publication of his first collection of verse), a complex form of attachment to religion that leaves him sensitive to the literary beauty of sacred writings despite his professed agnosticism, and a perennial taste for cynical logic. In a later entry, dated 1st January 1902, he further tries to redefine the pessimism he is accused of by describing it as a sort of safe wager, as if borrowing the logic of Pascal's famous reasoning on the existence of God:

> A Pessimist's apology.—Pessimism (or rather what is called such) is, in brief, playing the sure game. You cannot lose at it; you may gain. It is the only view of life in which you can never be disappointed. Having reckoned what to do in the worst possible circumstances, when better arise, as they may, life becomes child's play.[8]

Hardy's indignation at being presented as a pessimistic disillusioned poet was such that he sometimes directly requested magazines to "correct the misstatement," as one would ask about some factual misprint or chronological error. In December 1909, in reaction to the review by the London *Daily News* of his third collection of verse, he thus sent the following reply:

> Sir,
> I notice that, in reviewing *Time's Laughingstocks, and Other Verses*, after omitting the second part of the title, you say: "Throughout ... the outlook is that of disillusion and despair"—repeating the assertion more than once in slightly different words. If this were true it might be no bad antidote to the grinning optimism nowadays affected in some quarters; but I beg leave to observe that of the ninety odd poems the volume contains, more than half do not answer to the description at all—as can be seen by a mere glance through it—while of the remainder many cannot be so characterised without exaggeration. I shall, therefore, feel obliged if you will correct the misstatement.[9]

Here, Hardy voices his indignation at being presented as a pessimist, yet he simultaneously states in the clearest of fashions his contempt for conspicuous optimism. The position Hardy presents is indeed neither one nor the other: what other people perceive to be pessimism is to him an intermediate position of caution and safety, the position of a "meliorist." In an interview conducted by William Archer at Max Gate in February 1901, Hardy thus explained:

> [P]eople call me a pessimist; and if it is pessimism to think, with Sophocles, that "not to have been born is best," then I do not reject the designation. I never could understand why the word "pessimism" should be such a red rag to many worthy people; and I believe, indeed, that a good deal of the robustious, swaggering optimism of recent literature is at bottom cowardly and insincere. I do not see that we are likely to improve the world by asseverating, however loudly, that black is white, or at least that black is but a necessary contrast and foil, without which white would be white no longer. But my pessimism, if pessimism it be, does not involve the assumption that the world is going to the dogs, and that Ahriman is winning all along the line. On the contrary, my practical philosophy is distinctly meliorist. What are my books but one plea against "man's inhumanity to man"—to woman—and to the lower animals? [...] Whatever may be the inherent good or evil of life, it is certain that men make it much worse than it need be. When we have got rid of a thousand remediable ills, it will be time enough to determine whether the ill that is irremediable outweighs the good.[10]

More than twenty years later, despite the trauma and disenchantment which the Great War induced in the meantime, the preface to *Late Lyrics and Earlier* (1922) also famously exposed Hardy's meliorism:

> [W]hat is to-day, in allusions to the present author's pages, alleged to be "pessimism" is, in truth, only [...] "questionings" in the exploration of reality, and is the first step towards the soul's betterment, and the body's also.
> If I may be forgiven for quoting my own old words, let me repeat what I printed in this relation more than twenty years ago, and wrote much earlier, in a poem entitled "In Tenebris":
>> If way to the Better there be, it exacts a full look at the Worst:
>
> that is to say, by the exploration of reality, and its frank recognition stage by stage along the survey, with an eye to the best consummation possible: briefly, evolutionary meliorism.[11]

There does seem to be an ethical dimension to the meliorist quest here, yet Hardy also sounds ill at ease with the possible Christian implications of his definition. His apposed insistence that soul and body may equally be improved might indicate that his meliorism is both a moral and a pragmatic quest—or neither. Hardy's formulations remain obscure, yet what is definitely central is the poet's attachment to sincerity ("frank recognition," "full look") in his "exploration of reality."

But however sincerely professed, the "evolutionary meliorism" Hardy claimed as his own was never entirely convincing, especially as World War 1 clearly came to challenge such views of a possible betterment of mankind. I would argue that, supposing there *is* a "Hardy doctrine," rather than in meliorism it is to be found in a letter the author wrote to Dr. Arnaldo Cervesato (of Rome) on 20 June 1901:

> I do not think that there will be any permanent revival of the old transcendental ideals; but I think there may gradually be developed an Idealism of Fancy; that is, an idealism in which fancy is no longer tricked out and made to masquerade as belief, but is frankly and honestly accepted as an imaginative solace in the lack of any substantial solace to be found in life.[12]

As often in Hardy's personal writings and meditations on matters of a philosophical scope, the argument is unclear. Here, one is immediately tempted to try and find echoes of German philosophy, particularly of Kant ("the old transcendental ideals"), as well as connections with the Romantics, more precisely with Coleridge. Yet Hardy's words are misleading, because what the letter exposes is neither truly a reflection on German idealism, nor an adaptation of Coleridge's theory of imagination. It is rather, as I wish to demonstrate here, a complete expression of Hardy's aphilosophical uniqueness as a writer and of his abilities to absorb external ideas and make them his own.

One extremely relevant point to make is nonetheless that in the Spring and Summer of 1901, at the time the letter to Cervesato was written and sent, Hardy was indeed reading a fair amount of philosophy. This was partly done in preparation for the writing of *The Dynasts*, for which Hardy had already started taking notes in the 1890s. In the *Literary Notebooks*, a series of "Notes on Philosophy," headed as such by Hardy himself, thus contains extracts from several thinkers, and notably from Von Hartmann's *Philosophy of the Unconscious* which Hardy had bought some time after its publication in English in 1893.[13] Some of those entries do contain extracts from Von Hartmann's discussions of the German idealists—Kant, Schelling, Fichte—which might indeed have triggered Hardy's reflection on the future of "transcendental ideals," although this is mainly conjectural.

On the other hand, there isn't much, either, to be found in Hardy's writings to suggest that his reflection in the letter to Cervesato is primarily to be connected with the Romantic ideas of imagination. As the term "solace" suggests, in Hardy's eyes imagination seems rather to be taken as a refuge than celebrated for its creative powers. Such a need for comfort was also outlined in Hardy's own definition of his so-called pessimism, and is actually central to his "Idealism of Fancy" as we shall see, thus pointing Hardy's "doctrine" rather in the direction of individual affect than of ethics and aesthetics.

My aim here is therefore to try and show how that apparently uncertain notion of an "Idealism of Fancy" can be encountered with reasonable coherence in several instances of Hardy's poetic work. In no way is this study an attempt at pinpointing a "Hardyan philosophy." Rather than the mapping out of a theoretical system, what can be attained by an examination of Hardy's flirtations with philosophical concepts is an illustration of the combined uniqueness and plurality of his "idiosyncratic mode of regard."[14] As Robert Schweik comprehensibly notes, "elements of contemporary thought in Hardy's works tend to be embedded in a densely intricate web of imaginative connections and qualifications so complex that a consideration of them can hope only partly to illuminate the manifold ways they may have influenced his writings."[15] This is particularly true for the possible philosophical influences one may detect in Hardy's works, and even truer for Hardy's own attempts at metaphysical theorizing. It would indeed seem absurd to try and assign any philosophical coherence to a writer who himself admitted to finding none in metaphysics as a whole, as stated in the following note from the last day of the year 1901:

> After reading various philosophical systems, and being struck with their contradictions and futilities, I have come to this:—*Let every man make a philosophy for himself out of his own experience.* He will not be able to escape using terms and phraseology from earlier philosophers, but let him avoid adopting their theories if he values his own mental life. Let him remember the fate of Coleridge, and save years of labour by working out his own views as given him by his surroundings.[16]

In his letter to Cervesato, Hardy seems to consider that imagination offers the safest way to avoid the bitter experience of disillusionment. This could primarily appear as a form of escapism, and one might indeed read an echo of this in the poem "At Waking" (*Time's Laughingstocks*, 1909),[17] more specifically in the speaker's final appeal. Let us consider the first and the last stanzas:

> When night was lifting,
> And dawn had crept under its shade,
> Amid cold clouds drifting
> Dead-white as a corpse outlaid,
> With a sudden scare
> I seemed to behold
> My Love in bare
> Hard lines unfold.
>
> [...]
>
> O vision appalling
> When the one believed-in thing
> Is seen falling, falling,
> With all to which hope can cling.
> Off: it is not true;
> For it cannot be
> That the prize I drew
> Is a blank to me!

The dynamics presented here—the process through which the risk of disillusionment calls for an assertive preservation of the ideal—are also to be connected to other illusions of a wider scope. Despite Hardy's own opposition to that idea, I personally do see him as the poet of disillusionment (as Edmund Gosse saw him too), the poet of doubt—of the shattering of dreams against reality, particularly against the crude reality of a world lacking divine benevolence and of a violent post–Darwinian nature. As such, he often depicts in his poetry the dangers of dreams, hopes and ideals—one of humanity's main illusions being, in his eyes, that of religion. "God's Funeral" (*Satires of Circumstance*, 1914)[18] is among the most outspoken pieces on that point. One should be careful here to note, with T. R. Wright, that "Hardy's poem, of course, should not be read literally [...] as a statement of what he believed." Wright goes on to explain that Hardy "used often to complain that 'people *will* treat my mood-dictated writing as a single scientific theory.'"[19] Yet "God's Funeral" is indeed more about moods, affective and uncertain, than about a coherent asserted creed—more about what a poet felt and how he let his speaker express it, than about what he believed.

VI
"O man-projected Figure, of late
Imaged as we, thy knell who shall survive?
Whence came it we were tempted to create
One whom we can no longer keep alive?

VII
"Framing him jealous, fierce, at first,
We gave him justice as the ages rolled,
Will to bless those by circumstance accurst,
And longsuffering, and mercies manifold.

VIII
"And, tricked by our own early dream
And need of solace, we grew self-deceived,
Our making soon our maker did we deem,
And what we had imagined we believed.

The last line of the eighth stanza quoted here clearly features the equation between imagination and belief against which Hardy wrote in his letter to Cervesato ("what we had imagined we believed"; "an idealism in which fancy is no longer tricked out and made to masquerade as belief"). The poem indeed exposes the gradual process through which God, originally a dream, has been transformed into the "masquerade of belief" of Hardy's letter. Yet even in such an agnostic poem as this, one finds an obvious sense of nostalgia for the blissful ignorance of an unquestioning faith:

XI

> How sweet it was in years far hied
> To start the wheels of day with trustful prayers,
> To lie down liegely at the eventide
> And feel a blest assurance he was there!

In the final stanzas, the poem follows the speaker's constant wavering between his nostalgic impulse, his sympathy for and identification with all believers, and the sad but necessary realization of the loss. The syntax and punctuation thus carry the conflicting inclinations of a mind's internal struggles:

XIV

> I could not buoy their faiths: and yet
> Many I had known: with all I sympathized;
> And though struck speechless, I did not forget
> That what was mourned for, I, too, had long prized.

While the ensuing appearance of a "pale yet positive gleam" seen by the speaker and a "certain few" certainly stands for a glimpse of hope, the poem is carefully arranged so as to present the focus on that swelling small light as a possible mere answer to the "insistent question" on "how to bear such loss," an answer offered in order "to lift the general night." In other words, the only way to deal with the loss of an illusion will be to find another one to cling on to. This might seem to some as an overstretched reading; yet in any case, what remains in the poem's final lines is the irresoluble tension—imprinted on the alliterative style—that leaves the speaker in an in-between position of doubt, allowing him to embrace neither hope nor despair: "dazed and puzzled 'twixt the gleam and gloom."

That tension, and more particularly the speaker's paradoxical wish to believe and to retain the safe comfort of religious faith, appears regularly in Hardy's verse, quite famously for example in "The Oxen" (*Moments of Vision*, 1917),[20] a poem, Ross C. Murfin tells us, "in which the will to dream and to believe is as strong as the knowledge that all such beliefs are naïve."[21] That contradiction is indeed typical of Hardy's complex form of agnosticism, as mentioned above.

Yet the desire to believe despite appearances is not just a religious one. Hence in the poem "Let Me Believe" (*Human Shows*, 1925),[22] this is how the speaker addresses the loved one whose behavior towards him has obviously been one of neglect and disregard: "Let me believe it, dearest./ Let it be/ As just a dream—the merest—." Similarly, in the emblematic turn-of-the-century piece "The Darkling Thrush" (*Poems of the Past and the Present*, 1901),[23] the wish to believe sustains the end of the poem, as the speaker imagines that the thrush's song might actually bear a hidden message of hope. To this I would also add the paradox of "waiting in unhope" which famously concludes part I of one of Hardy's darkest poems, "In Tenebris" (which, interestingly enough, also contains Hardy's definition of his meliorism), as it is precisely of the same sort: an in-between position of willful hope, of conscious deliberate dreaming—*despite* reality.

In her book *Black Sun: Depression and Melancholia*, Julia Kristeva has a very useful definition of such a process of conscious dreaming, which we can directly relate to the form featured here in Hardy's verse:

> Indeed, we sense the imaginary experience not as theological symbolism or secular commitment but as flaring-up of dead meaning with a surplus of meaning, in which the speaking subject first discovers the shelter of an ideal but above all the opportunity to play it again in illusions and disillusion ... [...] This is a survival of idealization—the imaginary constitutes a miracle, but it is at the same time its shattering: a self-illusion, nothing but dreams and words, words, words.... It affirms the almightiness of temporary subjectivity—the one that knows enough to speak until death comes.[24]

The vision of imagination as first offering "the shelter of an ideal" can enlighten us as to the importance of the power of *solace* underlined by Hardy. A similar process of self-persuasion, or *self-illusion* as Kristeva names it (distinct from the *self-deception* featured in "God's Funeral"), surfaces repeatedly in Hardy's verse. The poem "Middle-Age Enthusiasms" (*Wessex Poems*, 1898),[25] written by Hardy for his sister Mary, is mainly built around that idea. It even seems to advocate a form of resilience which at once celebrates the joys of illusion and recalls the awareness of the bitter truth that life never holds its promises.

> We passed where flag and flower
> Signalled a jocund throng;
> We said: "Go to, the hour
> Is apt!"—and joined the song;
> And, kindling, laughed at life and care,
> Although we knew no laugh lay there.

The first stanza quoted here, like each stanza in the poem, ends with a tetrameter couplet bearing an obvious sense of disruption ("laughed" / "no laugh"; "And" / "Although"). Similarly, the central run-on line ("'Go to, the hour / Is apt!'") adds disorder to the impressions of ease and heedlessness of the first lines and of the exclamation. The very "aptness" is indeed contradicted by the intersected line and syntax. The speaker of the poem thus wavers between a full awareness of reality and the deliberate choice of make-believe, in what appears as an obstinate struggle against death, as Paul Zietlow points out:

The characters face the indifferent world by consciously making the best of things despite their awareness of approaching death. [...] Their lives are willed dramas, in which they consciously play the roles of hopeful people, deliberately assuming such roles as a means of defying the threat of mortality.[26]

Beyond the choice of deliberate illusion, or beyond the knowingly paradoxical advocacy of a hope that is clearly presented as vain, it seems logical that returning to the power of illusion should actually also translate, in Hardy's writing, into an almost mystical belief in the power of dreams, of some conscious controlled form of dreaming.

I would argue that *there* lies precisely Hardy's "Idealism of Fancy." Another poem conveys that "doctrine" even more explicitly and rhetorically. "On a Fine Morning" (*Poems of the Past and the Present*, 1901)[27] does so by relying on some form of common-sense philosophy,[28] and brings us, in Edmund Gosse's gently ironic words, "as far towards optimism as Mr. Hardy can let himself be drawn"[29]:

I

Whence comes Solace?—Not from seeing
What is doing, suffering, being,
Not from noting Life's conditions,
Nor from heeding Time's monitions;
    But in cleaving to the Dream,
    And in gazing at the gleam
    Whereby gray things golden seem.

II

Thus do I this heyday, holding
Shadows but as lights unfolding,
As no specious show this moment
With its iris-hued embowment;
    But as nothing other than
    Part of a benignant plan;
    Proof that earth was made for man.

In the quest of the first stanza—a quest instigated by the opening question— the unexpected presence of the verb "cleave" seems to encapsulate the strength of the speaker's belief in that soothing dream. Thanks to the combined use of definite article and capital D, "*the* Dream" itself is indeed magnified and glorified into what could be taken as a philosophical concept or even a divine allegory. The verb "cleave" tells us how strong the adherence to the conviction is, but it also necessarily echoes the notion of breaching, the rift or splitting, which the term carries in its most common meaning. As such, it points to the inner contradiction between illusion and disillusion which characterizes in Hardy's writing the celebration of such conscious dreaming. The systematic syntactic shifts ("Not from" / "But in"; "As no" / "But as") seem to map out some separate reality in which the speaker is eager to believe, something the *contre-rejet* (the first part of the run-on line) "holding" confirms: it leaves the syntax in a state of suspension, as if nothing could disturb the belief implied by the term. The trochaic rhythm, together with the catalexis of the last three line of each stanza (*Būt ăs | nŏthĭng | ōthĕr | thān*) candidly reveals how artificial that benevolent world is, while conversely pointing to the pure subtlety of the poetic language which gives substance to that Dream: note the refined craftsmanship of such a phrase as "iris-hued embowment," showing how the magic of poetic expression can turn one thing into its opposite, darkness into light. Under the symmetrical pattern and the metrical simplicity of the lines, lie the complexity and the tensions of the articulation, within the same poem, of those two discourses—the magic of poetic craft in a false universe—both contradictory and compatible.

That is why "On a Fine Morning," which can indeed be termed a poem of hope, is to be found next to the bitterest poems within the same collection, *Poems of the Past and the Present*—next to some "philosophical" pieces such as "The Mother Mourns" or "I Said to Love." And indeed, in the same collection, inserted between the two bleak dialogues of "The Lacking Sense" and "Doom and She," one may read the poem "To Life": "O Life with the sad seared face,/ I weary of seeing thee,"[30] the poet exclaims. The first two stanzas depict, in a dramatic mode, the speaker's bitter disenchanted mood, only to open in the third stanza onto an explicit call for the comfort of make-believe:

> But canst thou not array
>   Thyself in rare disguise,
> And feign like truth, for one mad day,
>   That earth is Paradise?
> I'll tune me to the mood,
>   And mumm with thee till eve;
> And maybe what as interlude
>   I feign, I shall believe!

The deliberate choice of embracing illusion ("feign," "mumm") appears as a strategy through which the speaker is trying to regain a perfect harmony ("I'll *tune* me to the *mood*"). The paradoxical nature of that deliberate illusion can be read in the parallel positions of "feign" and "believe" in the last line. Hardy's poetry thus celebrates a dreaming that is fully awoken ("for one mad day," "till eve") and that will come to substitute for a disappointing reality, allowing the poet to shift from a painful consciousness to a soothing *vision*.

However awkwardly put, Hardy's "Idealism of Fancy" thus appears as more coherent than one might have first considered. By arguing in favor of conscious dreaming, Hardy celebrates the virtues of illusion by distinguishing it from *delusion,* where fancy is indeed "tricked out and made to masquerade as belief." This is where one might after all link Hardy back to Coleridge. According to *The Life and Work,* Hardy's diary entry for 26 January 1882 has the following note: "Coleridge says, aim at *illusion* in audience or readers— i.e., the normal state when dreaming, intermediate between complete *de*lusion (which the French mistakenly aim at) and a clear perception of falsity."[31] Hardy's poetic defense of his "Idealism of Fancy" does resemble that intermediate position between pernicious delusion and stark disillusionment which he seems to have taken from Coleridge's theory of dramatic illusion. One may also perceive with further clarity the fundamental distinction between *self-illusion* and *self-deception.*

Hardy's "Idealism of Fancy" can thus be considered as post-romantic in that it believes in the power of the individual mind to create parallel realities, without letting itself be "tricked by its own dreams," i.e., remaining alert to the illusory nature of such creations. Yet what it celebrates is rather the futile powers of imagination than the grandeur of artistic creation. The illusion it promotes does not aim at creating phantasmagorias of limitless scope, but rather mere adjustments of reality to the desires and hopes of individuals. In most of the poems quoted above, such hopes are of a teleological and epistemological scope ("Proof that earth was made for man," in "On a Fine Morning") and testify to the helplessness of a disbelieving spirit, of a consciousness left numb by the disappearance of God. Self-illusion is indeed the way to retrieve the pre–Darwinian fullness of the meaning of existence. Kristeva's "flaring-up of dead meaning" is thus particularly relevant in the context of the nineteenth-century crisis of faith. Hardy's poetic response to that context and that crisis was perhaps given undue a-topicality because his verse only appeared publicly at the turn of the twentieth century. Yet he had started writing poems and forging his artistic sensitivity—his "idiosyncratic mode of regard"—at the same time as Swinburne and Arnold were voicing their own doubts. Hardy's "Idealism of Fancy," though not directly related to either the German or British schools of idealism,[32] thus appears clearly as a product of the Victorian era. Hardy's position is, in that respect, particularly close to that of Swinburne, for whom he had the highest admiration. In his book *Swinburne, Hardy, Lawrence, and the Burden of Belief,* R. C. Murfin describes Swinburne's and Hardy's ambiguous relation to faith in these terms:

> Swinburne and Hardy were raised on Christianity and romanticism—their youthful devotions are a matter of record—and their heroic, pre-eminently modern labours to raze the temples of all dead or doubtful gods seem almost fated to end in a second spiritual and aesthetic crisis, in a "return" to some

"form of" an old faith to fit "the mood" of their "age,"³³ in decadence, for their joy is not in the faith but in the form, not in the mysteries of which their songs sing but, rather, in the mysteries of song, the power of poetry to fantasize worlds so sweet that they almost seem real.³⁴

Murfin shows how both poets followed the same type of evolution from early to mature verse, from "a period of agonized, anti-romantic protest into a new period of post-romantic affirmation,"³⁵ "transitions from agony to acceptance."³⁶ "[I]n Hardy's later poetry," Murfin further explains, "the will to believe is not a frustrated, insatiable drive, as it was in the 1865–67 poems. It is, rather, a delicate *pose*, a "romantic" fiction that makes life bearable, even lovely, but that always remains a pleasant fiction."³⁷ Though I do not fully concur with Murfin's vision of Hardy's early poetry as being "anti-romantic," I find his perception of a poetry of *acceptance* particularly relevant to my present concern. This is indeed what Hardy's position, whether that of meliorism or his "Idealism of Fancy," is about, the former a "frank recognition" of reality, the latter "frankly and honestly accepted" as the only source of solace. Hardy's formulation is not truly a search for a metaphysical truth. Rather than the elaboration of a theoretical system of reasoning, it is a practical mode of adaptation to reality. And indeed, did not Hardy himself present his meliorist approach as a "practical philosophy"? His "Idealism of Fancy" is just as practical—it aims at adjusting reality rather than modifying it entirely, in order to restore the balance "between what things are and what they ought to be."³⁸

Hardy's enlightened pursuit of the dream is therefore the pursuit of what *remains* a dream or an illusion—the pursuit of the *impossible*. One of Hardy's very last poems, "We Are Getting to the End" (*Winter Words*, 1928),³⁹ thus laments the coming of "the end of dreams," and interestingly equates it with "the end of visioning/ The impossible within this universe." Beyond the soothing powers of conscious dreaming, the poem here seems to be celebrating the poet's own gift of vision and creation, again encapsulated in Hardy's linguistic craftsmanship, and particularly in the word "visioning."⁴⁰ Offering such a paradoxical power as that of "*visioning the impossible*" is just what Hardy's poetry does. It is, indeed, what Murfin calls "the power of poetry to fantasize worlds so sweet that they almost seem real."

Hardy's own unassuming declaration that his poems were merely "fancies, or poems of the imagination"⁴¹ cannot truly hide the reflexive, conceptual, if not philosophical nature of much of his writing, particularly his verse. As the quotation from his letter outlining his notion of an "Idealism of Fancy" proves, Hardy was much better at constructing a metatextual discourse via the means of poetic writing than by any form of prose theorizing. One final example will help further demonstrate that point and illustrate in verse how much the Hardyan idealistic "doctrine" is inseparable from poetic expression itself. Published in 1922 in *Late Lyrics and Earlier*, but bearing the much earlier date of 1867, "A Young Man's Exhortation"[42] can be interpreted in several ways, mostly because of the temporal shift indicated by the post-scripted date: one can read it as the exhortation of a young man by the experienced poet; as that of the reader by the poet who at that time *was* a relatively young man (of 36); or as an exhortation of the young poet by himself. In that piece, one finds again an obvious celebration of make-believe, as is mostly shown by the aphoristic ending whereby the speaker affirms the importance of "the passing preciousness of dreams;/ That aspects are within us; and who seems/ Most kingly is the King." The exhortative mode is more than clear in that poem: in the excessively alliterative style of the young poet serving the assertion of his fierce willpower ("determined deftness"); the recurrent use of run-on lines; the anaphoric devices (for example in the second stanza the epanorthosis which transforms "glee" into "Blind glee"). Being acutely aware of the brevity of life ("the hour/ That girdles us"; "soon"; "moment after moment"; "passing"), the speaker seeks for the satisfactions of excess ("Dear as excess"; "fill it full"; "excelling"; "limitless"). The poem's exhortation is therefore meant as an attempt to transform reality ("charm Life's louring fair"), one instance of Kristeva's "flaring-up of dead meaning," a transformation that can only be operated when imagination offers its endless resources up to poetic creation: "Send up such touching strains/ That limitless recruits from *fancy*'s pack/ Shall rush upon your *tongue*."

Celebrating the virtues of illusion also amounts to admitting to the weakness of man's position, and to the tediousness of existence without dreams. The "Hardy doctrine" might thus find another proper echo in that of Conrad's Marlow in *Lord Jim*: "it is respectable to have no illusions—and safe—and profitable—and dull."[43] There surely is no pessimism about such a standpoint.

Notes

1. E. K. Chambers's review for *Wessex Poems* (1898), *Athenaeum* (14 January 1899), in *Thomas Hardy: The Critical Heritage*, ed. R. G. Cox (London: Routledge & Kegan Paul, 1970), 325.
2. Unsigned review, *Saturday Review* (11 January 1902), *ibid.*, 329.
3. T. H. Warren, *Spectator* (5 April 1902), *ibid.*, 333.
4. Edmund Gosse, "Mr. Hardy's Lyrical Poems," *Edinburgh Review* (April 1918), *ibid.*, 451.
5. *Ibid.*, 454–455.
6. The references of Hardy's quotations are respectively to Rm 8,22, Jb 14,1, Jb 14,10 and Ps 109,22.

7. Thomas Hardy, *The Personal Notebooks of Thomas Hardy*, ed. Richard H. Taylor (London: Macmillan, 1979), 28.

8. Thomas Hardy, *The Life and Work of Thomas Hardy*, ed. Michael Millgate (London: Macmillan, 1989), 333–34.

9. Thomas Hardy, *Thomas Hardy's Public Voice. The Essays, Speeches, and Miscellaneous Prose*, ed. Michael Millgate (Oxford: Clarendon Press, 2001), 306–307.

10. William Archer, "Real Conversations: Conversation II.—With Mr Thomas Hardy," *Pall Mall Magazine* 23 (April 1901, 527–537) in *Thomas Hardy Remembered*, ed. Martin Ray (Aldershot: Ashgate, 2007), 35–36.

11. Thomas Hardy, *The Complete Poems*, ed. James Gibson (Basingstoke: Palgrave, 2001), 557. In the short story "An Imaginative Woman," published in 1894 in the collection *Life's Little Ironies*, Hardy also gives such qualities of "frank" explorer of reality to the poet Robert Trewe: "Neither *symboliste* nor *décadent*, he was a pessimist in so far as that character applies to a man who looks at the worst contingencies as well as the best in the human condition." Thomas Hardy, *Collected Short Stories* (London: Macmillan, 1988), 383.

12. *The Life, op. cit.*, 333.

13. Though Hardy was always careful to minimize the impact of Schopenhauer on his writing of *The Dynasts* and enhance that of Von Hartmann, he also bought *The Four-Fold Root of the Principle of Sufficient Reason* around 1890 in its first translation into English (London: George Bells & Sons, 1889). More importantly, as Carl J. Weber carefully demonstrated, the copy clearly attests to Hardy's reading of it (Carl J. Weber, "Hardy's Copy of Schopenhauer" in *Colby Quarterly* 4:12 [November 1957]: 217–224).

14. See Hardy's notebook entry from the Spring of 1890: "Art consists in so depicting the common events of life as to bring out the features which illustrate the author's idiosyncratic mode of regard; making old incidents and things seem as new." *The Life, op. cit.*, 235.

15. Robert Schweik, "The Influence of Religion, Science, and Philosophy on Hardy's Writings" in *The Cambridge Companion to Thomas Hardy*, ed. Dale Kramer (Cambridge: CUP, 1999), 54.

16. *The Life, op. cit.*, 333 (Hardy's own emphases).

17. *The Complete Poems, op. cit.*, 224. The poem bears the mention "Weymouth 1869."

18. *Ibid.*, 326–329. The poem is dated 1908–1910.

19. T. R. Wright, "The Victorians" in *The Oxford Handbook of English Literature and Theology* (Oxford: Oxford University Press, 2007), 158. Wright quotes from Thomas Hardy, *The Life, op. cit.*, 441.

20. *The Complete Poems, op. cit.*, 468.

21. Ross C. Murfin, *Swinburne, Hardy, Lawrence and the Burden of Belief* (Chicago: The University of Chicago Press, 1978), 156.

22. *The Complete Poems, op. cit.*, 711.

23. *Ibid.*, 150.

24. Julia Kristeva, *Black Sun: Depression and Melancholia*, transl. Leon S. Roudiez (New York: Columbia University Press, 1989), 102–103.

25. *The Complete Poems, op. cit.*, 63.

26. Paul Zietlow, *Moments of Vision: The Poetry of Thomas Hardy* (Cambridge, MA: Harvard University Press, 1974), 11.

27. *The Complete Poems, op. cit.*, 129–130. The poem is dated February 1899.
28. The expression is not to be taken as a reference to the Scottish School of Common Sense philosophy, but in a more casual understanding—though the two are indeed inextricable.
29. Edmund Gosse, "Mr. Hardy's Lyrical Poems," *Edinburgh Review* (April 1918), in Cox, *op. cit.*, 449.
30. *The Complete Poems, op. cit.*, 118.
31. *The Life, op. cit.*, 157 (Hardy's own emphases).
32. There's ample evidence that Hardy was fully informed of the bases of British idealism, both in the first generation of philosophers (he quoted from F. H. Bradley's *Appearance and Reality* in his own *Literary Notebooks*) and in its later developments (he and E. McTaggart became friends). Yet nothing suggests any sort of direct connection in Hardy's own understanding of the term "idealism" as used by him in the letter to Cervesato.
33. See Hardy's notebook entry from 1880: "Romanticism will exist in human nature as long as human nature itself exists. The point is (in imaginative literature) to adopt that form of romanticism which is the mood of the age" (*The Life, op. cit.*, 151). Hardy thus sought to adapt Romanticism—to "tune it to the mood" of the *fin de siècle*.
34. Murfin, *op. cit.*, 159. I am extremely grateful to Bernard-Jean Ramadier for pointing the parallel out to me and suggesting the relevance of Murfin's analysis.
35. *Ibid.*, 91.
36. *Ibid.*, 100.
37. *Ibid.*, 157.
38. "Poem—the difference between what things are & what they ought to be (stated as by a god to the gods—i.e., as god's story.)" (*The Personal Notebooks, op. cit.,* 59).
39. *The Complete Poems, op. cit.,* 929.
40. As Felicity Currie points out: "It is surely the emphatic placement of this word in its first function as verbal noun which makes it so innovatively and unequivocally positive—it has no great affirmative history, semantically." Felicity Currie, "Hardy's Sonnet: 'We Are Getting to the End' Reconsidered" in *Thomas Hardy Journal* 15.1 (February 1999): 79.
41. Letter to Alfred Noyes from 19 December 1920 (*The Life, op. cit.,* 439).
42. *The Complete Poems, op. cit.,* 601–602.
43. Joseph Conrad, *Lord Jim* (New York: Norton, Norton Critical Edition, 1996; first edition, 1900), 136.

Works Cited

Conrad, Joseph. *Lord Jim*. New York: Norton, Norton Critical Edition, 1996.
Cox, R. G., ed. *Thomas Hardy: The Critical Heritage*. London: Routledge & Kegan Paul, 1970.
Currie, Felicity. "Hardy's Sonnet: 'We Are Getting to the End' Reconsidered," in *Thomas Hardy Journal* 15.1 (February 1999): 79–83.
Hardy, Thomas. *Collected Short Stories*. London: Macmillan, 1988.
_____. *The Complete Poems*. Ed. James Gibson. Basingstoke: Palgrave, 2001.
_____. *The Life and Work of Thomas Hardy*. Ed. Michael Millgate. London: Macmillan, 1989.

_____. *The Personal Notebooks of Thomas Hardy*. Ed. Richard H. Taylor. London: Macmillan, 1979.
_____. *Thomas Hardy's Public Voice. The Essays, Speeches, and Miscellaneous Prose*. Ed. Michael Millgate. Oxford: Clarendon Press, 2001.
Kristeva, Julia. *Black Sun: Depression and Melancholia*. Trans. Leon S. Roudiez. New York: Columbia University Press, 1989.
Murfin, Ross C. *Swinburne, Hardy, Lawrence and the Burden of Belief*. Chicago: University of Chicago Press, 1978.
Ray, Martin, ed. *Thomas Hardy Remembered*. Aldershot: Ashgate, 2007.
Schweik, Robert. "The Influence of Religion, Science, and Philosophy on Hardy's Writings," in *The Cambridge Companion to Thomas Hardy*. Ed. Dale Kramer. Cambridge: Cambridge University Press, 1999.
Weber, Carl J. "Hardy's Copy of Schopenhauer," in *Colby Quarterly*, 4:12 (November 1957): 217–224.
Wright, T. R. "The Victorians," in *The Oxford Handbook of English Literature and Theology*. Oxford: Oxford University Press, 2007, 158.
Zietlow, Paul. *Moments of Vision: The Poetry of Thomas Hardy*. Cambridge, MA: Harvard University Press, 1974.

III

Specters of Doubt and Faith

Agnosticism and Freethinking
The Influence of Leslie Stephen
Ilaria Mallozzi

Agnosticism evolved in an era of transition, during which many important social and cultural changes clashed with apparent public and economic stability. A major influence among Victorian agnostic intellectuals was played by Charles Darwin, whose scientific narrative seemed to respond to a large and varied context of uncertainties and doubts about ethics that actually came before, or maybe were part of, his discoveries. As Gillian Beer points out, "Darwin's ideas have come to have so dominant a role in the construction of social domains apparently remote from biological"[1]; this was probably because Darwin's theory also presented a collective "voyage into the past."[2] In Darwin's own words: "I look at the natural geological record, as a history of the world imperfectly kept, and written in a changing dialect; of this history we possess the last volume alone, relating to two or three countries."[3] Darwin made Victorians realize how little they knew about the world and its biological narration, and, at the same time, he introduced the possibility to look at time and history in their physical relations.

In *Jude the Obscure*, Thomas Hardy's eponymous character speaks about the irregularity and plurality which founded "the original idea" in Gothic architecture. Jude's words certainly unveil scientific and metaphorical implications that effortlessly match with Darwin's biological scheme. In restoring Gothic churches, Jude finds out the irregular pattern of primogenial art: "there in the old walls were the broken lines of the original idea; jagged curves, disdain of precision, irregularity, disarray."[4] However, as we shall see, it is more in his poems than in his novels that Hardy probes into social and psychological matters and openly discusses with his age. Darwin's perspective produced indeed a storm in terms of morality and religion; nineteenth-century intellectuals, like Thomas Hardy, lived in a period of religious uncertainty and had to adapt their moral views to a new horizon. Victorian society was truly exposed to a radical change, as Jonathan Smith explained:

> [I]t is not only that the Darwinian method leads to inversions and paradox, but that it points to a generally mixed mode, in a world where, indeed, values are turned upside down (since Darwin was to argue for the material basis of both art and morality) and where conventional properties about the body, and expectations of unified identity, consistent behaviour and feeling, are constantly disappointed.[5]

From this perspective, the "Darwinian method" allowed a less constrained area of scientific and moral wandering, where those who re-thought their ideas after Darwin were able to work out a new sensibility. As the influence of Leslie Stephen's freethinking on Thomas Hardy's poems can show, agnosticism was part of this revolution, and my contention is that it was actually a sensible ideological instrument to evaluate the place of mankind in History, taking into account morality and religion in a less dogmatic way.

C. W. Dockrill's pioneering investigation of the English Free-Thought traces a first significant agreement between science and empiricism among English agnostics that inevitably also affected the Victorian art domain.[6] Agnosticism was first introduced to take a position in terms of faith and atheism, in search of a possible and safe escape from dualistic interpretations of Darwin's theories on mankind's evolution. However, as A. O. Cockshut puts it, "when we hear of the failure of authority, the collapse of standards and the death of God, we learn more about the speaker than about the time."[7] Actually each agnostic had his own definition of this radical change and, as Cockshut points out, agnosticism led to a more personal intellectual approach in dealing with religion. In Frederick Harrison's words, agnosticism was "a state of no-religion."[8] On the other hand, the first person who used this term was T. H. Huxley, who also probably coined it. In fact in Huxley's words agnosticism was "a confession of ignorance,"[9] expressing the scientific impossibility to face and respond to moral themes when dealing with evolutionary aspects of life (Romanes Lectures, "Evolution and Ethics," 1893). Agnosticism was actually propagated through T. H. Huxley's a-religious use of the word, and progressed by Leslie Stephen who provided the term with a philosophical and experienced insight. According to Ralph Pite, the Victorian sage who "combined religious doubt and moral resolve"[10] was essentially Leslie Stephen.

As Rosemarie Morgan perfectly sums up, Stephen was

> one of the century's most eminent sages: Sir Leslie Stephen—biographer, historian of ideas, literary critic, editor of the *Cornhill Magazine* and of the highly distinguished work: *The Dictionary of National Biography*. For an unknown author who has not yet lost his anonymity, and who will not do so

until *Far From the Madding Crowd* comes into volume publication later in 1874, this elite connection is more than fortunate, it is highly prestigious.[11]

Stephen's influence on Hardy left visible and very interesting traces, which actually are expanded and discussed in some of his poems. Renowned author of *The History of English Thought in the Eighteenth Century* (1876), *The Utilitarians* (1900), and *English Literature and Society in the Eighteenth Century* (1903, 1904), among other works, Stephen also wrote a number of essays that defined what agnosticism represented for his generation: *Essays on Free Thinking and Plain Speaking* (1873), *The Science of Ethics* (1882) and *An Agnostic's Apology* (1900). In the latter, he poignantly stated that agnosticism was "the frame of mind which [...] would restrain the human intellect from wasting its powers on the attempt to galvanise into sham activity this *caput mortuum* of old theology."[12] Leslie Stephen aimed to leave apart what refused to be unified, not only science and religion but also history and morality, in order to narrate history and social changes taking into account these significant separations.

The turning point was probably the Industrial Revolution—that, in Stephen's words, started during a period in which dwelled "a curious contrast between the political stagnancy and the great industrial activity."[13] Stephen's critical insight in the study and narration of British history made his books inexhaustible sources of social and political information; this is the reason why his personal interest and development of the Free-Thought was actually vital to the Victorian age. Similarly, his consistent writing production stands a document of his indisputable influence on the development of the nineteenth-century English disbelief. Agnosticism was a profitable term twice, as from the first impasse it was provided with a second philosophical life. Dockrill indicates 1862, when Spencer published *First Principles*, as a crucial year for the circulation of agnostic approach in thinking.[14] Most English agnostics found in Darwin's theory a conclusive and inevitable separation from some religious attitudes and expectations, but to observe how agnosticism also pervades English poetry, the debate around science and religion may not be enough. I would argue that a humanistic substratum has to be counted among its components, and Leslie Stephen can be observed as a leading humanistic presence in the Pantheon of Victorian agnostics. As Pite points out, Stephen filled agnosticism with "intellectual rigour," up to the point to give it a sort of "physical strength."[15] The definitions concerning agnosticism let us perceive how agnosticism was produced within the Victorian religious debate, whereas it was mostly adopted by intellectuals like Leslie Stephen who wanted to attain new humanistic concerns in an epoch of trepidation and disconcert.

Agnosticism in writing is not an easy ground to explore, mainly because agnostic authors often present significant differences in dealing with this term. Critics plunged into Victorian agnostic narrative in search of ruptures, separations and changes. Authors such as T. H. Huxley, C. Darwin, L. Stephen, A. H. Clough, George Eliot and Thomas Hardy have been investigated through their letters, autobiographies, novels, essays and poetry. They all maintained original interpretation and re-use of their agnostic literary thoughts. Regarding poetry in particular, S. D. Shaw came to the conclusion that

> [t]hese poets' full, unstable signs demystify the analogy between the human and the divine Word. They expose the divine Word as a distortion of the human word, and the human word as a mere alias of God. Words about the Word are no longer analogies that hide what they reveal. They are perpetual aliases, false names for God, designed to hide the scandal of His flight from the world.[16]

Victorian agnostic authors often explored language in order to describe what their eyes recorded; however, they also preserved a sort of irreplaceable symbolism. History and imperfection were finally jointed in Clough's verses, and consequently his tormented vision could only be expressed through his famous predilection for hexameters, a vanished metrical measure (except in translation from the Classics) that Clough never ceased to impart. This oxymoron in terms of metric and content was common to Thomas Hardy as well. In particular, Hardy's exactness and geometry in verse may offer a further dimension to Shaw's observation of the agnostic poetry in Victorian age. Hardy's poems are often dressed with restrained rhythms, whereas his lexicon suggests a vastness which is impossible to define and express in its entirety, a sort of precise infinity. As in his poem "Heredity,"[17] Hardy's verses seem to struggle to combine his love for ancient times with his appetite for adapting and expanding language borders:

> I am the family face;
> Flesh perishes, I live on,
> Projecting trait and trace
> Through time to times anon,
> And leaping from place to place
> Over oblivion.
>
> The years-heired feature that can
> In curve and voice and eye
> Despise the human span
> Of durance—that is I;
> The eternal thing in man,
> That heeds no call to die.

Hardy's predilection for universal terms like "oblivion," "eternal," "flesh," are balanced with the technical use of "human span," "durance," or the geometric rhythm in images like "in curve and voice and eye," which make this poem a sort of fainted portrayal of a living organism whose essence struggles between hereditary continuity and certain finitude. Hardy witnessed the Victorian theological and social turmoil, and also recorded many views in his journals and poems. In Geoffrey Harvey's words, "[a]lthough Hardy's agnosticism was less forceful than Stephen's, significantly it was Hardy whom he chose to witness his renunciation of Holy Orders on 23 March 1875."[18] It is therefore out of question that Hardy's friendship with Leslie Stephen played a very strong role in terms of religious and intellectual influence; Hardy declared himself agnostic during his collaboration with *The Cornhill Magazine*, whose director, at the time, was Stephen himself. From this perspective, there may be a separation between Hardy's earlier classical and Swinburnian agnosticism in poetry, characterized by a sculpted rigor, and his mature independent and more daring modern agnosticism.[19] However, Hardy's agnosticism is somehow allied to his curiosity and, unlike Clough, he could refine his questioning over the following century, giving his post–Darwinian sight a chance to get adapted to a new scenario.

Concerning the affinities between Victorian Darwinism and Victorian agnosticism, Stephen Jay Gould maintained that agnosticism was not entirely originated by Darwin's theory, but mainly treated by literary minds. Gould significantly mentioned one of Thomas Hardy's juvenile poems, "Nature's Questioning,"[20] as an example to explain Victorian pre-existing anxiety.[21] In Thomas Hardy's literary notebooks, we read a quotation from Leslie Stephen that Hardy himself considered far more interesting than Spencerian Darwinism or Mill's Positivism: "History depends upon the relation between the organism & the environment."[22] The humanistic flavor, necessary to make the post–Darwinian world less difficult and perhaps disappointing, was actually a major contribution made by Leslie Stephen. His influence on the debate about English agnosticism truly established a new relation between individual and history in terms of moral perception and human intellect. This influence is particularly interesting in Hardy's case; he learned from Stephen how to face the rigor of Nature and how to stand in opposition to historical obliteration, mainly through the means of a tactile memory and vigorous writing. As we can read in his *Apology*, Stephen firmly asserts that:

> The free-will hypothesis is the device by which theologians try to relieve God of the responsibility for the sufferings of His creation. It is required for another purpose. It enables the Creator to be also the judge. Man must be partly independent of God, or God would be at once pulling the wires and

punishing the puppets. So far the argument is unimpeachable; but the device justifies God at the expense of making the universe a moral chaos. Grant the existence of this arbitrary force called free-will, and we shall be forced to admit that, if justice is to be found anywhere, it is at least not to be found in this strange anarchy, where chance and fate are struggling for the mastery.[23]

The "strange anarchy" was produced by the deliberate juxtaposition of fortuitous and doomed, new and old views on life. To Stephen, Darwin's evolution, based on accident more than environmental circumstances, veritably drew a line under human predestination. On one side, in Leslie Stephen's words, "the crude empiricism was transformed into evolutionism"[24]; on the other, evolutionism also permitted to see that "human nature is radically irregular, and therefore beyond the sphere of reason."[25] In other words, there was more space for questioning old assumptions and proposing new ones. However, to some extent, agnosticism also lessened Victorian optimism and imposed a border between the demonstrable and the unnoticeable. When Leslie Stephen declared that "The Agnostic is one who asserts—what no one denies—that there are limits to the sphere of human intelligence,"[26] he seemed to suggest that the language of feelings and emotions had to adapt itself to a sort of platform for evidences that Victorian authors modeled each in their own personal way. Not to kill phantasy or restrain transcendental images, but to refurbish human mind with new and more tangible dwellings in order to make authors' writings more effective and durable on society. Further on, Stephen deepens his position:

> Dreams may be pleasanter for the moment than realities; but happiness must be won by adapting our lives to the realities. And who, that has felt the burden of existence, and suffered under well-meant efforts at consolation, will deny that such consolations are the bitterest of mockeries? Pain is not an evil; death is not a separation; sickness is but a blessing in disguise. Have the gloomiest speculations of avowed pessimists ever tortured sufferers like those kindly platitudes? Is there a more cutting piece of satire in the language than the reference in our funeral service to the "sure and certain hope of a blessed resurrection"? To dispel genuine hopes might be painful, however salutary. To suppress these spasmodic efforts to fly in the face of facts would be some comfort, even in the distress which they are meant to alleviate.[27]

Stephen's *Apology* is an infinite source of commentary if read beside some of Thomas Hardy's poems. As Tess Cosslett pointed out, Hardy adopted and re-adapted Stephen's short-story "A Bad Five Minutes in the Alps" (significantly part of his *Essays on Free Thinking and Plain Speaking*) in some of his novels, with the intent of stressing the "Victorian agnostic man in this perilous, cliff-hanging attitude."[28] The intellectual task energetically fabricated by Stephen was absorbed by Hardy who made the most out of it. However, a similar strength is often visible also in Hardy's poems. In particular, "In

Time of 'The Breaking of Nations,'"[29] although laconic and short, offers an insightful vision of human time as seen through personal and historical memory. The poem starts with Hardy's typical diminished intonation: "Only a man harrowing clods/ In a slow silent walk" and ends with "War's annals will cloud into night/ Ere their story die." Hardy's peasant is accompanied by his old horse, and their minuscule existence seems to stand in opposition to the authority of "Dynasties" that make their entrance in the following stanza: "Yet this will go onward the same/ Though Dynasties pass." In order to reinforce this sense of human impotency and silence, Hardy repeats the same pattern in the third and last part of the poem, where he locates "a maid and her wight" whose personal story is annihilated by "War's annals" and clouded by a symbolic "night." Although Hardy's last human portrayal seems to offer no space for hope and justice, his all-inclusive pessimism does suggest also a human relief in remembering them. His perception, without denying or edulcorating human sorrow, gave a place to uneventful existence and tried to comfort individuals. Hardy's awareness of the importance of layers in individual life and collective history seems to recall the origins of Victorian agnosticism when Leslie Stephen looked for a new humanism.

"At the Entering of the New Year,"[30] "He Wonders About Himself,"[31] and "Fragment,"[32] among others, can attest to Hardy's concerns with this new humanism. With regard to "Fragment," the poem was published in *Moments of Vision* in 1917, however, the composition date is unknown. As we shall see, this poem clearly moves into agnostic considerations about mankind and history. As is often the case with Hardy's lyrical production, these poems were often written at the end of the nineteenth century, few decades before he actually revised and published them. The reason why Hardy's poetic work presents such a long *décalage* is not only due to his predominant and necessary career as a novelist; I would argue that another possible explanation may concern his interest in observing events and places in a longer perspective before making them into writing. A major difference between Wordsworth's well-known "recollection in tranquillity" and what we may call Hardy's "recollection in distress" can be the idea of History as an ongoing process of reflection and re-consideration of events in the light of their historical and social consequences. It is not a coincidence that Hardy was indeed a key figure for the British War poet generation, who addressed his poetry for they could see in it the distance between a manifold reality, which is History, and the individual life. Poetry is the finest instrument to investigate Time, and, following Stephen's agnostic lesson, Hardy looked for physicality and strength in writing to represent it. In his poem "He Wonders About Himself," Hardy questioned his conscience in search of sensible fulfillment in living:

> No use hoping, or feeling vext,
> Tugged by a force above or under
> Like some fantocine, much I wonder
> What I shall find me doing next!
>
> Shall I be rushing where bright eyes be?
> Shall I be suffering sorrows seven?
> Shall I be watching the stars of heaven,
> Thinking one of them looks like thee?
>
> Part is mine of the general Will,
> Cannot my share in the sum of sources
> Bend a digit the poise of forces,
> And a fair desire fulfil?

The strophe in the middle of the poem presents an anaphoric rhythm and, as anaphors usually convey irony and bitterness, Hardy here put all his mordant doubts to the extent of overwhelming himself with his own sense of impotency and rationality. Hardy ends his poem with a question, as if to reinforce his reluctance to give up. The powerful and somehow liturgical aspects of Hardy's verses can be actually seen as agnostic questions. Poetry is indeed mentioned in Stephen's agnostic writing as a tangible sign of human impulse to celebrate and protect grief and joy. Poems are seen not as vehicle of comfort, but as a way to become acquainted with the world. Another extract from Stephen's *Apology* simplifies his ideas and presents strong similarities with Hardy's poetic philosophy:

> No poetry lives which reflects only the cheerful emotions. Our sweetest songs are those which tell of saddest thought. We can bring harmony out of melancholy; we cannot banish melancholy from the world. And the religious utterances, which are the highest form of poetry, are bound by the same law. There is a deep sadness in the world.[33]

Stephen's agnosticism did not expunge optimism as such; it interrogated Victorian optimistic vision of human possibilities and took into account social differences and opportunities, showing the world as irregular as it appears to his agnostic eyes. He broke the ground for the effects of the late *fin de siècle* melancholia, but above all he intended to warn individual confidence. Although not openly declared, Stephen aimed to contradict the after-life of Rousseau's philosophy over the fundamental candor of men's thoughts and actions, and he wanted to re-shape man's place in Nature. As he wrote in his *Apology*, "man knows nothing of the Infinite and Absolute; and that, knowing nothing, he had better not be dogmatic about his ignorance."[34] Hardy embraced Stephen's poignancy about man's disgraced presence in the world, as his poem "Fragment" can attest. Here the poet imagines a queue of men waiting for God. The poet questions them about the meaning of their waiting, and in the poem a sense of impotency and finality come out to switch their expectations off.

Fragment

At last I entered a long dark gallery,
    Catacomb-lined; and ranged at the side
    Were the bodies of men from far and wide
Who, motion past, were nevertheless not dead.

    "The sense of waiting here strikes strong;
Everyone's waiting, waiting, it seems to me;
    What are you waiting for so long?—
        What is to happen?" I said.

"O we are waiting for one called God," said they,
    "(Though by some the Will, or Force, or Laws;
    And, vaguely, by some, the Ultimate Cause;)
Waiting for him to see us before we are clay.
    Yes; waiting, waiting, for God to know it." ...
        "To know what?" questioned I.
"To know how things have been going on earth and below it:
    It is clear he must know some day."
    I thereon asked them why.
        "Since he made us humble pioneers
        Of himself in consciousness of Life's tears,
        It needs no mighty prophecy
        To tell that what he could mindlessly show
        His creatures, he himself will know.

    "By some still close-cowled mystery
    We have reached feeling faster than he,
    But he will overtake us anon,
        If the world goes on."

Men are "humble pioneers," and as Hardy wrote "we have reached feelings faster than he"; once again, the poet not only interrogates his doubts but makes it evident that it is a human struggle to survive the death of religious comfort. Furthermore in this poem, questions have a remarkable role. Hardy also plays with names designed to address the divinity: "God, [...] the Will, or Force, or Laws, [...] the Ultimate Cause." As well as the title of the poem, "Fragment," Hardy points to the fragility of mankind. Humanity seems to be lost in waiting for God, and there is no trace of that Beckettian sarcasm that characterized the twentieth-century religious uncertainty. Hardy's setting is grave; echoing a Dantesque infernal scenario, the poet acts as a lost poet who "needs no mighty prophecy." God's "creatures" live in an unresolved mystery which cannot be disentangled by a human mind. Hardy ventured even further: he seems to accept God's own lack of omniscience in a world subjected to an unattainable truth. As observed by Murfin, Hardy's early poems already included his distinctive view on life. "Amabel" is the title of a poem written by Hardy in 1865–67, when he was in his mid-twenties; nevertheless, his youth could not prevent him from avoiding any embellishment about the inescapability of disillusions in human life.

> Hardy's early poems, like Swinburne's, exist in a world so bleak and faded that its inhabitants have to occasionally suspect that it is rife with hounds of "Time and Fate, Gods without pity." It is a place in which men and women who are all too human fail to achieve or maintain either their high ideals or some transcendental state of being, in any case, their "Amabels."[35]

Overall, Hardy's poems often envisioned a large overview of a universe under the control of mindless forces, in which humans are hapless pawns. However, poems like "Fragment" and "In Time of 'The Breaking of Nations'" also manifest awareness and strength in facing the world as it appeared to Victorians. Stephen's lessons in freethinking and agnosticism surely reinforced and developed Hardy's investigations on human unattainable truths. Going back to Hardy's "Fragment," we can see how the poet's imagination used this symbolic figure to define mankind from many perspectives: from a Darwinian point of view (fragments as inherited traits), from a philosophical point of view (Bergson's fragments as atoms of memory),[36] from an architectural point of view (above all in his experience of church restoration when he discovered a pagan and religious architecture made of a combination of *fragments/relics*). In "Fragment," he enucleated an important speculation about the superiority of human feelings in comparison with God's lack. Bailey supposed that the title of the poem, "Fragment," was in reality a philosophical and unfinished thought[37]; moreover, it seems to me that the idea of fragment pervades Hardy's personality, also causing his typical agnostic hesitation.

Whereas some agnostics seem to belong exclusively to Victorian Free-Thought, Hardy's agnostic eyes looked over the nineteenth century and, as we are about to see, contributed to influence some of the twentieth-century social contradictions and intellectual questionings in poetry. Some of his expressions—which sometimes coincide with his poems' titles such as "Hap," "The Impercipient," "The Lacking Sense," and vibrant phrases like "Time's unflinching rigour" ("At Castle Boterel"), "immense Mortality" ("At a Lunar Eclipse"), "the Spinner of the Years" ("The Convergence of the Twain")— seem to "hide what they reveal," as Shaw puts it. They convey abstraction and grandeur while expressing specific states of mind, they identify detailed situations regarding time and people. Moreover, Hardy's withdrawing/revealing attitude in poetry shows a coordinated dialogue between his poetic self and his lucid imagination that never ceased to grow during his old age, as we can also see in his literary notes. In his collection of extracts from letters, essays, books, magazines, Hardy managed to comprehend social and intellectual doubts and stages of his age. Here Darwin, Huxley, Spencer, Stephen and many others cohabit on the same page, as they contributed to expand his inner debates and helped him to fruitfully spend their ideas in his poetry. An example can be found in his poem "The Convergence of the Twain,"[38] where the image of the seabed is somehow assimilated to a microscopic observation:

> IV
> Jewels in joy designed
> To ravish the sensuous mind
> Lie lightless, all their sparkles bleared and black and blind.

A quotation from J. G. Wood's *Insects at Home* (London, 1872)—"some of our dullest and most insignificant little insects are, when placed under the revealing lens of the microscope, absolutely blazing with natural jewellery"—collected in Hardy's notebooks,[39] exemplifies the influence and reception of scientific methods in writing poetry. In particular, "The Convergence of the Twain" seems to show Hardy's ability to use his Victorian meticulous look to illustrate episodes of the twentieth century, like the atrocious sinking of the Titanic.

Hardy's scientific and creative writing has been hugely investigated and profitable ideas have been enucleated through his poems. However, Hardy's microscope in verses also suggests his habit to observe and describe his images from a very short distance. Moreover, his agnosticism was often another instrument to express what his sight recorded without judgment. This way to consider life and death was inconceivable before scientific discoveries, or at least, it was entirely addicted to religion and religious rites. As Stephen points out in his essays on agnosticism:

> We must admit, to be frank, that "belief in God" is a phrase covering so many radically different states of mind, that a categorical yes or no can hardly be given to the question. At the present day it is too often used to mean disbelief in man. It connotes, at least, the opinion that reason is a delusion, and progress a sham. But if, in a more philosophical sense, belief in God means belief in a "general stream of tendency," Darwinism, so far from weakening that belief, helps us to map out some small part of the stream, though its source and its end be hidden in impenetrable mystery. On the other hand, Darwinism is clearly opposed to the more popular conceptions of theology. [...] The eye and the ear are no longer to be regarded as illustrating the cunning workmanship of the Divine artificer, but as particular results of the uniform operation of what are called the laws of nature.[40]

Through Stephen's writing, Hardy discovered and understood the benevolent side of scientific writing; during a period in which nature was suddenly perceived as cruel and vengeful, Hardy looked at human intellect as an instrument to face grief and, at the same time, as a new territory for his philosophical speculations. Nature had to be respected in its ancestral rules and, at the same time, it has to be seen as a representation of reality also in terms of violence and hostility. Stephen's "anecdote" on the Alps is profoundly emblematic: the author climbs a mountain while suddenly he loses his balance and thinks he is only waiting to die, to be swallowed up by nature itself. Hardy seems to go even further, as he later realized that human progress is often a social barrier and significantly affects human lives. His poems collect what Stephen called "the deep sadness of the world,"[41] not to comfort humanity, but to collect human memories, collective and personal events, to resist time's oblivion.

Actually, Hardy's poetic reputation as a free-thinker is also visible thanks to his influence on later generations of poets, Sassoon, Blunden and Grave, but also Auden, Larkin and Nicholson, among others. Auden's "In Praise of Limestone"[42] offers a tribute to "the poet," "Admired for his earnest habit of calling/ The sun the sun." In that poem, Auden reconstructs "poetically" the images of the significant change, Jurassic coast included, formed around the rise of agnosticism in poetry and prose, and he gave Hardy a privileged position on his beloved cliffs as an "antimythological" presence in a celestial setting. Hardy certainly owed much to the post–Darwinian world and its renewed sense of time and history, and, unlike Hopkins, he is not "isolated [...] by an utter personal, theological and historical aloneness,"[43] but totally accommodated into the images of the new collective past. Hardy's poetry led to the creation of new definitions to outline the human past, aims and expectations. The opening to agnosticism was necessary to avoid the risk of any likelihoods either with French Positivism as enunciated by Comtean philosophy, or with Mill's empiricism, as proposed in his *System of Logic* (1843) and *Utilitarianism* (1861). It was probably mainly Stephen's influence that played a freethinking role on Hardy's literary mind. Moreover, as Stephen's encyclopedic work *The English Utilitarians* can illustrate, agnosticism became also a way to interpret history by mapping out changes and turning points with a different, and possibly more consistent, language. In Thomas Hardy's poetry, as Ross C. Murfin noticed in "The Lacking Sense," "The Mother Mourns," "God's Funeral," "A Plaint to Man," "Agnosti Teoi," or "God-Forgotten":

> Hardy [...] implicitly acknowledges that, just as "romantic" men tend to "shape" a spiritual world, usually benevolent but occasionally malign, according to the random pleasures, hopes, or disappointments they feel in the moment, so "religious" men (for Hardy, as for Swinburne, Carlyle and Arnold, they are much the same) "frame" various "phantasies" of a personal God or "Fate" or "Doom" according to their own temporary doubts, dreams, or dis-

satisfactions. Thus, in these poems of agnostic acknowledgment, Hardy manages to "frame" himself in the act of "framing" or "shaping" weak fantasies, that is to say, he manages to step outside of the agonized agnosticism of his own past and thus emerge from it, moving himself as well as his reader beyond disappointment, beyond fantasies, "beyond church."[44]

The influence of Darwin's theory and the incisiveness of Stephen's essays produced an insightful echo in Hardy's poetics and language, as he wrote in his "ghosted" biography: "the most far-reaching consequence of the establishment of the common origin of all species is ethical."[45] Hardy claimed his position of agnostic and offered a new "empiric" and individual gaze, without rejecting his transcendentalist-romantic background and sometimes sentimental imagination. In this respect, agnosticism was a valuable passport to understand and explain "almost every aspect of the universe,"[46] but not its social and emotional consequences, or as Hardy puts it in *Tess of the D'Urbervilles*, in the transition between old and modern times, people did experience "the ache of modernism."[47] In this respect, Stephen might be seen as a bridge and, at the same time, as a social and cultural barrier for Hardy's ideas, since the latter witnessed the consequences and developments of modernity.

However, the connections between Stephen and Hardy seem to be not only visible when their sensibilities agree, but also when they collide. Stephen's influence on Hardy clarifies the important negotiation of Hardy's Victorian and modern personality with the construction of a humanistic agnosticism. Thomas Hardy's determination in writing and his mature decision to devote his mind entirely to poetry shows above all his yearning for emotions as well, and maybe his nostalgia too. Hardy's sentiments—sometimes buried into his personal or local memory, sometimes majestically observed through his psychological and cerebral microscope—seem to review obsessively the past, in search of Stephen's "deep sadness [of] the world" in order to oppose and resist it.

Notes

1. Charles Darwin, *The Origins of Species*, introd. Gillian Beer (Oxford: Oxford University Press, 1998; first edition, 1859), ix.
2. *Ibid.*, xii.
3. *Ibid.*, 251.
4. *Jude the Obscure* (Boston: Houghton Mifflin, 1965; first edition, 1895), 68.
5. Jonathan Smith, *Charles Darwin and Victorian Visual Culture* (Cambridge: Cambridge University Press, 2006), 181.
6. David William Dockrill, "The Origin and Development of Nineteenth Century English Agnosticism" in *The Historical Journal* 1:4 (February 1971): 3–31.

7. A. O. J. Cockshut, *The Unbelievers* (London: Collins, 1964), 40.
8. Bernard Lightman, *The Origins of Agnosticism: Victorian Unbelief and the Limits of Knowledge* (Baltimore: Johns Hopkins University Press, 1987), 1.
9. *Ibid.*, 13.
10. Ralph Pite, *Thomas Hardy: The Guarded Life* (London: Picador, 2006), 213.
11. Rosemarie Morgan, "'The Rugged Trim.' Leslie Stephen's Occasional Letters to Thomas Hardy" in *Days to Recollects: Essays in Honour of Robert Schweik*, ed. Rosemarie Morgan (Hew Haven, CT: The Hardy Association Press, 2000), 97.
12. Leslie Stephen, *An Agnostic's Apology and Other Essays* (London: Smith, Elder, & co., 1903; first edition, 1900), 7.
13. Leslie Stephen, *The English Utilitarians*, volume 1 (London: Duckworth, 1900), 57.
14. Dockrill, *op. cit.*, 3.
15. Pite, *op. cit.*, 212.
16. W. David Shaw, "The Agnostic Imagination in Victorian Poetry" in *Criticism* 22:2 (Spring 1980): 131.
17. *The Complete Poems*, ed. James Gibson (London: Macmillan, 1976), 434. Published in *Moments of Vision* in 1917.
18. Geoffrey Harvey, *The Complete Critical Guide to Thomas Hardy* (London: Routledge, 2003), 23.
19. "In poetry, the agnostic afflatus is traceable in Swinburne's poetic imagination," as Margot K. Louis points out in her book *Swinburne and His Gods: The Roots and Growth of an Agnostic Poetry* (Montreal: McGill-Queen's University Press, 1990), 10. Swinburne's poetic agnosticism had its roots in his reception and modulation of Romanticism, especially his constant confrontation with William Blake's imagination. It was also conveyed by his mythological imagination and classical competences. Swinburne's "Hymn of Man" solemnly exemplifies a new unsettling perspective regarding human questionings on faith.
20. *The Complete Poems, op. cit.*, 66–67. Published in *Wessex Poems* in 1898.
21. Stephen Jay Gould, *I Have Landed: The End of Beginning in Natural History* (New York: Harmony Books, 2002), 94–96.
22. *The Literary Notebooks of Thomas Hardy* (New York: New York University Press, 1985), 132.
23. Stephen, *An Agnostic's Apology, op. cit.*, 21–22.
24. Stephen, *The English Utilitarians, op. cit.*, 375.
25. Stephen, *An Agnostic's Apology, op. cit.*, 27–28.
26. *Ibid.*, 1.
27. *Ibid.*, 3–4.
28. Tess Cosslett, *The "Scientific Movement" and Victorian Literature* (Brighton: The Harvester Press 1982), 136.
29. *The Complete Poems, op. cit.*, 543. The poem was published in *Moments of Vision* in 1917, but probably written in 1915 as the post-scripted date suggests.
30. *Ibid.*, 639–640. Published in *Late Lyrics and Earlier* in 1922, probably written in 1917 (the post-script reads: "December 31. During the War").
31. *Ibid.*, 510. Published in *Moments of Vision* in 1917; the post-script sends either the composition or at least the prompting idea back to November 1893.
32. *Ibid.*, 513–514.

33. Stephen, *An Agnostic's Apology, op. cit.*, 35–36.
34. *Ibid.*, 41.
35. Ross C. Murfin, *Swinburne, Hardy, Lawrence and the Burden of Belief* (Chicago: University of Chicago Press, 1978), 84.
36. See Tim Armstrong, *Haunted Hardy: Poetry, History, Memory* (Basingstoke: Macmillan, 2000).
37. J. O. Bailey, *The Poetry of Thomas Hardy: A Handbook and Commentary* (Chapel Hill: University of North Carolina Press, 1970), 404.
38. *The Complete Poems, op. cit.*, 306–307. Published in *Satires of Circumstance* in 1914; written in 1912.
39. *Literary Notebooks, op. cit.*, 281.
40. Stephen, *Essays on Freethinking and Plainspeaking* (London: Longmans, 1873), 99–100.
41. Stephen, *An Agnostic's Apology, op. cit.*, 35–36.
42. W. H. Auden, *Selected Poems* (New York: Random House, 2007), 189.
43. Shaw, *op. cit.*, 139.
44. Murfin, *op. cit.*, 108–109.
45. Florence Hardy, *The Life of Thomas Hardy 1840–1928* (London: Macmillan, 1965), 349.
46. Dockrill, *op. cit.*, 8.
47. *Tess of the D'Urbervilles* (London: Penguin Classics, 2003; first edition, 1891), 19.

Works Cited

Armstrong, Tim. *Haunted Hardy: Poetry, History, Memory*. Basingstoke: Macmillan, 2000.
Auden, W. H.. *Selected Poems*. Ed. E. Mendelson, NY: Random House, 2007.
Bailey, J. O. *The Poetry of Thomas Hardy: A Handbook and Commentary*. Chapel Hill: University of North Carolina Press, 1970.
Cockshut, A. O. J. *The Unbelievers*. London: Collins, 1964.
Cosslett, Tess. *The "Scientific Movement" and Victorian Literature*. Brighton: The Harvester Press, 1982.
Darwin, Charles. *The Origins of Species* (1859). Ed. Gillian Beer, Oxford: Oxford University Press, 1998.
Dockrill, David William. "The Origin and Development of Nineteenth Century English Agnosticism," in *The Historical Journal* (University of Newcastle) 1:4 (February1971): 3–31.
Gould, Stephen Jay. *I Have Landed: The End of Beginning in Natural History*. New York: Harmony Books, 2002.
Hardy, Florence. *The Life of Thomas Hardy 1840–1928*. London: Macmillan, 1965.
Hardy, Thomas. *The Complete Poems*. Ed. James Gibson. London: Macmillan, 1976.
_____. *Jude the Obscure* (1895). Ed. Irving Howe. Boston: Houghton Mifflin, 1965.
_____. *The Literary Notebooks of Thomas Hardy*. Ed. Lennart A. Björk. 2 vols. New York: New York University Press, 1985.
_____. *Tess of the D'Urbervilles* (1891). Ed. Tim Dolin. London: Penguin Classics, 2003.
Harvey, Geoffrey. *The Complete Critical Guide to Thomas Hardy*. London: Routledge, 2003.

Lightman, Bernard. *The Origins of Agnosticism: Victorian Unbelief and the Limits of Knowledge*. Baltimore: Johns Hopkins University Press, 1987.
Louis, Margot K. *Swinburne and His Gods: The Roots and Growth of an Agnostic Poetry*. Montreal: McGill-Queen's University Press, 1990.
Morgan, Rosemarie. "'The Rugged Trim.' Leslie Stephen's Occasional Letters to Thomas Hardy," in *Days to Recollects: Essays in Honour of Robert Schweik*. Ed. Rosemarie Morgan. Hew Haven, CT: The Hardy Association Press, 2000, 91–111.
Murfin, Ross C. *Swinburne, Hardy, Lawrence and the Burden of Belief*. Chicago: University of Chicago Press, 1978.
Pite, Ralph. *Thomas Hardy: The Guarded Life*. London: Picador, 2006.
Shaw, W. David. "The Agnostic Imagination in Victorian Poetry," in *Criticism* 22:2 (Spring 1980): 116–139.
Smith, Jonathan. *Charles Darwin and Victorian Visual Culture*. Cambridge: Cambridge University Press, 2006.
Stephen, Leslie. *An Agnostic's Apology and Other Essays* (1900). London: Smith, Elder, & Co., 1903.
_____. *The English Utilitarians*. 3 vols. London: Duckworth, 1900.
_____. *Essays on Freethinking and Plainspeaking*. London: Longmans, 1873.

The Shadow of God in
Poems of the Past and the Present
Stéphanie Bernard

In his Preface to *Poems of the Past and the Present* published in 1901, Thomas Hardy explains that the volume gathers "a series of feelings and fancies written down in widely differing moods and circumstances, and at various dates. It will probably be found, therefore, to possess little cohesion of thought or harmony of colouring."[1]

To Hardy, though, this is no defect. Conversely, it allows for a wider expression of the thoughts and sentiments of the poet. The contradictions inherent in such a loose mode of writing and publishing give way to the rich and varied rendering of life: "I do not greatly regret this. Unadjusted impressions have their value, and the road to a true philosophy of life seems to lie in humbly recording diverse readings of its phenomena as they are forced upon us by chance and change."[2] Philip Larkin seemed to share this point of view for he wrote: "One can read him for years and years and still be surprised."[3] Hardy's poetry is characterized indeed by "its resistance to belongingness."[4] There is "a sense of the lyric's placelessness in his poetry, of its ability to unsettle and disorient both its speakers and readers, and to achieve [...] a music of wondrous strangeness."[5]

Hardy's treatment of the question of faith and religious belief contributes to the unsettling strangeness of the writing. As Timothy Hands puts it in his work entitled *Thomas Hardy: Distracted Preacher?*: "Though stridently anti–Christian on the one hand, Hardy's religious impulse is also a more complex mixture of conflicting viewpoints, a war between intellect and emotion which necessitates an artistically fructifying indecision."[6] A metaphorical war takes place under the reader's eyes as soon as he or she tries to trace a coherent system of ideas in Hardy's thought as it is expressed in the poems, especially in *Poems of the Past and the Present*. The collection creates a feeling of indeterminacy, not only in so far as style, form and subject-matter are concerned—Hardy's "little cohesion of thought or harmony of colouring"—but also as regards the notion of the passing of time, of the now and then contained in the title. The conjoined evocation of the past and the present suggests a blurring of limits and a need to turn towards the past in order to be, or speak, in the present. Is the past the origin, the cause that gives life to the present? Or is it the shadow that darkens the present and tints every moment with the hues of loss and withering?

These questions are also those Hardy seems to ask about God. Is he the Creator, the Cause? Or the Destructor? Is God really God? In asking such questions, Hardy baffles the Victorian reader, challenges religious dogmas and undermines the notion of sacredness. But how daring is the poet? How far does he travel on that road of human self-reliance in a rejection of transcendence?

The Refusal of the Sacred

The themes of the poems inside the collection confirm the impression of strangeness and tension which is characteristic of Hardy's poetry: some texts are about the disasters of war ("Embarcation," "The Colonel's Soliloquy"), others about the disillusions of lovers ("The Well-Beloved," "A Broken Appointment," "The Supplanter"). Others at last, like "The Mother Mourns," "The Subalterns," "To an Unborn Pauper Child," tend to evoke a bleak vision of life in general, and to convey a disenchanted philosophical outlook, derived from a loss of faith.

The reading of most poems begets an overall impression of nostalgia, i.e., a feeling that the text insists on what is lost but still longed for (whereas elegy would notify the loss as irrecoverable and definitive). In the very same manner, Thomas Hardy's loss of faith when he was a young man in London was never a thing of the past, so that most of his writings are haunted by the Scriptures and the question of belief. As Claire Tomalin explains: "He could no longer believe, but he cherished the memory of belief."[7]

Brought up in a Christian family, Hardy read the Bible and sang Christian hymns. He went to church regularly and was well aware of the differences that existed within the Anglican Church. Indeed, the parish of Stinsford to which Hardy belonged was High Church, so that he was accustomed to the ceremonial of the service there. But the rest of Dorset was chiefly Low Church, that is to say Evangelical: this meant a close reading of the Scriptures and rituals being brought to a minimum. As an apprentice in architecture in Dorchester, Hardy met Henry Robert Bastow who was a staunch Evangelical;

the correspondence they kept with each other allowed for discussions on Christian dogmas, and rites such as baptism. Hardy fluctuated between the edges of Anglicanism: in London, he would "attend a strangely polarized mixture of churches allied to established religious extremes."[8] It may have been a foreshadowing of his later abandonment of faith and church attendance. Yet, at the same time, the hesitation can signal renewed attempts to find a suitable church and show how significant religion was to him; it suggests what impact the rejection of belief could have on his life and art—what a void it could have left. As for the writings, they are imbued with contradictory feelings of rejection and nostalgia as regards Christian belief. Indeterminacy pervades the whole of Hardy's creation. His lyrics notably oscillate between a rendering of prosaic reality and epiphanic "moments of vision,"[9] between the despondency of loss and the joy of past regained.

An example of that oscillation can be found in the poem "The Self-Unseeing."[10] The first stanza emphatically opposes the past and the present, to underline what used to be in the place described and consequently what has been lost:

> Here is the ancient floor,
> Footworn and hollowed and thin,
> Here was the former door
> Where the dead feet walked in.

Yet this vision of death allows for a revival of the past, a nostalgic re-enactment of youth's innocence and joy in the rest of the poem:

> She sat there in her chair,
> Smiling into the fire;
> He who played stood there
> Bowing it higher and higher
>
> Childlike, I danced in a dream;
> Blessings emblazoned that day;
> Everything glowed with a gleam;
> Yet we were looking away!

This revival can be interpreted as a moment of vision. The "dream" gives life to phantoms of the past: we see a smile, a dancing child, a violin player. Suddenly, through the melodious rhythm of the first two lines in the last stanza, one can *hear* the music, the footsteps of the child (/t/, /d/ and /b/ sounds), and the vibrations of the violin (/s/ sound): "_Ch_ildlike, I dan_c_ed in a _d_ream;/ Ble_ss_ings em_b_lazoned tha_t d_ay."[11] The plain reality depicted—the floor, the fireplace—allows for some sort of revelation and almost preternatural recreation of what no longer exists.

Hardy's vision, therefore, does not exclude the spiritual or the supernatural. The short story "The Withered Arm," for instance, illustrates the intrusion of the supernatural into the harsh reality of plain rural life. Several poems, too, evoke the manifestation of something that is normally invisible or ungraspable. However those manifestations are emptied of any sacredness: they have to do with "A Dream" (in "The Dream-Follower"[12]) or a "Shape" (in "The Well-Beloved"[13]), with "Shades" (in "I Have Lived with Shades"[14]) and "Memory" (in "Memory and I"[15]), but not with God's presence or with faith.

What exists beyond grasp and beyond sight resurfaces in Hardy's writing. The movements in nature, the coming and passing of life, the presence of light and shade, the recurrent evocation of the past and memory, constitute means of representing, or at least suggesting, that not all that exists can be seen, touched or depicted. But to Hardy the ungraspable is not of God, it is of nature rather. It is not transcendent but immanent.

The consequence of immanence rather than transcendence as the origin of life is that death is no hope at all. In the poem entitled "To Life,"[16] nothing is to be expected outside life itself. There is no hope to foster on any account, except the illusory one "That Earth is Paradise." The dead therefore haunt those who survive. They haunt the only space that can be haunted. This could be the reason why the figure of the specter is recurrent in Hardy's writing.[17] In the poem "The Self-Unseeing" quoted above, "the mind's ear hears the absent footfall at the end, the last, emphatic, ghostly tread"[18] through the evocation of the "dead feet" in the first stanza. In the poem "The Well-Beloved,"[19] the speaker falls in love with a sprite who is the very ghost of his bride. When he meets the latter again, it seems that "her soul had shrunk and died,/ And left a waste within." She has become the unsubstantial specter.

Paul Volsik stresses that ghosts are central to the poetry of Thomas Hardy. He argues that on the one hand the ghost shows that Hardy belongs to the nineteenth century, his art appearing under the influence of the Romantics. But "the ghost is powerful also in that he—or especially she—gives direct access to the psychological, the dimension that the twentieth century will insist upon in several ways."[20] This psychological approach to the specter can be traced in the poem entitled "His Immortality."[21] Here, the poet envisions after-life as the continuation of a man's existence through the traits and memory of those he has left:

I

I saw a dead man's finer part
Shining within each faithful heart
Of those bereft: Then I said: "This must be
His immortality."

But as the descendants grow old and die, the man disappears into oblivion, which could be the true meaning of death in Hardy's sense,[22] his own version of "the second death" mentioned in the Book of Revelation (2:11; 20:6,14; 21:8), but here emptied of its sacred, Christian meaning.

The Death of God

Hardy empties the Christian religion of its message of hope. He often discredits or mocks the priests who may appear in his texts: to him they cannot cure the soul. Religion cannot soothe suffering mankind because it is cut off from the reality of human life. In fact, Hardy negates the foundation of Christian theology: Jesus-Christ, the Son of God. The *Encyclopaedia Britannica* first defines Christianity as "stemming from the life, teachings, and death of Jesus of Nazareth (the Christ, or the Anointed One of God)," then adding that:

> [f]ew Christians, however, would be content to keep this reference merely historical. Although their faith tradition is historical—i.e., they believe that transactions with the divine do not occur in the realm of timeless ideas but among ordinary humans through the ages—the vast majority of Christians focus their faith in Jesus Christ as someone who is also a present reality.[23]

Accordingly the Church of England insists on the relationship with Jesus Christ in its definition of "Being a Christian":

> Christian life is lived in relationship with God through Jesus Christ and, in common with other Christians, seeking to deepen that relationship and to follow the way that Jesus taught. [...].
> How do we know that "God is for us"? Because Jesus Christ, the one human being who is completely in tune with God—with what God wants and what God is doing—has carried the burden of our human betrayals of God and running away from goodness. He has let himself be betrayed and rejected, executed in a humiliating and agonising way, and yet has not turned his back on us. *Death did not succeed in silencing him or removing him from the world. He is alive*; and that means that his love is alive, having survived the worst we can do.[24]

In his approach to religion, Hardy does seem to silence Jesus Christ by not mentioning the Resurrection and by obliterating the notions of hope, life, and communion that are characteristics of Christian faith. As an example, "The Bedridden Peasant,"[25] who is agonizing on his deathbed, addresses God, "the Maker." He sounds submissive and reverent in the end: "I'll praise Thee as were shown to me/ The mercies Thou wouldst show." However he does not mention the very core of orthodox Christian faith, never alluding to Jesus, the Savior. He praises "an Unknowing God," as the subtitle indicates, which heightens the tragedy and hopelessness of his situation:

> But Thou, Lord, giv'st us men our day
> In helpless bondage thus
> To time and Chance, and seem'st straightaway
> To think no more of us!—

There are indirect echoes of the Gospel in the poem. "But Thou, Lord, giv'st us men our day" recalls Jesus's prayer in Luke 11.3: "Give us day by day our daily bread." The expression "For Thou art mild of heart" that appears line 16 alludes to Matthew 11.29: "I am gentle and humble in heart." But these occurrences tend to heighten the subversive and even provocative irony of the painful whimper. The poor peasant seems culturally imbued with Christian teachings without being personally convinced or truly grasped by the essence of the belief, so that his conventional Christianity makes him feel abandoned by the powerful God who should be all-loving and all-knowing.

Similarly, "The Respectable Burgher"[26] who decides to "sit on Sundays in [his] chair,/ And read that moderate man Voltaire," rejects the contents of the Old and New Testaments: he expresses doubts about the veracity of the stories of several prophets and Biblical characters; more strikingly he refuses to name Jesus Christ. Although the speaker pretends to omit the name for the sake of respect ("but for shame I must forbear"), the effect of the two long dashes that signal the place left vacant by the omission is to empty the Biblical message of its substance. Christianity is hollowed out of its gospel of love: the absence of the moment when God offers his son to save humanity (John 3:16)—in other words, the negation of incarnation—means depriving the Gospel of its meaning and denying its historical and human dimension.

Logically, therefore, God appears as a distant and potentially cruel entity, cut off from the humanity he has made. In the last line of the poem entitled "The Sick Battle-God"[27] the poet declares: "The Battle-god is god no more." On first reading, the "Deity" may recall the God of the Old Testament, especially in the first stanza:

> I
>
> In days when men found joy in war,
> A God of Battle sped each mortal jar;
> The peoples pledged him heart and hand,
> From Israel's land to isles afar.

This last line, however, shows that Hardy does not refer narrowly to a Judeo-Christian context. The "isles afar" designate other religious traditions and Hardy's thought underlines the universality of the urge to oppose, destroy and dominate. The author denounces man's idolatry more than the god in question. The Battle-God, who is "god no more," announces "the Monarch" of "God's Funeral"[28] in the later collection of poems entitled *Satires of Cir-*

cumstance. The said Monarch is a "man-projected Figure" described as "jealous, fierce, at first" and who was then given "justice as the ages rolled." The story of that god is in reality the history of humanity. Hence, each poem deprives its god of any sacredness or grandeur, and suggests that men are the creators of the divinity, urged by a need to revere and believe.

On the one hand, both poems could be read as daring, revolutionary, even blasphemous pieces. On the other hand, the displacement of the focus onto man and his idolatry undermines the argument and relocates the core of the subject: the absence of transcendence results in human tragedy. Man is mistaken and errs in a universe that surpasses him. The poet himself is mistaken: the hope for a better world and for the weakening of the war spirit expressed in "The Sick Battle-God" acquires a tragic and pessimistic dimension in the light of later events, such as the two World Wars. The irony which is so typical of Hardy now turns against the poet himself.

These several aspects could leave the reader with the impression of a desperate philosophical thought, of a nihilistic and pessimistic vision of life. The impact of Nietzsche's thought can be discerned in the description of a crowd weeping over the death of God as well as in the title "God's Funeral." The poem could be read as a rewriting of the so-called "parable of the madman" in Nietzsche's *The Gay Science* published in 1882:

> Haven't you heard of that madman who in the bright morning lit a lantern and ran around the market-place crying incessantly, "I'm looking for God! I'm looking for God!" Since many of those who did not believe in God were standing around together just then, he caused great laughter. Has he been lost, then? asked one. Did he lose his way like a child? asked another. Or is he hiding? Is he afraid of us? Has he gone to sea? Emigrated?—Thus they shouted and laughed, one interrupting the other. The madman jumped into their midst and pierced them with his eyes. "Where is God?" he cried; "I'll tell you. We have killed him—you and I! We are all his murderers."[29]

Both texts enact the death of God and denounce man's foolishness in revering an idol. They also express man's distress after losing his way and his points of reference with the disappearance of God. Indeed, the parable ends up with a series of questions: "Where are we moving to? Away from all suns? Are we not continually falling? Backwards, sidewards, forwards, in all directions? Is there still an up and a down? Aren't we straying as though through an infinite nothing?"[30] These questions are echoed by stanza XII in Hardy's poem:

> "And who or what shall fill his place?
> Wither will wanderers turn distracted eyes
> For some fixed star to stimulate their pace
> Towards the goal of their enterprise?" ...

Nevertheless the feeling of disillusion and disorientation is not equivalent in both texts. While in Nietzsche's story the laughter of the people standing in the marketplace resounds, deriding the madman and stressing the ridicule of the situation, Hardy's speaker insists on the memory of what has been lost and cannot be regained. There is no notion of radical nihilism[31] in Hardy who found him "incoherent"[32] and had "an unfavorable opinion of Nietzsche, which paralleled that of a greater part of the English community in the early twentieth century."[33] So that, even in "God's Funeral," a feeling of doubt and sadness gradually replaces the intimation of blasphemy that can be derived from the reading at first, for the speaker eventually joins the procession of mourners, "'twixt the gleam and gloom."

Blasphemy or Disenchantment?

This movement that takes poet and reader away from philosophical considerations and cold irony, and closer to the condition and moods of man, appears clearly in the poem entitled "The Church-Builder" published in *Poems of the Past and the Present*.[34] The vision is no longer that of an anonymous "I," but of the dismayed church-builder, arousing and encouraging the reader's empathy. The denunciation of religion is conveyed through the personal testimony, the intimate story of pain and failure of one particular man. The general effect is much closer to blasphemy than in the two previous poems. The *mise en scène* of his suicide in this place of communal worship—suicide being condemned by the church and Christianity at large as a transgression of the sixth commandment "Thou shalt not kill"—is "mockery" in the face of society and religion.

The church-builder's abandonment of faith is complete and definitive, but it also has undertones of tragedy. The man spent all his money, neglected his family, and wasted his strength in order to realize the dream of his life. But, like the dream of *Jude the Obscure*, "the whole scheme had burst up, like an iridescent soap-bubble, under the touch of a reasoned inquiry."[35] The new awareness has undertones of the absurd:

VIII

My gift to God seems futile, quite;
    The world moves as erstwhile;
And powerful Wrong on feeble Right
    Tramples in olden style.
        My faith burns down,
      I see no crown;
But Cares, and Griefs, and Guile.

The story of that man turns out to be a tale of self-destruction. The irony of the situation is extreme as all his efforts and "stintless pains" (stanza I) to build an incredible edifice of "ashlared masonry" (stanza II) and "ivoried Rood" (stanza IV), "emblazoned glass" and "jewels" (stanza III) attract the others' scorn and deprive him of all hope and faith. The last stanza, dramatizing the probable reactions of those who will find the dead man's body in the church, sums up his predicament in poignant terms:

XII

> Well: Here at morn they'll light on one
>   Dangling in mockery
>   Of what he spent his substance on
>   Blindly and uselessly! ...
>   "He might," they'll say,
>   "Have built, some way,
>   A cheaper gallows-tree!"

The ending of the poem is all the more ironical as the church-builder turns the mockery against those who used to laugh at him. He is now the one to "sneer and smirk" (stanza VII), very like the Conrad character of Kayerts who, in *An Outpost of Progress*, "was hanging by a leather strap from the cross" and "irreverently [...] putting out a swollen tongue."[36] By writing his own end in advance, he defies God, becoming the creator of his own story. Yet the denunciation targets men and society again, as much as it targets God who is not addressed directly but appears to be absent and uncaring.

    The individualization of the outlook humanizes the rebellion and de-rationalizes the argument. The doubt so common in Hardy's texts and which recalls his agnosticism, the insistence on the particularity of an individual's vision, as well as the numerous versions of the representation of God in the poetry, do not allow for a systematic discourse on religion, or for a clear-cut and methodical denunciation of God on scientific grounds.

    So, the poet continues his quest. He does not announce, after all, the death of God but the disappearance of man's belief in God or in a man-created image of God. He asserts the coming of a new, godless and disenchanted age, in an orphan world. Hardy's writings, in other words, resist the diktats of philosophy, relying more on impressions and intimations that emphasize the tragedy of loss and endow the poems with nostalgia.

    The absent keeps returning in Hardy's texts through the memory of those who are still present—often through the voice and gaze of a solitary figure that can be that of the poet himself. "The dominant figure for his art is the voice of the absent person, lost or dead,"[37] and so is it with God whose absence is enigmatic and does not allow for a final answer to the question of his existence and his attributes. Is God absent or unconscious? Is he malevolent or simply not caring? Senseless or merely clumsy? The obsession with the question of God, of the origin of life, of suffering, makes it impossible for Hardy to be satisfied with a monolithic answer. This accounts for what could appear as incoherence in the discourse but allows for the never-ending quest of the poet whose imagination seems to be inhabited by the specter of the ungraspable divine.

One of the answers offered by the poet in response to this endless questioning is that humanity has been abandoned and is now "God-Forgotten"[38]:

> —"The Earth, sayest thou? The human race?
> By Me created? Sad its lot?
> Nay: I have no remembrance of such place:
>   Such world I fashioned not."—

In the poem God's forgetfulness is almost wish fulfillment. The poet's hope for a creator who would suddenly remember his creatures is but a "childish thought," for God remains, as in James Joyce's *Portrait of the Artist as a Young Man*, "invisible, refined out of existence, indifferent, paring his fingernails."[39]

The absent creator in Joyce's meaning is God, but also the artist himself. Irony surges if we apply the quotation to Hardy, for while he reproaches God with creating a world he abandons, he does the same in his fiction from which he seems absent and in which the characters are the victims of fate. The narrator is what Nathalie Bantz calls "a figure of the absent" in the short stories.[40] In the novels, the narrator is more intrusive, often infusing the text with his own view of event and character. Yet the narrative voice fades further away with each new novel. In the poems, the first person is more present, revealing itself through a mosaic of personae and stances, making the ambivalence of the position toward God even more blatant. A doubt remains, which is inscribed in the fluctuating narrative standpoint in the various works and in the artistic commitment of the author.

This suggests that Hardy cannot go as far as Joyce in his denunciation of God. Hardy's craft largely amounts to countering the disappearance of meaning and the absence of form that characterize the universe and human existence in his eyes, and to making up for that loss through artistic creation. While Joyce or Conrad attempt to say the unspeakable, Hardy depicts what can be represented in order to suggest what is hidden and ungraspable. Hesitating between the Victorian age and the dawn of modernity, he offers a multiple vision that gives birth to numerous images of God in *Poems of the Past and the Present*.

A Ghostly Presence

Sometimes God is presented as a careless weaver or clumsy mother. The effect is that God is repeatedly feminized and deprived of the unlimited power conferred on him by the traditional view of an omniscient, all-powerful masculine presence. The poem "The Sleep-Worker,"[41] for instance, delineates a mother-god who has "unwittingly" blundered in her creative gesture. The world she has created is a mixture of joy and pain, of "right enmeshed with wrong," "of ache and ecstasy," that seems beyond all comprehension. The poet's perplexity is reinforced by the absence of an answer, the silence of the "Sleep-Worker."

The same idea of the unconsciousness of God informs the poem "Doom and She,"[42] in which the creator is represented as a blind "Matron": "Unlit with sight is she." Deprived of one of her senses, she is nonetheless full of empathy for her "clay-made creatures" and wishes she could see what she has done. She addresses her male companion, who personifies the very Hardyan concept of "Doom," asking him to be her vision:

> IV
> "The fate of those I bear,
> Dear Lord, pray turn and view,
> And notify me true;
> Shapings that eyelessly I dare
> Maybe I would undo.
>
> V
> "Sometimes from lairs of life
> Methinks I catch a groan,
> Or multitudinous moan,
> As though I had schemed a world of strife,
> Working by touch alone."
>
> VI
> "World-Weaver!" he replies,
> "I scan all thy domain;
> But since nor joy nor pain
> It lies in me to recognize,
> Thy questionings are vain.

Unfortunately "Doom" is blind *at heart*: "Vacant of feeling he," reads the text. This heartless lord cannot fulfill the "World-Weaver"'s wish:

> VIII
> —Unanswered, curious, meek,
> She broods in sad surmise....
> —Some say they have heard her sighs
> On Alpine height or Polar peak
> When the night tempests rise.

The last stanza with the repetition of the sound /ai/ allows us to hear her sincere and heart-breaking "sighs" as they are echoed by the "Alpine height" and the tempests that "rise." The pair here depicted give a strange image of the creator and this undermines the notion of a powerful and omniscient God. This tale of a blind, vulnerable mother and a heartless, unfeeling father as the origin and cause of humanity leaves an impression of powerlessness and, indeed, doom. The image of the couple is all the more sarcastic as one may think of Hardy's conception of marriage as a mere contract rather than as a sacred union or at least a love match. In the first stanza of the poem entitled "The Conformers,"[43] Hardy's narrator voices similar disillusion as his wedding with his beloved will inevitably put an end to the couple's "mad romance":

> Yes; we'll wed, my little fay,
> And you shall write you mine,
> And in a villa chastely gray
>   We'll house, and sleep, and dine.
>   But those night-screened, divine,
>   Stolen trysts of heretofore,
> We of choice ecstasies and fine
>   Shall know no more.

In the last of the *Poems of the Past and the Present*, whose Greek title is "ἈΓΝΩΣΤΩΙ ΘΕΩΙ,"[44] the character named "Doom" is echoed by the "Willer masked and dumb,"

> Who makest Life become,—
> As though by labouring all-unknowingly,
> Like one whom reveries numb.
>
> How much of consciousness informs Thy will,
> Thy biddings, as if blind,
> Of death-inducing kind,
> Nought shows to us ephemeral ones who fill
> But moments in Thy mind.

These personae lead us back to the notion of immanence for they are alternative versions of the universal cause that, in the later poem "The Convergence of the Twain,"[45] Hardy will reduce to the senselessness of the "Immanent Will that stirs and urges everything." The Will is initially alluded to in the opening of *The Dynasts*, Hardy's epic drama about the Napoleonic Wars (1904–1908). One character of the tragic chorus says:

> [...] like a knitter drowsed,
> Whose fingers play in skilled unmindfulness,
> The Will has woven with an absent heed
> Since life first was; and ever will so weave.[46]

To counter this "skilled unmindfulness" that gives birth to a cruel reality torn apart by antagonistic forces, Hardy uses his own artistic will, his visionary power to shape a sensible rather than a senseless world. The life he creates becomes meaningful in an artistic way, as opposed to the meaninglessness of real life. So that through writing Hardy infuses consciousness and form into creation—at least into his creations, and more particularly in the poetry, with its insistence on sound, rhythm and structure. For, to him, "[t]o find beauty in ugliness is the province of the poet."[47]

The fabric of the universe has been loosely knitted, while it should have been the work of a delicate embroiderer. This is what Joseph Conrad will suggest some years later in a letter to R. B. Cunninghame Graham in which he develops the concept of the knitting machine:

> There is—let us say—a machine. It evolved itself (I am severely scientific) out of a chaos of scraps of iron and behold!—it knits. I am horrified at the horrible work and stand appalled. I feel it ought to embroider—but it goes on knitting. [...] And the most withering thought is that the infamous thing has made itself: made itself without thought, without conscience, without foresight, without eyes, without heart. It is a tragic accident—and it has happened...
> It knits us in and it knits us out. It has knitted space, time, pain, death, corruption, despair and all the illusions—and nothing matters.[48]

The echoes between this quotation and the extract from *The Dynasts* hint at the modernity of Thomas Hardy. The terms chosen by each writer suggest a strange connection with Joseph Conrad, one of the fathers of modern fiction. Besides, the correlation highlights the fact that Hardy's stance, as stated above, is that of the poet and not that of the philosopher. If Schopenhauer's influence can be traced in the notion of the Will, it is the never-ending quest and the need to turn it into words and worlds that prevail—the need for the poet and novelist to "embroider" where the senseless machine "knits."

Moreover, it is necessary to bear in mind that, at the time of the writing of *Poems of the Past and the Present*, the notion of the Immanent Will was not yet defined. Several texts give rise to philosophical or metaphysical questions. Nevertheless, most poems in the collection convey an impression rather than assert a theory: they convey the impression that something is happening beyond the veil of words, outside the reality described or the story told, as if word after word the vision "is turning ghost."[49]

The texts are inhabited by an indefinable force that seems to infuse every line. Most poems reveal an invisible but powerful presence, the ghostly shadow of God. In "God-Forgotten,"[50] for instance, the speaker is addressing God while denying His existence. The poem even opens on the image of the narrator standing "within/ The presence of the Lord Most High." The image may well be a mirage; it nevertheless initiates a dialogue between himself and his creator. The latter's answers are imagined only and unheard in reality; however they are printed on the page.

In the same way, the three sad and meditative poems that make up "In Tenebris"[51] are headed by quotations from the Book of Psalms. Each of the three extracts from the Psalms expresses alienation and despair, instead of offering hope and relief. The epigraph to "In Tenebris III" reads: "Heu mihi, quia incolatus meus prolongatus est! Habitavi cum habitantibus Cedar. Multum incola fuit anima mea" (Psalm 120:5). The translation in the King James Version is the following: "Woe is me, that I sojourn in Mesech, that I dwell in the tents of Kedar! My soul hath long dwelt with him that hateth peace." The verse casts a gloomy and woeful shadow on every remembered scene in the poem, in the very same manner as the repeated evocation of "the ending" that might "have come" places the specter of death at the heart of the text. The reader, therefore, seems to be the witness of inverted moments of vision. The potentially blissful episodes turn out to be sad and pale; the atmosphere is growing darker as on "a winter-wild night"[52]: those moments blind rather than reveal. God's words quoted in the epigraph no longer bring light, yet they remain "Written indelibly," as the Lord says in "By the Earth's Corpse."[53]

In that poem the irony becomes tragic nostalgia: the creator repents too late of what he has done. Life on earth has disappeared and he regrets

> [...] all the wrongs endured
> By Earth's poor patient kind,
> Which my too oft unconscious hand
> Let enter undersigned.

Hardy reverses the traditional notion of hell: it is God who now repents for the wrongs he has done ("it still repenteth me!"). His own version of Christianity is subversive: because of his "eternal mind," God is doomed to remember and regret "that late earthly scene"—what used to be and is no more.

God becomes tragic. He is paradoxically presented in a very human way: the uncaring maker is now torn by a feeling of shame and regret. This strangely recalls Hardy's own experience after the loss of his wife Emma. The mixture of regret and desire that Hardy felt for the wife from whom he had been estranged so many years is quite similar to the nostalgia expressed in the poems about God. Besides, just as the "Poems of 1912–13" are infused by Emma's ghost-like presence, so the *Poems of the Past and the Present*—and many other poems too—are imbued with the ghost-like presence of God.

The reader, therefore, is invited to go beyond appearances. God's silence does not mean he *is* actually absent. On the contrary, most texts that seem to mock or at least question religion lead to "an irrefutable experience of transcendence even though the poet refuses to credit belief in any transcendent domain."[54] This is true of the poems that give voice to God in spite of Hardy's loss of faith, or that let the dead speak although nothing seems to be expected after this earthly life. This is true of other texts, as is suggested notably by the short story "The Withered Arm," in which the irrational and the supernatural gradually overpower the characters, the diegesis, and the text as a whole.

The shadowy, specter-like presence of God haunts Hardy's writing. Even in his re-writing of the creation, he can never entirely get rid of the Biblical intertext. Hence, in "The Lacking Sense"[55] which conjures up again the image of the blind mother weaving "her world-webs," the reference to an "angel fallen from grace" shows that the writer cannot get free of the influence of the Christian religion. The priest in "The Lost Pyx"[56] *must* answer the call he has received and *must* look for the pyx he has lost. Similarly, Hardy *must* return incessantly to that call he received in his youth but rejected when he lost faith.

Religion is inescapable as Hardy himself knew. In the "Apology" he wrote in 1922 on the occasion of the publication of *Late Lyrics and Earlier*, he contends that "poetry and religion touch each other, or rather modulate into each other; are, indeed, often but different names for the same thing."[57] The amount of poems written suggests therefore their author's never-ending quest for form and reasons to believe—recalling the enduring hope of the narrator of "The Oxen"[58] in spite of "the gloom"—, and this until "he resolved to say no more."[59]

Notes

1. Thomas Hardy, *The Complete Poems*, ed. James Gibson (Basingstoke: Palgrave, 2001), 84.
2. *Ibid.*
3. Philip Larkin is quoted by James Gibson in his "Introduction" to *The Complete Poems, op. cit.*, xxxv.
4. DeSales Harrison, "Reading Absences in Hardy's Lyrics" in *The Ashgate Research Companion to Thomas Hardy*, ed. Rosemary Morgan (Burlington, VT: Ashgate, 2010), 403.
5. *Ibid.*, 404.
6. Timothy Hands, *Thomas Hardy: Distracted Preacher?* (Basingstoke: Macmillan, 1989), 117.
7. Claire Tomalin, *Thomas Hardy: The Time-Torn Man* (London: Penguin, 2006), 78.
8. Timothy Hands, "One Church, Several Faiths, No Lord: Thomas Hardy, Art and Belief" in Morgan (ed.), *op. cit.*, 203.
9. *Moments of Vision* is the title of Hardy's fifth collection of poems, published in 1917.
10. *The Complete Poems, op. cit.*, 166–167.

11. /t/, /d/ and /b/ sounds are underlined and /s/ sounds appear in italics in the quotation.
12. *Ibid.*, 143.
13. *The Complete Poems, op. cit.*, 133–135.
14. *Ibid.*, 184–185.
15. *Ibid.*, 185–186.
16. *Ibid.*, 118.
17. Already in the novels several characters are ghost-like: Jude who continues to be present in the text through Arabella's words about him after his death, or Tess who reappears under the features of her sister Liza-Lu.
18. John Hughes, "'Tune' and 'Thought': The Uses of Music in Hardy's Poetry" in Morgan (ed.), *op. cit.*, 280.
19. *The Complete Poems, op. cit.*, 133–135.
20. Paul Volsik, "'A Phantom of His Own Figuring.' The Poetry of Thomas Hardy" in *Études anglaises* 1, Tome 57 (2004): 109.
21. *The Complete Poems, op. cit.*, 143.
22. Following this train of thought, we could then say that Hardy has achieved immortality through his fame. This sheds an interesting and somewhat ironical light on Hardy's achievement.
23. "Christianity" in *Encyclopædia Britannica Online Academic Edition*, http://www.britannica.com/EBchecked/topic/115240/Christianity, accessed 14 July 2014.
24. Baron Williams of Oystermouth, "Being a Christian," http://www.churchofengland.org/our-faith/being-a-christian.aspx, accessed 14 July 2014. My italics.
25. *The Complete Poems, op. cit.*, 124–125.
26. *Ibid.*, 159–160.
27. *Ibid.*, 97–99.
28. *Ibid.*, 326–329.
29. Friedrich Nietzsche, *The Gay Science*, ed. Bernard Williams, trans. Josephine Nauckhoff (Cambridge: Cambridge University Press, 2001), 119–120.
30. *Ibid.*, 120.
31. "Rather than argue that God does not exist, Nietzsche claims that 'God is dead.' [...] That is, 'God is dead' because the timeless and universal standpoint of God has led to 'nihilism'—the viewpoint that there is essentially nothing meaningful to our world beyond a set of true facts" (Adrian Samuel, "Nietzsche and God" [Part I], in *Richmond Journal of Philosophy* 14 [Spring 2007], http://www.richmond-philosophy.net/rjp/back_issues/rjp14_samuel.pdf, accessed 14 July 2014).
32. Patrick Bridgewater, "English Writers and Nietzsche" in *Nietzsche: Imagery and Thought: a Collection of Essays*, ed. Malcolm Pasley (Berkeley: University of California Press, 1978), 225.
33. Barbara DeMille, "Cruel Illusions: Nietzsche, Conrad, Hardy, and the "Shadowy Ideal'" in *Studies in English Literature, 1500–1900* 30.4 (Autumn 1990): 699.
34. *The Complete Poems, op. cit.*, 170–172.
35. *Jude the Obscure* (New York: Norton, 1999; first edition, 1895), 138.
36. Joseph Conrad, *An Outpost of Progress* (Oxford: Oxford University Press, 1998; first edition, 1898), 34.
37. Harrison in Morgan (ed.), *op. cit.*, 404.
38. *The Complete Poems, op. cit.*, 123–124.

39. James Joyce, *A Portrait of the Artist as a Young Man* (Harmondsworth: Penguin, 1966; first edition, 1916), 245.
40. Nathalie Bantz, *Les Nouvelles de Thomas Hardy: Stratégies narratives d'une écriture sous contrainte* (Paris: Honoré Champion, 2011), 74 ("une figure de l'absent").
41. *The Complete Poems, op. cit.*, 121–122.
42. *Ibid.*, 118–120.
43. *Ibid.*, 229–230.
44. *Ibid.*, 186–187.
45. *Ibid.*, 306–307. The poem was written in 1912 after the loss of the Titanic and was published in 1914 in *Satires of Circumstance*.
46. *The Dynasts* (London: Macmillan, 1978), 22–23.
47. Florence Emily Hardy, *The Life of Thomas Hardy, 1840–1928* (London: Macmillan, 1962), 213.
48. C. T. Watts (ed.), *Joseph Conrad's Letters to R. B. Cunninghame Graham* (Cambridge: Cambridge University Press, 1969), 57.
49. "A Commonplace Day" in *The Complete Poems, op. cit.*, 115.
50. *Ibid.*, 123–124.
51. *Ibid.*, 167–169.
52. "In Tenebris III," *ibid.*, 169.
53. *Ibid.*, 126–127.
54. Hughes in Morgan (ed.), *op. cit.*, 272.
55. *The Complete Poems, op. cit.*, 116–118.
56. *Ibid.*, 173–175.
57. *Ibid.*, 561.
58. *Ibid.*, 468.
59. "He Resolves to Say No More," *ibid.*, 929.

Works Cited

Bantz, Nathalie. *Les Nouvelles de Thomas Hardy. Stratégies narratives d'une écriture sous contrainte.* Paris: Honoré Champion, 2011.
DeMille, Barbara. "Cruel Illusions: Nietzsche, Conrad, Hardy, and the 'Shadowy Ideal,'" in *Studies in English Literature, 1500–1900*, 30.4 (Autumn 1990): 697–714.
Hands, Timothy. *Thomas Hardy: Distracted Preacher?* Basingstoke: Macmillan, 1989.
Hardy, Florence Emily. *The Life of Thomas Hardy, 1840–1928.* London: Macmillan, 1962.
Hardy, Thomas. *The Complete Poems.* Ed. James Gibson. London: Macmillan, 2001.
_____. *The Dynasts.* London: Macmillan, 1978; first ed. 1904–1908.
_____. *Jude the Obscure.* New York: Norton, 1999, first edn 1895.
_____. *Tess of the D'Urbervilles.* Oxford: Oxford University Press, 1998, first edn 1891.
Hynes, Samuel. *The Oxford Authors. Thomas Hardy.* Oxford University Press, 1984.
Morgan, Rosemarie, ed. *The Ashgate Research Companion to Thomas Hardy.* Burlington, VT: Ashgate, 2010.
Nietzsche, Friedrich. *The Gay Science.* Ed. Bernard Williams, trans. Josephine Nauckhoff. Cambridge: Cambridge University Press, 2001.
Tomalin, Claire. *Thomas Hardy: The Time-Torn Man.* London: Penguin, 2006.
Volsik, Paul. "'A Phantom of His Own Figuring.' The Poetry of Thomas Hardy," in *Études anglaises* 1, Tome 57 (2004): 103–116.

Uncomfortably Numb
"In Tenebris"

ADRIAN GRAFE

The nature of poetry is to illuminate. It explores night, the night of the soul and the mystery in which human existence is shrouded. Obscurity is banished from its expression.—St John Perse[1]

Breakage, whatever its cause, is the dark complement to the act of making; the one implies the other.—Louise Glück[2]

By the time he entered determinedly on his career as a poet, Hardy was a wealthy man. Yet his poems rarely give off a feeling of comfort or ease. They suggest, even, a certain willed spiritual poverty, an openness to feelings, whether pleasurable or disturbing or mournful, an openness, too, to the world, the openness of a man endowed with Keatsian negative capability, who does not refuse to lead a life free of suffering. Hardy manages to infuse his poetic darkness, the damage he sometimes writes of, with the beauty of pathos that bears his own undeceived signature. He reveals something of his own fragility. Such fragility may be the mark of instability, but that very instability can by definition open the way to change and transformation since, by its very self, instability is precarious and ephemeral. Darkness can be transformative.

In the three poems which make up "In Tenebris,"[3] Hardy deepens his tragic vision, whether it be found in his novels or his poems. In Hardy's shadowlands the self, his self, both sees and becomes visible, while in his shadowlands, too, vision is or can be affectionate. But do such poems show Hardy to be addicted to misery? Naturally morbid, even? Or drawn, rather, to disturbing poetic spaces which inspire him to innovation and creativity?

If one looks up the poem in various selections, studies of Hardy or more general studies of poetry, one discovers that, despite the poem being arguably one of Hardy's most passionate creations, it has received little attention and that the line that has received most and, in some cases, all of it, is: "if way to the Better there be, it exacts a full look at the Worst."[4] Katherine Kearney Maynard's *Thomas Hardy's Tragic Poetry: The Lyrics and The Dynasts* refers to the poem on four separate occasions, but every time it does so the author quotes the one line about the Better and the Worst, as though it encapsulated or summarized both Hardy's outlook and the poem as a whole.[5] Andrew Motion's Everyman selection of Hardy's poems gives only "In Tenebris I."[6] Motion's introduction quotes the passage from Hardy's "Apology" to his *Late Lyrics and Earlier* in which Hardy quotes the "Better and Worst" line in order to defend what he (Hardy) perceives as his own spiritual realism and refute charges of pessimism.[7] Though Philip Larkin does not quote this particular line, he accepts Hardy's own position as regards his poetry and, as Motion notes, it is that position, with the quoted line as central to it, which lies behind Larkin's defense of Hardy in his influential piece, "Wanted: Good Hardy Critic."[8] Dennis Taylor's *Hardy's Literary Language and Victorian Philology* has three brief references to "In Tenebris II" and one equally brief one to "In Tenebris III."[9] In *Hardy's Poetry, 1860–1928*, Taylor alludes to "In Tenebris I" in a footnote (he mentions the fact that Hardy takes his epigraph from Psalm 101, but quotes to suit his purpose another line from that Psalm[10]). His only reference to "In Tenebris II" is the line I began with about the Better and the Worst; and there is no mention of "In Tenebris III." Finally, Tom Paulin in *Thomas Hardy: The Poetry of Perception* quotes from "In Tenebris" I and II on the same page, in order to comment on the poems' unrhetoricalness.[11] Hardy himself in his own selection from his verse, *Chosen Poems* (1929), included "In Tenebris II," the one with the Best and Worst line in it, thus implying that the poems can indeed stand apart from each other.

"In Tenebris" is the only case of Hardy attributing the same title to three different poems, or of his grouping three poems together in this way—the sign, perhaps, of an obsession. The second and third poems are dated 1895 and 1895–6 respectively, and the first is undated, perhaps as though Hardy thought of it as expressing something timeless or permanent for him. If it dates, too, from the mid–1890s, then Hardy could have included all three in *Wessex Poems* which came out in 1898, but decided to wait until *Poems of the Past and the Present* of 1902. Perhaps he considered them too melancholic for *Wessex Poems*. In terms of imagery one might compare "In Tenebris" with a poem from *Moments of Vision* entitled "In the Seventies." This is a poem of light gone dark, but which in its own way celebrates the light.

In the "In Tenebris" poems, Hardy blends Biblical darkness and late Gothic nocturnal angst, along with a possible hint of Shakespearean tragedy;

philosophical and possibly autobiographical considerations. The texts of the three poems do not refer or allude to each other in any way. They share, however, the same title and an epigraph, different each time, taken from the Psalms. Of the three poems, the first and third are especially intimate: the speaker is entirely alone in the first and second ones; he appears briefly alongside a woman in the third. In the second one, the speaker confronts a group of people with whom he does not share the same vision of the age. His inability to see what they see, and their failure to see what he sees, set him apart from them.

As just stated, the first poem stages its speaker entirely alone, barely feeling a cold indifference to death, and death's cold indifference. The speaker has as it were been inoculated against further suffering by previous bouts of it. So winter's effect on the natural elements of the first line of each stanza does not have the same impact on the speaker. Nevertheless the chiasmic rhyme scheme—the same rhyme scheme recurs in the third poem, though the lines there are much longer—and the implied cycle of the seasons hint at a possible regeneration. In the third stanza one notes the sheer beauty of the phrase "the lone frost's black length."

The tortuous syntax—"love can not make smart/ Again this year his heart/ Who no heart hath"—reflects the intolerable psychological burden. The speaker speaks from a space of deprivation, as seen in the peculiarly short lines. He is under emotional anesthetic, uncomfortably numb: part of the epigraph to Geoffrey Hill's poem "Tenebrae" seems apt: "he felt imprisoned in a cold region where his brain was numb and his spirit was isolated"[12]—the speaker in Hardy's poem has no pain, no strength, no fear, no heart, no doubt, no hope. But it seems only natural to look for some positive content in these poems. In the last three stanzas, the first-person speaker disappears from the poem to be replaced by "him" or "one who."

"In Tenebris II" takes this technique forward, shifting in the last line of each stanza from "I" to "he" or "one"; in the last stanza the "I" is entirely replaced by "he." Unlike the first poem, the tone of this one is jaunty, its long dactylic lines "breezily" echoing the viewpoint of the "stout upstanders." This second poem quits the space of sentiment and nature for more social and philosophical ground. It pits one man against a majority. It's not clear who or what "the First" in the Hardy poem is or are; but it might well be the "many and strong," a variant perhaps on the proverbial "strength in numbers," referred to in the first stanza of the poem, where the notion of "best" is introduced: "When the clouds' swoln bosoms echo back the shouts of the many and strong/ That things are all as they best may be, save a few to be right ere long." Hardy's speaker is not "the many," in all their anonymity, nor is he ever with "the many": he is "me alone," "one," "one born out of due time," "one shaped awry." The phrase "the many and strong" is picked up in the second stanza by "The stout upstanders" and "the potent." Hardy's speaker here is, or is with, the one and the weak. He is not many, strong, stout, or potent, apparently. That doesn't prevent him from castigating the herd instinct. He does not shirk the pain of not fitting in. The herd is capable of killing the "low-voiced Best." In an interview Hardy said: "much of the sniggering optimism of recent literature is cowardly and insincere."[13] The speaker presents himself as a man at war with his age. His age is in denial. Is the speaker applying the title to himself? Or, rather, does he not insinuate that it is his contemporaries, not he, who are "in tenebris"? One somewhat enigmatic note in his literary notebooks reads simply: "Persons with something of a vested interest in darkness."[14] Or, conversely, do they see the speaker as in intellectual darkness, threatening their adherence to reason? As one Gothic commentator says, "Darkness, metaphorically, threatened the light of reason with what it did not know."[15] The poet also depicts a situation in which the individual is seen as excluded from the group. Society is seen as exclusive, or there is an excess of differentiation on his part which is intolerable to the group. In the last line, the speaker perceives himself in the polemical position of "disturbing the order."

The first two poems are poems of the present. The third "In Tenebris" poem is the only one of the three to be devoted wholly to the past. It is a poem of lost illusions, and arguably the most personal of the three; the poem maintains the first person throughout. The three middle stanzas each depict a childhood moment of extreme intensity: the first two are in some sense ecstatic, the third deathly. The depiction of the speaker and a woman, possibly his mother, on Egdon Heath localizes the poem. In this respect, it is comparable to another poem of powerful bitterness, set on "Wessex Heights," a poem dated 1896 like "In Tenebris II" and "In Tenebris III," and like them written in unusually long—heptameter—lines. Both "In Tenebris II" and "Wessex Heights" pit a lone speaker against a group with whom he feels he has nothing in common and by whom he feels rejected.[16]

"In Tenebris III" is perhaps the most touching of the three "In Tenebris" poems because of the three glimpses in it of these moments in the speaker's childhood. He relates these three childhood moments with an affectionate but unflinching gaze. The penultimate stanza depicts the speaker at what would appear to be his most defenseless. Defenseless against what? In the "Apology" from *Late Lyrics and Earlier*, Hardy wrote: "we seem threatened with a new Dark Age,"[17] again using the imagery of darkness, and I wonder whether there is some sense of threat behind the "In Tenebris" poems—such as an intense emotional pressure bearing in on the poet—to which the poems form a three-pronged response.[18] In "In Tenebris III," the speaker looks back at times in his childhood, especially when he was "the smallest and feeblest of folk," and this seems to provide another suitable counterpoint to the many, strong, stout upstanders of the previous poem. Rilke's poem "The Man Watching" comes to mind, with its slightly Hardyesque title and its close: "Winning does not tempt that man./ This is how he grows; by being defeated decisively/ by ever greater things." The "ending" that "might have come" in the last line becomes at once the poem's chorus, first stated and repeated in the first stanza, an allusion to the speaker's death, and a witty way of ending the poem. It also carries an eschatological undertow that the quotation in line 18 from the Book of Revelation would support.

Among little to be cheerful about in "In Tenebris" is "delight." One can see light in "delight" for though the word derives from the Latin verb *delectare*, English has altered the Latin second syllable and replaced it with light. The speaker's enemies, the enemies of "delight," are not only people but "crookedness, custom, and fear." But the damage wreaked on delight can lead to creation. The speaker in this poem does not take on the "stout upstanders" directly—indeed, he lends them voice, and this ventriloquistic act is in itself creative. The "delight," the "delicate growth," is the creative act itself, even though the subject matter is strife between two antagonistic philosophies and the speaker's own standpoint is "awry"—that is, it does not and cannot mesh with that of "the many and strong." The very "cramping" of delight gives rise to delight: the delight of what Louise Glück in the second epigraph above calls "the act of making."

But to return to the particular character of the poems, we may examine more closely the title and epigraphs. It is the interference between the title, epigraphs and texts which, in a sense, makes the poem. When a quotation is a fragment, quotation is by definition a synecdochal art. The title and epigraphs here are all fragments, quotations from a larger whole. The fragment in literature at least bears a paradox within it: it is both a discrete text, and inevitably makes one think of the whole of which it is or was a part. At the same time, the quotation reminds one of its author and of its author's own aims, aims which may be deflected when the text is fragmented, decontextualised, then recontextualised in a new context and therefore made to serve the quoter's aims. I'll draw briefly on Antoine Compagnon's *La seconde main ou le travail de la citation*, in order to sketch out a framework for an examination of this dimension of the poem. Compagnon says that quotation is like an organ transplant: there are two operations involved: taking an organ, a passage of text, out of a body, and placing it in another body, another text.[19]

The phenomenon can be examined further by separating out the meaning of the quotation from the act of quoting. Quotation is a phenomenon in itself, independently of the meaning of the quotation. On the one hand, the act of quoting has a meaning. On the other, the meaning of the quotation arises, in part, from the new context in which the quotation is placed. The words of the quotation mean something different to what they meant in their original context. What does Hardy want from the quotations? What is he asking of the reader that he would not have been asking if he had omitted the quotation? Quotation is a form of repetition, like a chorus, suggests Compagnon.[20] Compagnon doesn't seem to consider the original context as much as he does the new one. On the other hand, in a discussion of allusions to Newman in Hardy's writing, L. Björk says that apart from the children singing "Lead, kindly Light" while Bathsheba watches the graves of Troy, Fanny Robin and their illegitimate child, "[t]he other quotations from the hymn, intended to comment on the past relationship between Bathsheba and Gabriel Oak, seem less fortunately used, since the meaning and emotional overtones of their original contexts have but superficial relevance to the scene in the novel."[21] The point here is not to discuss the role of quotation from Newman's hymn in the novel, but to stress the fact that Björk almost automatically expects the original contexts of the quotations from the hymn to be relevant to the new context, the novel.

If this is a legitimate critical view, then one can or should examine the "meaning and emotional overtones of [the] original contexts" from which the quotations from the Psalms are taken, to see if and how they are relevant to the "In Tenebris" poems.

To take the poem title first. Hardy's original title was "De Profundis," the first words of Psalm 130. Oscar Wilde's text of the same title was written about the same time as Hardy's "In Tenebris" poems, and published in the same year (1905). As Robert Gittings speculated, Hardy may have changed the poem's title to avoid confusion with Wilde's text.[22] The "De Profundis" is a penitential Psalm, a confession of faults, a cry for divine mercy.

"In Tenebris" does not have this penitential or at least confessional dimension.

The unattributed words "In Tenebris" make for a potentially richer title in the context of the poem than "De Profundis" because the phrase appears in both the First and the Second Testaments. It appears in at least two Psalms, Psalms 88 and 107, not those used for the epigraphs. Psalm 88 is one of the most despondent of all the Psalms, although the next one begins: "I will sing of the mercies of the Lord forever." In Psalm 107, those who "sit in darkness" are later in the text brought out of darkness. The term also appears in the first chapter of John: "And the light shineth in darkness; and the darkness comprehended it not."

Hardy's notebooks show him working through this theme in John as he copies out the following: "While ye have light believe in the light." John XII.36. "Walk while ye have the light, lest darkness come upon you." John XII.35.²³ If Hardy takes these injunctions as spiritually edifying, so be it. If he takes them as statements with not only spiritual but also poetic possibilities they can, I think, inflect our reading of the "In Tenebris" poems. Incidentally, one should not forget the darkness in the second verse of Genesis, which precedes the first creative word, the "fiat lux."

It is in this sense that one might consider the three epigraphs from the Psalms. What is the function of the Psalms quoted here? It is perhaps the poet Hardy reaching out to another poet who expressed for all time, with incomparable depth and accuracy, the ache of desolation—though not only that. For they also serve to remind us, in a perverse sort of way, that if Hardy's speaker himself waits in "unhope," the Psalmist waits, rather, in hope.

The epigraphs suggest then that the speaker, like countless others before and after him, finds that the poetry of the Psalms expresses his own deepest feelings. Hardy in a sense inscribes himself within the tradition of precedence by which Israel and the Christian churches, considered both ecclesially and from the viewpoint of the individual believer, have taken over and made their own the Psalmist's words and feelings. Hardy's epigraphs point to a broader, liturgical reality, a community reality, they are the voice of a lone speaker but are prayed by both individuals and worshipping communities. Hardy knew this experientially.

Liturgically, darkness always heralds light. Whether prayers of praise or supplication, what characterizes the Psalms is spiritual realism, rather than the denial Hardy accuses his contemporaries of being in. These poems see Hardy driving as far as possible into the heart of his own darkness, as the Psalmist does. However, given the mainly non-religious content of the poem and Hardy's well-known agnosticism, Hardy's speaker may be using the praying figure of the Psalmist, the Psalmist's voice and words, as a double, an Other for himself, with the Psalmist praying what he the poet cannot pray. The Psalmist's vitality is depleted, and this is why the site from which he writes is the dwelling-place of the dead.

In 1919, writing to the American poet and critic Amy Lowell, Hardy called his views on poetry as possibly old-fashioned, because he had written poetry nearly fifty years before. He went on to say: "Though of course in divine poesy there is no such thing as fashion old or new. What made poetry

2000 years ago makes poetry now."²⁴ I think that if we apply this argument to the "In Tenebris" group, Hardy is saying that he finds a correlative for his feelings in the Psalms. Nevertheless, despite the poetic artistry with which the Psalms are everywhere infused, I don't believe it was Hardy's intention to treat them as works of art alone: "poetry and religion touch each other, or rather modulate into each other; are, indeed, often but different names for the same thing."²⁵

The epigraphs from the Psalms dramatize the speaker's situation and intensify its status as a spiritual combat. If these three poems are poems of "unhope"—and I'm not sure that that is the overall impression I would take away from them—any "hope" has been cunningly hidden by Hardy out of sight from the reader of the poems but within the Psalms from which he gives us these gobbets. God, the speaker and the speaker's enemies (who are often God's enemies, too) make up the structural triangle of the Psalms of supplication. Hardy's quotations make no mention of God. The "In Tenebris I" quotation, taken from Psalm 101, in English reads: "My heart is smitten, and withered like grass." Psalm 102 has its own subtitle, or epigraph: "A Prayer of the afflicted, when he is overwhelmed, and poureth out his complaint to the Lord." However, the Psalm itself is not just a complaint but a call for help—"Hear my prayer, O LORD, and let my cry come unto thee."—as are all three Psalms from which Hardy takes his epigraphs. The first half of verse 4, which is what Hardy quotes, is from that part of the Psalm where the Psalmist explains why he is calling for help. The Psalm ends with a prayer to God to "take me not away in the midst of my days" and a declaration of faith in God's and His servants' everlastingness. The phrase "take me not away in the midst of my days" runs counter to the resignation dominant in the first poem, as well as the idea expressed in the third poem about the ending that might have come.

The second poem's epigraph reads, in English: "I looked on my right hand, and beheld, but there was no man that would know me ... no man cared for my soul" (Ps 141). One may draw a parallel between the "persecutors" in the Psalm who are "stronger than" the Psalmist, and the "many and strong" in Hardy's poem. Hardy may even possibly be making some kind of instrumental use of these Psalms, drawing on them in order to excoriate his enemies and critics.

The structure of this short Psalm (seven verses) is quite complicated. It begins with a recall of the speaker's cry to the Lord—"I cried unto the Lord with my voice," but then becomes a direct address to the Lord in which the speaker recounts his sorrow in the past—this part includes the verse quoted by Hardy. It addresses the Lord again in verse 6: "Attend unto my cry," and ends with a declaration of faith: "Bring my soul out of prison, that I may praise thy name/ the righteous shall compass me about; for thou shalt deal bountifully with me." Of the three Psalms from which Hardy takes his epigraphs, this one and the previous one end prospectively and, unlike the poems, hopefully.

As for the epigraph to "In Tenebris III," finally, Psalm 119, from which Hardy takes the whole of verse 5, "Woe is me, that my dwelling is prolonged, that I dwell in the tents of Kedar. My soul hath dwelt too long there." is, like Psalm 102, a call for help. But it begins by proclaiming the Psalmist's personal salvation: "In my distress I cried unto the LORD, and he heard me." Only after this, curiously enough, does the Psalm become a cry of distress. But the Psalm is also vitriolic, and the Psalmist turns on his enemy: "What shall be given unto thee, thou false tongue?" These kinds of emotion—both the joy of spiritual salvation, and acrimony—stand at odds with the wistfulness of "In Tenebris III."

The Psalms are religious texts and the Hardy poems themselves in their own right are not directly religious. If you remove the title and epigraphs the poems are almost devoid of any religious significance, except possibly for the capitalized "Voice" in the third poem. The quotation from St Paul in "In Tenebris II"—"one born out of due time"—and the words taken from Revelation in "In Tenebris III"—"sweets to the mouth in the belly are bitter"—complicate the reader's response to the poem. These quotations have a different status to the Psalms. They are in English, seamlessly woven into the texts of the poems themselves and unattributed, and the reader is expected to recognize them. The context for the first quotation is 1 Cor 15: 8: "And last of all he was seen of me also, as of one born out of due time.", and for the second, Revelation 10: 10: "And I took the little book out of the angel's hand, and ate it up; and it was in my mouth sweet as honey: and as soon as I had eaten it, my belly was bitter." Nevertheless, the original contexts are not decisive, and the quotations have a more proverbial ring to them than the texts from the Psalms.

One might, finally, shift the perspective slightly from quotation to allusion or possible allusion. The poem under discussion contains one of Hardy's most oft-quoted phrases: "If way to the Better there be, it exacts a full look at the Worst." As said above, Hardy quoted it himself in his prose "Apology" to his *Late Lyrics and Earlier*. The idea in the line seems to be that vision to be worth anything must be global not selective; only global vision enables one to discern what could be an improvement on present circumstances. The terms "the Better" and "the Worst" somehow call out to each other. At the same time, one notices an imbalance or rather asymmetry in the phrase, whereby the first capitalized term, the comparative "the Better," does not lead on to the comparative "the Worse," as one might expect, but rather to "the Worst."

The familiar lines from Yeats's "Second Coming"—"The best lack all conviction, while the worst/ Are full of passionate intensity."—restore the grammatical balance. If we reverse the argument and take "the Worst" as the reference point, then "the Worst" would require "the Best" in the first clause. But there is only "the Better," for "the low-voiced Best is killed by the clash of the First." Hardy brings together "First," "Best" and "Worst," echoing, perhaps not altogether unconsciously, Cordelia's first words of her last speech in *King Lear* (V, iii), that tale of the sort of wrongful banishment which is the theme of the second "In Tenebris" poem. Cordelia says: "We are not the first who with best meaning have incurred the worst." Cordelia is at this point taken prisoner with her father, the king, to whom she speaks and refers in the "we" of her statement. How are we to understand Cordelia's statement? Is it just a truism, a mere generality, stock philosophizing in distressing circumstances? Possibly, but then again possibly not. Who are "the first," if she and her father are "not the first"? This might be a veiled allusion on Shakespeare's part to religious or Catholic martyrdom. It could also be a reference to the Crucifixion, and it is a commonplace of Shakespeare criticism to see Cordelia as a Christ figure. This reading, if plausible, would put the Christian paradigm of the Passion at the heart of the poem, with all its implications for the speaker; it would draw together the title, the excerpts from the Psalms and the two allusions to the Second Testament into a single nexus, through which the whole of the poem could be interpreted. In short, this pattern would "fashion and furbish" the poems.

To refuse to acknowledge the existence of darkness is by definition to be in denial. To accept the vision of darkness is, then, to refuse denial. What Jung wrote seems relevant for Hardy: "One does not become enlightened by imagining figures of light, but by making the darkness conscious."[26] Once it becomes conscious, the bleak, forlorn winterscape of the first poem and last two stanzas of the third one takes its place in the natural cycle, moving beyond the "unhope" of the first poem, and a "spring-seeming order" emerges, quickening the poem. Literally standing behind the "unhope" here is the "blessed Hope" (with a capital H indicating a possible religious allusion) he attributes to the darkling thrush,[27] Hope of which the speaker in that poem claims to be unaware, which is not the same as saying that it does not exist, or that it is unreasonable. The speaker has not lost all sight of light and beauty as the second and third stanzas of "In Tenebris III" make clear. The poet's engagement with the history of the English language is absolute since according to

OED "unhope" had not been used in English writing for over four hundred years before Hardy resurrected it.

Poetically speaking, it would perhaps have been of little comfort to Hardy to learn that he was not alone in his nocturnal despondency. Only a few years before the composition of "In Tenebris," an English Jesuit living in Dublin, fond of Hardy's novels, was going through a dramatic confrontation with the night: "I wake and feel the fell of dark, not day./ What hours, O what black hours we have spent/ This night! What sights you, heart, saw [...]"; "Earnest, earthless, equal, attuneable, vaulty, voluminous, ... stupendous/ Evening strains to be time's vast, womb-of-all, home-of-all, hearse-of-all night.../ our night whelms, whelms and will end us [...] all is in an enormous dark drowned." There is something in Hopkins's "God's most deep decree" similar to Hardy's "the Voice that is law." And at least in one poem, Hopkins goes further into darkness than Hardy, for Hardy "exacts a full look at the Worst," while for Hopkins there *is* no worst. But Hardy, unlike Hopkins, was unable or unwilling to welcome the comfort of the Resurrection.

It is as esthetically viable to create poetry out of deprivation, as it is out of anything else. But we might consider an observation of Florence Hardy's in a letter of December 26th 1920. She told her correspondent her husband was "now—this afternoon—writing a poem with great spirit: always a sign of well-being. Needless to say it is an intensely dismal poem."[28] Let the "great spirit" stand as an antidote to the "intensely dismal."

Notes

1. St. John Perse, Nobel Prize Banquet Speech, 1960, http://www.nobelprize.org/nobel_prizes/literature/laureates/1960/perse-speech.html, accessed 14 July 2014.
2. Quoted by John O'Donoghue, *Divine Beauty: The Invisible Embrace* (London: Bantam, 2003), 171.
3. The poem title is Latin for "in darkness."
4. Thomas Hardy, *The Complete Poems*, ed. James Gibson (Basingstoke: Palgrave, 2001), 168; all quotations from "In Tenebris," 167–169. In reality, the "line" mentioned is not a full one: a few words at the beginning of the line are truncated. Stephen Tardif's discussion of these words in his essay in this volume is some of the most enlightening comment I have read on them.
5. See Katherine Kearney Maynard, *Thomas Hardy's Tragic Poetry: The Lyrics and The Dynasts* (Iowa City: University of Iowa Press, 1991).
6. Thomas Hardy, *Selected Poems*, ed. Andrew Motion (London: Everyman/Dent, 1998), 38.
7. *Ibid.*, xxix.
8. Philip Larkin, "Wanted: Good Hardy Critic" in *Required Writing: Miscellaneous Pieces 1955–1982* (London: Faber and Faber, 1983), 168–174.

9. Dennis Taylor, *Hardy's Literary Language and Victorian Philology* (Oxford: Oxford University Press, 1993).
10. Dennis Taylor, *Hardy's Poetry, 1860–1928* (New York: Columbia University Press, 1981), 173 note 79.
11. Tom Paulin, *Thomas Hardy: The Poetry of Perception* (London: Macmillan, 1975), 72.
12. Geoffrey Hill, *Collected Poems* (Harmondsworth: Penguin, 1985), 172.
13. Quotation from Trevor Johnson, *A Critical Introduction to the Poems of Thomas Hardy* (London: Macmillan, 1991), 153.
14. Lennart A. Björk (ed.), *The Literary Notebooks of Thomas Hardy* (London: Macmillan, 1985), 216.
15. Fred Botting, *Gothic* (London: Routledge, 1996), 32.
16. See "Wessex Heights," *The Complete Poems, op. cit.*, 319–320. The anonymous mother figure (if that's what she is) in the third stanza of "In Tenebris III" is comparable to the unnamed compassionate woman in the second stanza of "Wessex Heights."
17. Thomas Hardy, "Apology" to *Late Lyrics and Earlier*, in *Selected Poems*, ed. Harry Thomas (London: Penguin Books, 1993), 199–206 (203).
18. The early-to-mid 1890s were a time of depression for Hardy, and this period also corresponds to the publication of *Tess* (1891) and the violent critical attacks the novel's author came in for.
19. Antoine Compagnon, *La seconde main ou le travail de la citation* (Paris: Seuil, 1979), 29.
20. *Ibid.*, 37.
21. See Bjork (ed.), *The Literary Notebooks of Thomas Hardy, op. cit.*
22. Robert Gittings, *The Older Hardy* (London: Penguin Books, 1980; first edition 1978), 121.
23. Both quotations from Bjork (ed.), *op. cit.*, 97.
24. See Paul Turner, *The Life of Thomas Hardy: A Critical Biography* (Oxford: Blackwell, 1998), 237.
25. "Apology" from *Late Lyrics and Earlier*, in *Selected Poems, op. cit.*, 199–206 (204).
26. Quoted by John O'Donoghue, *op. cit.*, 189.
27. See "The Darkling Thrush," *The Complete Poems, op. cit.*, 150.
28. James Gibson, *Thomas Hardy: A Literary Life* (London: Macmillan, 1996), 179.

Works Cited

Björk, Lennart A., ed. *The Literary Notebooks of Thomas Hardy*. London: Macmillan, 1985.
Botting, Fred. *Gothic*. London: Routledge, 1996.
Compagnon, Antoine. *La seconde main ou le travail de la citation*. Paris: Seuil, 1979.
Gibson, James. *Thomas Hardy: A Literary Life*. London: Macmillan, 1996.
Gittings, Robert. *The Older Hardy*. London: Penguin Books, 1980; first edition 1978.
Hardy, Thomas. "Apology" in *Selected Poems*. Ed. Harry Thomas. London: Penguin Books, 1993, 199–206.
_____. *The Complete Poems*. Ed. James Gibson. Basingstoke: Palgrave, 2001.
_____. *Selected Poems*. Ed. Andrew Motion. London: Everyman/Dent, 1998.

Kearney Maynard, Katherine. *Thomas Hardy's Tragic Poetry: The Lyrics and* The Dynasts. Iowa City: University of Iowa Press, 1991.
Hill, Geoffrey. *Collected Poems*. Harmondsworth: Penguin, 1985.
Johnson, Trevor. *A Critical Introduction to the Poems of Thomas Hardy*. London: Macmillan, 1991.
Larkin, Philip. "Wanted: Good Hardy Critic," in *Required Writing: Miscellaneous Pieces 1955–1982*. London: Faber and Faber, 1983, 168–174.
O'Donoghue, John. *Divine Beauty: The Invisible Embrace*. London: Bantam, 2003.
Paulin, Tom. *Thomas Hardy: The Poetry of Perception*. London: Macmillan, 1975.
Perse, Saint-John. Nobel Prize Banquet Speech, 1960. http://www.nobelprize.org/nobel_prizes/literature/laureates/1960/perse-speech.html, accessed 14 July 2014.
Taylor, Dennis. *Hardy's Literary Language and Victorian Philology*. Oxford: Oxford University Press, 1993.
_____. *Hardy's Poetry, 1860–1928*. New York: Columbia University Press, 1981.
Turner, Paul. *The Life of Thomas Hardy: A Critical Biography*, Oxford: Blackwell, 1998.

IV

Poetic Craft and Accidentals

Messy Feelings, Tidy Forms
"Poems of 1912–13"
EMILY TAYLOR MERRIMAN

The somewhat unexpected death of Thomas Hardy's wife Emma in 1912 provoked in the poet a volcanic eruption of complicated feelings and accompanying creative energy. Although the Hardys were married and living in the same house for decades after a romantic if not uncomplicated courtship, the couple had been estranged for many years. The sequence of eighteen poems (plus three added later) that Hardy wrote in the wake of Emma's decease is distinguished by a strong disparity between the tumultuous feelings that they describe and the carefully constructed forms that seek to contain as well as express those feelings. Hardy tries to control a storm of conflicting emotions in a series of meticulously crafted rhyming and metrical verses, each different from one another. Such care for and variety of form are characteristic of Hardy as a poet. The poems are a series of tightly pressurized verbal soundshapes at once appealing and disturbing.

Many critics have analyzed and praised aspects of the effectiveness of Hardy's versification in "Poems of 1912–13." Dennis Taylor in particular has made a thorough study of Hardy's entire prosody, pointing out that "he wrote poems in more metrical forms [over 700] than any other major English poet."[1] Cecil Day Lewis noted in 1951 about "Poems of 1912–13": "The variety of emotion is equaled by that of stanza-form: it is as though the diverse moulds had been preparing through a lifetime, and now those scenes from the past ran freely into them, each recognizing its own."[2] It is worth surveying how the sequence as a whole uses the structural features of verse, including Hardy's expertise in rhyme and meter, to house the poet's conscious and unconscious reactions to his grief, his hatred, and his memories of destroyed love. (The sequence was originally published as part of the volume *Satires of Circumstance* so they also form part of a larger sequence.) The sometimes unusual verse forms create the sequence's ghost-story strength: the building is sturdy and sometimes beautiful, but there are mysterious banging noises and doors keep opening unexpectedly. A couple of surprising inter-texts can also be heard rattling around. Under apparently stone-solid, engraved declarations of love lie smoldering resentments that can suddenly spring into motion. Although several critics have argued that there is a loose plot to the sequence's overall structure—a distancing from the raw grief, a lessening sense of the deceased woman's haunting presence, a movement towards a degree of reconciliation[3]—the range of verse structures complicates this development, and the overall sequence is more disquieting than generally perceived. It is elegiac in the sense that it memorializes the dead, but its lamentations are often ambiguous and its consolations few.

The critical reputation of Hardy's "Poems of 1912–13" has grown over the past century. Although the sequence received little notice on first appearance,[4] it is now generally described as a "great elegiac series."[5] Neil Wenborn declares that the poems are "some of the most powerful poems of love and loss in the English language."[6] Suzanne Keen claims they "achieve miracles of reanimation" while resisting "metaphysical consolations."[7] For Tim Armstrong the poems are "Hardy's great mourning sequence."[8] Peter Sacks speaks of their "formal brilliance" and "superb control of personal voice" and declares them "among the most affecting lyrics in the language."[9] Later twentieth-century poets Donald Davie and Tom Paulin have written poems directly inspired by "Poems of 1912–13" as well as important critical works.[10] A recent enthusiast is Hardy's biographer Claire Tomalin, who also edited a small volume that publishes the sequence, plus a selection of other poems about Emma. Tomalin's *Unexpected Elegies*,[11] with its matching portraits of Emma and Thomas on the front cover, is a curious little book that cushions the poetry with an introduction, images, and selections for further reading. Like the cat curled up on the older Emma Hardy's lap pictured in the section "Photographs and Illustrations," the volume looks sweet and soft, but conceals teeth and claws. It is true that the poems are love poems, and elegies, and an attempt at making amends. Hardy wrote to Florence Henniker: "Some of them I rather shrink from printing—those I wrote just after Emma died, when I looked back at her as she had originally been, and when I felt miserable lest I had not treated her considerately in her latter life. However I shall publish them as the only amends I can make, if it were so."[12] But the love is convoluted, the elegizing unconventional, and the amends problematic.

Any individual poem in "Poems of 1912–13" can be read on one level as a poignant if wry tribute from Hardy to his dead wife. However, when they are read together, especially aloud, the level of emotionality and the self-torment in particular start to sound excessive even to the sad facts. The risk Hardy runs in writing and re-writing his guilt and grief is that he can be accused of protesting too much. Given the biographical circumstances, on some level it must have been a huge relief when his wife died, but the speaker of the poems will not overtly acknowledge this. Hardy is aware of the risks of sentimentality of course, and there are aspects of the poems that seek to hold it at bay. The classical epitaph sets the work in an ancient literary context. Even the title of the sequence is emotionally neutral, merely a demarcation of dates that supposedly set a beginning and an end to the composition of the poems. The poems will not be contained within those chronological bounds, however. The events in the poems go back at least to 1870, and Hardy added more poems to the published sequence in 1919 (and continued to write about the subject for many years). This is one small example of how Hardy fails (perhaps self-consciously) to isolate and thereby control at least his literary response to his marriage and his loss.

Jahan Ramazani states that the "psychological work" accomplished by the structure of the sequence is "its supplanting of a guilt-ridden present with an idealized past."[13] Rather than psychological "work," this may be better considered psychological repression, or at least suppression, as Hardy seeks relief from the painful feelings of guilt and hatred aroused by this deceased wife, their failed relationship, and her death. At moments, his degree of elevation of her as beloved feminine figure appears strikingly like a "reaction formation"—in the field of psychology a well-recognized defense mechanism in which someone expresses repressed feelings in contrasting, and even over-accentuated, opposing, forms.

Underscoring this possibility, there is a small but vital textual change Hardy made in "The Voice,"[14] which now begins, "Woman much missed," but originally read "O woman weird." Claire Tomalin says of this: "You might think he had written down what was in his heart immediately, but the manuscript shows that his first draft suggested something more complicated and even sinister."[15] She concludes that he made the amendment in the interests of "simplicity." However, "O woman weird" probably *does* indicate what was "in his heart immediately," and he made the change to cover up those negative feelings, at least from public view if not from his own awareness.

"O woman weird" is not only sinister, it evokes the "Weird Sisters" of *Macbeth*, especially in the context of a clause three lines later: "when our day was fair." "Foul" is what the Hardys' day had changed to, and perhaps he could not help but think of Emma as a bit of a witch—an accusation she had actually made about his own sisters and mother. In 1896 she wrote to his sister Mary: "You are a witch-like creature & quite equal to any amount of evil-wishing & speaking—I can imagine you, & your mother & sister on your native heath raising a storm on a Walpurgis night."[16] In the preceding poem, "The Haunter,"[17] the speaker is the dead woman. She claims to "Hover and hover a few feet from him," just as the Weird Sisters "Hover through the fog and the filthy air."[18] In this Shakespearean context, the beautiful "original air-blue gown" of "The Voice" seems stained in the present, although it may have been pristine once. The second half of the poem is occupied by "breeze" and "wind," the weather force summoned up for evil mischief by the weird sisters on their second appearance in *Macbeth*.[19] Even if the voice is not merely a wind-created figment of the narrator's imagination, the woman cannot be trusted to be telling the truth that she is now as she was in the early days of courtship. Her calling voice evokes the archetype of the siren, and the narrator's sudden vision of her restored to her youthful appearance suggests the witch's fairy-tale ability to shape-shift from her true appearance as an ugly hag into a beautiful young woman. The poem's eerie power, as others have pointed out, is emphasized by the shortened lines of the final stanza in which the speaker has been brought to mental and physical extremis by his vision of past love, his loss of that before she died, his further loss of the once-beloved woman to death, and his tortured recollections, hopes and fears:

> Thus I; faltering forward,
> Leaves around me falling
> Wind oozing thin through the thorn from norward,
> And the woman calling.

The word "weird" actually appears later in the published sequence, in the phrase "wild weird Western shore" in "Beeny Cliff."[20] Phillip Mallett points to this poem's allusion to "La Belle Dame Sans Merci," with Keats's portrayal of the enchanting but evil woman who captivates the man.[21] The end of "Beeny Cliff," which talks about the woman who "will laugh there nevermore" also echoes Edgar Allan Poe's "The Raven," a poem worth comparing to Hardy's poems in this sequence. "The Raven" is melodramatic while "Poems of 1912–13" are not, but they share plot elements, and the male narrator of many of Hardy's poems has something of Poe's narrator's self-tormenting style. A year after "The Raven" was published, Edgar Allan Poe wrote: "the death [...] of a beautiful woman is, unquestionably, the most poetical topic in the world—and equally is it beyond doubt that the lips best suited for such topic are those of a bereaved lover."[22] Hardy came upon the same vein of poetical richness over fifty years later, and, as Ramazani says, he made "poetic gain of personal loss."[23]

Further evidence that Hardy associated his dead wife with the witches in *Macbeth*, or at the very least with bewitchment, can be found in one of the poems that Tomalin adds to *Unexpected Elegies*, "Once at Swanage,"[24] in which the "incantation scene" of the couple's falling in love, hand in hand, in front of the ocean and under the half-moon is lit up by a green light, "As a witch-flame's weirdsome sheen." The ocean's roar not only echoes the power of the romantic moment but also "symboled the slamming of doors." When Hardy and Emma fell in love, a spell was cast that led to suffering. Even the end of "Where the Picnic Was,"[25] which concludes "Poems of 1912–13" in its revised version, suggests the gathering of the Weird Sisters, although it is "we four" (rather than "we three") who "made the fire." This poem ends with the one who "has shut her eyes/ For evermore," once again subtly evoking Poe's raven's "nevermore" and that poem's theme of supernatural torment. Even the flames of the sequence's Virgilian epigraph "Veteris vestigia flammae" could be reinterpreted as the remnants of a spell-casting fire, not just an allusion to renewed feelings of love (originally spoken by Dido after meeting Aeneas). In "A Dream or No,"[26] the echoes of "La Belle Dame Sans Merci" can be heard again, as the speaker has been bewitched by "Some strange necromancy" and the illusion of masculine control shows itself to have been under feminine power: "quickly she drew me/ To take her unto me,/ And lodge her long years with me." Under the illusion that she was his captive, he has in fact been trapped by her.

In this context of evil enchantresses, it becomes difficult not to hear an undertone of resentment in the male narrator's voice in many of these poems, despite the endearments and authentic memories of great love lost. The first poem "The Going,"[27] begins with the complaint that the deceased did not give warning of her death. "Without Ceremony,"[28] five poems on, deals with the same theme in lighter mode. In the third stanza of "The Going," the speaker complains that the deceased causes him to imagine he sees her for a moment. Halfway through the poem the speaker recalls her beauty and, touchingly, with an encompassing vision, the joy they once shared: "While Life unrolled us its very best," and he then includes himself among the wrongful parties in the third complaint: why didn't we try to remember and even revisit our early love? The most distinctive formal feature of the six-stanza poem is the dimeter rhyming couplets that precede each stanza's closing line. They give the poem a lyrical lightness at the same time as they create a sensation of tightness: the varying line lengths (sometimes two, sometimes three, sometimes four stresses, all in a regular pattern) create a rhythm that oscillates between an opening out into spaciousness and a closing down. This rhythm mirrors some of the evident concerns of the poem. The opening out has its terrors, leading to a sense of vertigo and even nausea, for it leads to the unboundedness of death: "Till in darkening dankness/ The yawning blankness/ Of the perspective sickens me!" Yet the sense of containment or closing down is also stultifying: "I seem but a dead man held on end/ To sink down soon...."

These alternating feelings of agoraphobia and claustrophobia, the speaker's ambivalence about boundaries and freedom, inside and outside, as well as Hardy's ambivalence about his wife, surface repeatedly in other poems. Most eerily, "I Found Her Out There"[29] associates the deceased woman with the precipitous space of the sea-cliff and the liminal space of the coast. The narrator seems to feel some implicit guilt about taking her from her beloved home territory and confining her, ultimately in the grave, "a noiseless nest," "her loamy cell." He remembers her in her former windy haunts (literally, those "haunted heights"). Most striking is the final stanza, in which he imagines her ghost finding its way through the confines of the earth back to the sea. This image manages to convey simultaneously a sense of claustrophobia, and a sense that things that should be spiritually—and materially—contained have escaped their proper bounds.

> Yet her shade, maybe,
> Will creep underground
> Till it catch the sound
> Of that western sea
> As it swells and sobs
> Where she once domiciled,
> And joy in its throbs
> With the heart of a child.

The heavily enjambed two-stress lines echo the human heartbeat. In addition these few words evoke the sobbing of grief, perhaps the pleasures of sex, and—in the last line's unexpected finale—something of the character of the woman who has died. The introduction of a "child," even a metaphorical one, is surprising at the end of a poem all about death, nature's wildness, unboundedness, and hauntings. It is not quite enough to lighten the dark mood, and so the phrase "heart of a child" is itself somewhat shadowed. Dennis Taylor points out that there is a "release" in this final line as the iambic-anapaestic lines turn to an anapaestic one.[30] This ambivalent release achieves both a letting go of tension, and a removal of reassuring limits. Children can be delightful, but one would not want to be married to one.

Tomalin conjectures that the Hardys might have been happier had they had children of their own.[31] This is scarcely addressed in these poems, but perhaps some subtle exploration of the topic occurs in one of the poems that Hardy later added to the sequence, "The Spell of the Rose."[32] The poem has its literal elements (Hardy never planted a rose at Max Gate, but before she died Emma did), but it reads on one level like a fairy-tale or a fantasy. We see the woman figure of the poems actually casting a "spell," although supposedly in the interests of good, to "mend these miseries." The lines that suggest fertility problems are spoken by the poem's third person narrator (the poem has three voices, the man, the woman, and the narrator): "Since he had planted never a rose/ And misconceits raised horrid shows,/ And agonies came thereof." If the rose, the "flower of love," symbolizes the child that the husband never planted in his wife, then the failures of conception led to bloody and painful menstruation. The poem preceding "I Found Her Out There," "Rain on a Grave,"[33] also sees the deceased woman in her grave, but ends with a vision of her like a child, loving daisies—the flower traditionally used for the game of "he loves me; he loves me not" (a question at stake in "Poems of 1912–13"). In one reading this stanza offers a loving moment in traditional elegiac mode, in which the body of the dead person is transformed into the beauties of nature:

> Soon will be growing
>   Green blades from her mound,
> And daisies be showing
>   Like stars on the ground,
> Till she form part of them—
> Ay—the sweet heart of them,
> Loved beyond measure
> With a child's pleasure
>   All her life's round.

The superficial message is that she is his "sweet heart," also loved beyond measure, and that he can find some consolation and she can find some peace, as she becomes the flowers on the earth and the stars in the sky. However, there is a subtle accusation of narcissism. The flower may be the daisy, not the narcissus, but the woman who will become daisies herself loved daisies; the poem suggests that her love is subtly for herself rather than for another human being. John Paul Riquelme comes to a similar conclusion about the poem, which he sees as mixing "sexual implications and a vengeful attitude." He points out that she becomes the daisies' sweetheart, not the speaker's, and he sees a "less than consoling" circularity in the final line, and no traditional elegizing in her incorporation into "vegetative death and growth," because it brings her no closer to adult love.[34]

Phillip Mallett points out that the second poem of the sequence, "Your Last Drive,"[35] is a poem "founded on negatives."[36] In fact, this could describe almost the entirety of "Poems of 1912–13." The negatives are especially central in this poem, however, in which each of the six-line stanzas is rounded off with a neat concluding couplet that often emphasizes the one stark certainty of the piece: the primary addressee is dead. The poem's tone is a curious combination of the conversational and the formal, reinforced by the poetic diction and rhythms. What is quite unusual in the poem, which reads rather like a condensed section of a novel, is that there are two speakers. The dead woman's voice can be heard in seven lines, including the entire fourth stanza. Her words are harsh—but they are only imagined. Even if the main speaker had been with her as she neared her unexpected death, he would not have "read the writing upon your face." The imagined utterance on the page says:

> "I go hence soon to my resting-place;
> You may miss me then. But I shall not know
> How many times you visit me there,
> Or what your thoughts are, or if you go
> There never at all. And I shall not care.
> Should you censure me I shall take no heed,
> And even your praises no more shall need."

The vision is bleak: no consciousness after death is envisioned, and the deceased is as uncaring in death as perhaps she was in life. These lines are remarkably monosyllabic, which risks making the rhythm plod. Hardy is such a master of meter, however, that the effect instead is of clipped sharpness: the voice of a discontented spouse. Despite her overt claims to eternal oblivion, she is still disturbing her husband's peace from beyond the grave.

What unites the first three poems of the sequence is that they all are spoken primarily by the bereaved husband to the deceased wife. These characters are deduced from the overall sequence and biographical situation—in fact, neither the word "husband" nor "wife" is mentioned in the sequence. The pronouns "you," "I" and "me" therefore take on a particular weight. One might say of them as Geoffrey Hill does of the pronouns in "The Love Song of J. Alfred Prufrock" that the distinction between them is "a proper distinction in pitch."[37] Although as in Prufrock (though nearly not to the same degree), the exact identities of the "you" and the "I" are not clear (is the "I" really "Hardy"? is the "you" the real woman he married?[38]), the differences between them, and the degree of their separation, are very clear. The third poem of the section, "The Walk,"[39] even bears comparison to Eliot's "Prufrock"—a poem composed just a year or two previously—in other ways. Structurally the poems could hardly be any more different. One is long and free verse; the other composed of two very tightly compressed rhyming, metrical stanzas. One is set in the country, one in the city. One is past tense, one present. "Prufrock" begins with movement forwards; "The Walk" with stasis. Notwithstanding these differences, they share a male narrator whose primary emotional state is loneliness. The women come and go, the mermaids will not sing to Prufrock, and Hardy's narrator goes from being "alone" and content with that in the first stanza to lonely in the last one. I hear "lonely" as a word that echoes from the opening "only" and the "l" alliteration of the poem's last two lines: "Only that underlying sense/ Of the look of a room on returning thence." The two iambs following the two anapests in the last line give a satisfactory sense of aesthetic closure, but the words "returning" and "thence" throw the reader back to "there," the "hill-top tree" at the beginning of the poem (a place described with admirable compression).

The ultimate effect is unsettling: the consciousness of the enclosed space of the room haunts the outdoor open area, and the room acquires an aura of the hill walk. The narrator did not think of his wife "as left behind" when she was alive. Ironically, it is when she is dead that he thinks of her this way. Louisa Hall argues that because so many of the poems take place outside, and because there is no overall structural symmetry to the sequence, that in "Poems of 1912–13" Hardy resists what she calls "architectural monumentalizing," a typical elegiac mode in which the poem itself serves as a visible monument.[40] She sees even in the individual poems a "dismantling of symmetrical soundness."[41] Much in Hall's argument is compelling, but soundness doesn't necessarily depend on symmetry. Hardy, ghost-writing through his second wife, describes what architecture taught him about the tremendous value of "cunning irregularity" in poetry.[42] In any case there remains much symmetry in "Poems of 1912–13" despite the variations and irregularities. In fact, Hardy works with the creative dynamic between stasis, monument and closure on the one hand, and impermanence, loss, and openness on the other.

Peter Sacks emphasizes the "open" side of the dialectic between openness and closure at the heart of this work; he praises "the unsheltered nature of these poems, their openness to loss, and their apparent insistence on remaining outside the borrowed comforts of the [elegiac] genre."[43] He goes on to argue that read as a whole the poems nonetheless perform some of the work of elegizing. He points out how the "intricacy of form" not only controls "the emotional release" but "has more precisely elegiac properties."[44] He argues that the sequence accomplishes the conventional tasks of an elegy: "proving the reality of loss, confronting guilt and anger, recollecting and then severing attachments to the dead, establishing substitutive figures for the lost object of love, curbing the mourner's desires by an act of self-purification that both redefines and reinforces his continuing identity."[45]

Yet, the purifying and reinforcing aspects of the elegy are strained and constrained in Hardy's Emma poems in a way that in a magnificent poem like "During Wind and Rain" (published in *Moments of Vision*, 1917)[46] they are not. Dennis Taylor has written eloquently about the extraordinarily effective prosody of this poem, which Hardy himself thought "possibly among the best I have written."[47] Admittedly, this superb elegy could not have been written without everything Hardy had learned from writing so much poetry of mourning in the wake of his wife's death. But in its vision of the immitigable transience of earthly pleasures, however dear, it is more generally applicable to everyone than any of the "Poems of 1912–13." The greater distance of the narrator from the human beings whose mortality is portrayed enables Hardy to speak with a voice of poetic authority that establishes the inevitability of loss. The scene in "During Wind and Rain" when the family moves house and the "Clocks and carpets and chairs" are "On the lawn all day" echoes the imagined party scene from "Lament"[48] in "Poems of 1912–13," in which "With table and tray/ And chairs on the lawn/ Her smiles would have shone." The rain-drop of the final line of "During Wind and Rain" incorporates the traditional elegiac correlation between rain and tears, but it also shows that even the carved names on the stones are impermanent; slowly they will be weathered away. The poem's plot moves in two opposing directions that make its evocation of loss even more poignant: in the first part of each stanza something joyful and increasingly *less* ephemeral is described (music, plants, animals, houses and furniture). In the counterplot, the one that wins, the end of each stanza shows seasons, plants, and finally human beings coming to their end.

> They sing their dearest songs—
>   He, she, all of them—yea,
>   Treble and tenor and bass,
>   And one to play;
>   With the candles mooning each face....
>   Ah, no; the years O!
> How the sick leaves reel down in throngs!
>   They clear the creeping moss—
>   Elders and juniors—aye,
>   Making the pathways neat
>   And the garden gay;
>   And they build a shady seat....
>   Ah, no; the years, the years,
> See, the white storm-birds wing across.
>
>   They are blithely breakfasting all—
>   Men and maidens—yea,
>   Under the summer tree,
>   With a glimpse of the bay,
>   While pet fowl come to the knee....
>   Ah, no; the years O!
> And the rotten rose is ript from the wall.

> They change to a high new house,
> He, she, all of them—aye,
> Clocks and carpets and chairs
> On the lawn all day,
> And brightest things that are theirs....
> Ah, no; the years, the years
> Down their carved names the rain-drop ploughs.

Partly in reference to "During Wind and Rain" and to the Emma poems, John Paul Riquelme claims, "Hardy rewrites the elegiac tradition" by no longer portraying the dead as continuing on in some form "especially as speaking subjects or as spirits in a landscape."[49] This is and is not true of "Poems of 1912–13," for Emma certainly remains as a speaking subject in the poet's mind, one that he projects out into a haunted world and a haunted landscape (including Cornwall, the scene of their courtship, which he revisited in the spring after her death). The sequence keeps claiming that she is no more, and then refuting its own claims. For example, the end of "Lament" declares the woman to be entirely closed off from life and what she enjoyed of it. The repetitions and the trio of masculine rhymes emphasize the case:

> She is shut, she is shut
> From the cheer of them, dead
> To all done and said
> In her yew-arched bed

But in the very next poem, we hear her talking: "He does not think that I haunt here nightly" ("The Haunter"[50]). Dead as alive, the poet's spouse exceeds his understanding of who, where, or how she ought to be.

The eighteen-plus-three elegiac poems that Thomas Hardy wrote after the death of his wife Emma are stable and attractive containers for emotions that are anything but stable and attractive. They employ something of what Donald Davie attributes to Hardy of an "allusive deviousness" that allows him to "convey and cloak his meanings" at the same time.[51] Although each poem has a difference structure, and the variations are impressive, they share a reliance on the locking effects of rhyme and on variations in line length in order to create their effects. They also employ his principle (especially in how he works with meter) "that inexact rhymes and rhythms now and then are far more pleasing than corrections."[52] The carefully crafted verses themselves were written to last (and they are still read a century after their composition), yet they dwell on impermanence, especially the tragic impermanence of human love and human life. From the biographical point of view, they convey above all a sense of tragic irony: when she was with me I didn't love her as I should have done, and now that she's gone I love her! The poems house Hardy's complex feelings, including love, anger, guilt, regret, resentment, loneliness, and loss, but those feelings exceed the semantic and formal confines of any individual poem. Just as the couple's early feelings about each other changed, and just as Emma is no longer bodily in their marital home, and just as she even leaves the grave to wander as a ghost (at least in Hardy's imagination), so the bounds of the poems cannot hold her youthful energy, the Hardys' romance and its fading, or his memories and meditations. As the environmental features inherent to the landscape of the poems—rivers, oceans, and cliffs, as well as domestic spaces—involve ever-shifting boundaries and energetic flux, so aspects of the verse itself dramatize the changing emotional and physical states of the two protagonists of the sequence. Hardy the trained architectural assistant uses the structural features of metrical verse in such a wide variety of carefully designed forms in order to articulate, shape and so manage his private feelings of grief; he also ends up demonstrating that love, relationships, death, and many emotional responses exceed the limits of human control, defying fixity.

Notes

1. Dennis Taylor, *Hardy's Metres and Victorian Prosody: With a Metrical Appendix of Hardy's Stanza Forms* (Oxford: Clarendon Press, 1988), 4.

2. Cecil Day Lewis, "'The Lyrical Poetry of Thomas Hardy': The Warton Lecture on English Poetry, 6 June 1951," reprinted in *Thomas Hardy, Poems: A Casebook*, eds. James Gibson and Trevor Johnson (London: Macmillan, 1979), 157.

3. See for example Melanie Sexton, "Phantoms of His Own Figuring: The Movement Toward Recovery in Hardy's 'Poems of 1912–13,'" *Victorian Poetry* 29:3 (Autumn 1991): 209–226; William W. Morgan, "Form, Tradition, and Consolation in Hardy's 'Poems of 1912–13,'" *PMLA* 89 (1974): 496–505; and Peter Sacks, *The English Elegy: Studies in the Genre from Spenser to Yeats* (Baltimore: Johns Hopkins University Press, 1985).

4. Claire Tomalin, *Thomas Hardy* (New York: Penguin Press, 2007), 320.

5. Dennis Taylor, "Hardy as a Nineteenth-Century Poet" in *The Cambridge Companion to Thomas Hardy*, ed. Dale Kramer (Cambridge: CUP, 1999), 200.

6. Neil Wenborn, *Reading Thomas Hardy: Selected Poems* (Penrith, CA: HEB Humanities E-Books, 2012), 65.

7. Suzanne Keen, "Psychological Approaches to Thomas Hardy" in *The Ashgate Research Companion to Thomas Hardy*, ed. Rosemarie Morgan (Farnham, Surrey: Ashgate, 2010), 290.

8. Tim Armstrong, "Sequence and Series in Hardy's Poetry" in *A Companion to Thomas Hardy*, ed. Keith Wilson (Malden, MA: Wiley-Blackwell Pub, 2009), 390.

9. Sacks, *op. cit.*, 235.

10. Donald Davie, "Thomas and Emma" in *Poems and Melodramas* (Manchester: Carcanet, 1996); Tom Paulin, "Love's Bonfire" in *Love's Bonfire* (London: Faber and Faber, 2012).

11. Thomas Hardy, *Unexpected Elegies: Poems of 1912–13, and Other Poems About Emma*, ed. Claire Tomalin (New York: Persea Books, 2010).
12. *The Collected Letters of Thomas Hardy*, ed. Richard L. Purdy, and Michael Millgate (Oxford: Clarendon Press, 1978), V, 37.
13. Jahan Ramazani, *Poetry of Mourning: The Modern Elegy from Hardy to Heaney* (Chicago: University of Chicago Press, 1994), 49.
14. Thomas Hardy, *The Complete Poems*, ed. James Gibson (Basingstoke: Palgrave, 2001), 346.
15. *Unexpected Elegies, op. cit*, xv; Tomalin, *op. cit.*, xx.
16. Emma L. G. Hardy, *Letters of Emma and Florence Hardy* (Oxford: Oxford University Press, 1996), 7–8.
17. *The Complete Poems, op. cit.*, 345–346.
18. William Shakespeare, *Macbeth* (act I, sc. 1, l. 11) in *The Oxford Shakespeare: The Complete Works*, eds. Stanley Wells and Gary Taylor (Oxford: Clarendon Press, 1988, repr. 1998), 977.
19. *Ibid.*, 978 (act I, sc. 3).
20. *The Complete Poems, op. cit.*, 350–351.
21. Phillip Mallett, "'You were she': Hardy, Emma and 'Poems of 1912–13'" in *Thomas Hardy Journal* 20:3 (2004): 57.
22. Edgar Allan Poe, "The Philosophy of Composition" in *Graham's Magazine* 28:4 (April 1846), http://www.eapoe.org/works/essays/philcomp.htm, accessed 18 July 2014.
23. Ramazani, *op. cit.*, 53.
24. *The Complete Poems, op. cit.*, 783–784.
25. *Ibid.*, 357–358.
26. *Ibid.*, 348.
27. *Ibid.*, 338–339.
28. *Ibid.*, 343.
29. *Ibid.*, 342–343.
30. Taylor, *Hardy's Metres, op. cit.*, 156.
31. *Unexpected Elegies, op. cit.*, xi.
32. *The Complete Poems, op. cit.*, 355–356.
33. *Ibid.*, 341–342.
34. John Paul Riquelme, "The Modernity of Thomas Hardy's Poetry" in Kramer ed., *op. cit.*, 216.
35. *The Complete Poems, op. cit.*, 339–340.
36. Mallett, *op. cit.*, 58.
37. Geoffrey Hill, *Collected Critical Writings* (Oxford: Oxford University Press, 2008), 377.
38. As Ross C. Murfin points out, Emma's name never appears in these "twenty-one troubled 'elegies'" ("Moments of Vision: Hardy's 'Poems of 1912–13'" in *Victorian Poetry* 20.1 [1982]: 79).
39. *The Complete Poems, op. cit.*, 340–341.
40. Hall, Louisa, "An Alternative to the Architectural Elegy: Hardy's Unhoused 'Poems of 1912–13'" in *Victorian Poetry* 50:2 (Summer 2012): 211.
41. *Ibid.*, 217.
42. Thomas Hardy, *The Life and Work of Thomas Hardy*, ed. Michael Millgate (Athens: University of Georgia Press, 1985), 300.

43. Sacks, *op. cit.*, 235.
44. *Ibid.*, 237.
45. *Ibid.*, 235.
46. *The Complete Poems, op. cit.*, 495–496.
47. Taylor, *Hardy's Metres, op. cit.*, 157–158, quoting Thomas Hardy, *The Collected Letters of Thomas Hardy, op. cit.*, VI, 96.
48. *The Complete Poems, op. cit.*, 344–345.
49. Riquelme, *op. cit.*, 215.
50. *The Complete Poems, op. cit.*, 345–346.
51. Donald Davie, *Agenda: Thomas Hardy Special Issue* (London, 1972), 151.
52. *The Life, op. cit.*, 108.

Works Cited

Armstrong, Tim. "Sequence and Series in Hardy's Poetry" in *A Companion to Thomas Hardy*. Ed. Keith Wilson. Malden, MA: Wiley-Blackwell, 2009, 378–94.
Davie, Donald, ed. *Agenda: Thomas Hardy Special Issue*. London, 1972.
_____. *Poems and Melodramas*. Manchester: Carcanet, 1996.
_____. *With the Grain: Essays on Thomas Hardy and Modern British Poetry*. Manchester: Carcanet, 1998.
Gibson, James, and Trevor Johnson, eds. *Thomas Hardy, Poems: A Casebook*. London: Macmillan, 1979.
Hall, Louisa. "An Alternative to the Architectural Elegy: Hardy's Unhoused 'Poems of 1912–1913,'" *Victorian Poetry*, 50:2 (Summer 2012): 207–225.
Hardy, Emma L. G., and Florence E. Hardy. *Letters of Emma and Florence Hardy*. Ed. Michael Millgate. Oxford: Oxford University Press, 1996.
Hardy, Thomas. *The Collected Letters of Thomas Hardy*. Ed. Richard L. Purdy, and Michael Millgate. Oxford: Clarendon Press, 1978.
_____. *The Complete Poems*. Ed. James Gibson. Basingstoke: Palgrave, 2001.
_____. *The Life and Work of Thomas Hardy*. Ed. Michael Millgate. Athens: University of Georgia Press, 1985.
_____. *Unexpected Elegies: Poems of 1912–13, and Other Poems About Emma*. Ed. Claire Tomalin. New York: Persea Books, 2010.
Hill, Geoffrey. *Collected Critical Writings*. Ed. Kenneth Haynes. Oxford: Oxford University Press, 2008.
Keen, Suzanne. "Psychological Approaches to Thomas Hardy," in *The Ashgate Research Companion to Thomas Hardy*. Ed. Rosemarie Morgan. Farnham, Surrey: Ashgate, 2010, 285–300.
Kramer, Dale, ed. *The Cambridge Companion to Thomas Hardy*. Cambridge: Cambridge University Press, 1999.
Lewis, Cecil Day. "'The Lyrical Poetry of Thomas Hardy': The Warton Lecture on English Poetry, 6 June 1951," in *Thomas Hardy, Poems: A Casebook*. Eds. James Gibson and Trevor Johnson. London: Macmillan, 1979.
Mallett, Phillip. "'You were she': Hardy, Emma and 'Poems of 1912–13,'" *Thomas Hardy Journal* 20:3 (2004): 54–75.
Morgan, Rosemarie, ed. *The Ashgate Research Companion to Thomas Hardy*. Farnham, Surrey: Ashgate, 2010.

Morgan, William W. "Form, Tradition, and Consolation in Hardy's 'Poems of 1912–13,'" *PMLA* 89 (1974): 496–505.
Murfin, Ross C. "Moments of Vision: Hardy's 'Poems of 1912–13,'" *Victorian Poetry* 20.1 (1982): 73–84.
Paulin, Tom. *Love's Bonfire*. London: Faber and Faber, 2012.
_____. *Thomas Hardy, the Poetry of Perception*. Totowa, NJ: Rowman and Littlefield, 1975.
Poe, Edgar Allan. "The Philosophy of Composition," *Graham's Magazine*, 28:4 (April 1846): 163–167. <http://www.eapoe.org/works/essays/philcomp.htm>. Accessed 18 July 2014.
Ramazani, Jahan. *Poetry of Mourning: The Modern Elegy from Hardy to Heaney*. Chicago: University of Chicago Press, 1994.
Riquelme, John Paul. "The Modernity of Thomas Hardy's Poetry," in *The Cambridge Companion to Thomas Hardy*. Ed. Dale Kramer. Cambridge: Cambridge University Press, 1999, 204–223.
Sacks, Peter M. *The English Elegy: Studies in the Genre from Spenser to Yeats*. Baltimore: Johns Hopkins University Press, 1985.
Sexton, Melanie. "Phantoms of His Own Figuring: The Movement Toward Recovery in Hardy's 'Poems of 1912–13,'" *Victorian Poetry*, 29:3 (Autumn 1991): 209–226.
Taylor, Dennis. "Hardy as a Nineteenth-Century Poet," in *The Cambridge Companion to Thomas Hardy*. Ed. Dale Kramer. Cambridge: Cambridge University Press, 1999, 183–203.
_____. *Hardy's Metres and Victorian Prosody: With a Metrical Appendix of Hardy's Stanza Forms*. Oxford: Clarendon Press, 1988.
Tomalin, Claire. *Thomas Hardy*. New York: Penguin Press, 2007.
Wenborn, Neil. *Reading Thomas Hardy: Selected Poems*. Penrith, CA: HEB Humanities E-Books, 2012.
Wilson, Keith, ed. *A Companion to Thomas Hardy*. Malden, MA: Wiley-Blackwell, 2009.

Challenging Time
Philological and Lexicographical Landscape
Emilie Loriaux

Hardy's poetic work began towards the end of the Victorian era, a time which had been one of intensive debates around language, linguistics and dictionaries. When Dennis Taylor writes that "Hardy's main interest is in the history of the word, [...] its antedating and pedigree,"[1] he underscores the fact that Hardy was indeed a historian—the historian of Wessex, of its culture and therefore of its language. This is true to some extent, but Hardy was more than just a historian. He was a poet and a philologist in a more elementary, affective sense. A look at "his most important tool,"[2] the *OED*, reveals that the word "philology" means the "love of learning and literature; the study of literature, in a wide sense, including grammar, literary criticism and interpretation."[3] Hence one does find in philology this elementary aspect of "loving letters," which is naturally intrinsic to Hardy's sensibility. He himself, in relation to his prose method, wrote:

> The whole secret of a living style and the difference between it and a dead style, lies in not having too much style—being, in fact, a little careless, or rather seeming to be, here and there.... It is, of course, simply carrying into prose the knowledge I have acquired in poetry—that inexact rhymes and rhythms now and then are far more pleasing than correct ones.[4]

This means Hardy's possible linguistic inaccuracies are aesthetic and cannot be totally explained from the point of view of the history of language.

Hardy was avidly curious and his sources of inspiration were diverse. His greatest local influence was the Dorset poet-philologist William Barnes (1801–1886). As Robert Gittings, in his biography *The Older Hardy*, reveals: "Hardy wrote nearly two dozen letters to the Press in 1907 and 1908 after he had finally laid aside *The Dynasts*. He comes very well out of the correspondence, hard-working, meticulous as an editor, patient about copyright difficulties, but above all intensely loyal to Barnes's poetry and the selection itself."⁵ In his obituary of Barnes, Hardy wrote that the latter was "probably the most interesting link between the present and past forms of rural life that England possessed."⁶ In Barnes's dialect poetry one can find an entire repertory of the life, language, customs and folklore of pre-industrial England.⁷

Hardy was a close friend of Barnes's, and from him he learnt grammar, philology, poetry and linguistics. When Barnes died on 7 October 1886, Hardy lost a major figure in his life. If one considers Hardy's interest in dictionaries, two other men had an impact on him, particularly revealed after their deaths: lexicographers Robert Scott and Henry George Liddell, who died in 1887 and 1898. As Hardy continued his career as a writer well after their deaths, one is tempted to look for signs of preservation of their memory as philologists and lexicographers in his essential "love of letters." More precisely, how, in Hardy's poems, do the linguistic relics of the past live on and how do they intertwine with the present?

Part of the answer, on Barnes's side, might lie in *The Life*:

> Hardy's walk across the fields to attend the poet [Barnes]'s funeral was marked by the singular incident to which he alludes in the poem entitled "The Last Signal."⁸ He also wrote an obituary notice of his friend for the *Athenæum*, which was afterwards drawn upon for details of his life in the *Dictionary of National Biography*. It was not till many years after that he made and edited a selection of Barnes's poems.⁹

The latter writings are the ultimate tributes from Hardy to his friend, and such materials helped, and help, perpetuate Barnes's life and work. Hardy's *Complete Poems* includes eleven poems which feature the word 'last' in their titles, a reminder, perhaps, of how keenly aware Hardy's poetry is, of the brevity of all earthly things. As to Robert Scott and Henry George Liddell, though there was no personal connection between Hardy and the two lexicographers, Hardy also wrote a poem dedicated to them, "Liddell and Scott: *On the Completion of their Lexicon*." Therefore, it seems appropriate to focus on those two poems in praise of men whom Hardy admired, in order to study their nature as possible linguistic tributes.

The first poem, mentioned in *The Life*, is "The Last Signal" written in 1886 and published in 1917 in *Moments of Vision and Miscellaneous Verses*. This is an accolade to William Barnes and a memory of Dorset's linguistic history. The poem, which explicitly bears the date of Barnes's funeral, 11 October 1886, and the subtitle "A Memory of William Barnes," describes the progress of Barnes's funeral cortège from the poet's viewpoint. The second poem, "Liddell and Scott: *On the Completion of their Lexicon*," appeared in

Hardy's last (and posthumous) collection of verse in 1928, *Winter Words in Various Moods and Metres*, but was written, as Hardy's note beneath its subtitle says, after the death of Liddell in 1898, Scott having died about ten years earlier. This is a tribute to the first edition of Liddell and Scott's Greek-English dictionary, entitled *A Greek-English lexicon based on the German work of Francis Passow* and published in 1843. Robert Scott (1811–1887) was an English academic philologist, clergyman and a fellow of Balliol College. He served as Dean Ireland's Professor of the Exegesis of Holy Scripture at Oxford (1861–1870). Henry George Liddell (1811–1898) was the headmaster of Westminster school (1846–1855) and the vice-chancellor and dean of Christ Church at Oxford University (1855–1891).[10] Other names are mentioned by Hardy in this poem. "[O]ld Donnegan" (l. 26) is a reference to James Donnegan's Greek and English lexicon of 1826, a book which is in itself an inheritance as it is based on a Greek and German lexicon, the *Griechisch-Deutches Wörterbuch* (J. Schneider, 1798). This type of dictionary covers dialectal varieties, poetic diction, terms or expressions particular to writers and more specifically classical writers, with examples. The "Liddell and Scott" dictionary, then, is a lexicon with a past, as it is inspired by Donnegan's dictionary and also by Francis "Passow"'s (l. 45), itself first published in 1824. In writing poems to Barnes and to Liddell and Scott, Hardy thus restores the landscape of lexicography and philology of past generations—the word "landscape" being intentionally used here in the sense of a "depiction or description of something in words."[11] The poet thus extends this landscape to depict the legacy of two English lexicographers and one English philologist-poet in their research, respectively, into Greek and Anglo-Saxon.

Written around the turn of the 20th century, both poems are testimonies and farewells to the Victorian era. They also mark a turning point for the English language: on the one hand, the death of Barnes signals the end of an era in itself, on the other hand, Liddell and Scott's dictionary presents itself as a lexicographic milestone; and with Barnes, Liddell and Scott all dead, a new page can be written.

The register of these two affectionate, light-hearted tributes is different in each case. While "Liddell and Scott" is entirely written as a humorous dialogue between the two men, "The Last Signal" is more serious and full of symbolism, which is quite expected given Hardy's longstanding personal relationship with Barnes. These two poems can be linked and perceived as formal, prosodic and verbal artifacts, and also related to the referents outside the poems: Barnes, Liddell and Scott. This combines poetic artistry with the intellectual context.

The Last Signal
(11 Oct. 1886)
A Memory of William Barnes

    Silently I footed by an uphill road
      That led from my abode to a spot yew-boughed;
Yellowly the sun sloped low down to westward,
        And dark was the east with cloud.

    Then, amid the shadow of that livid sad east,
      Where the light was least, and a gate stood wide,
Something flashed the fire of the sun that was facing it,
        Like a brief blaze on that side.

    Looking hard and harder I knew what it meant—
      The sudden shine sent from the livid east scene;
It meant the west mirrored by the coffin of my friend there,
        Turning to the road from his green,

    To take his last journey forth—he who in his prime
      Trudged so many a time from that gate athwart the land!
Thus a farewell to me he signalled on his grave-way,
        As with a wave of his hand.

Winterborne-Came Path[12]

    The memory of Hardy's friend is not only perceptible throughout the poem and through the vivid image of the "coffin" (l. 11), but also through Hardy's choice of words. They sometimes echo each other: the verb "signalled" in "Thus a farewell to me he signalled on his grave-way" (l. 15) is a working-out of the noun "signal" from the poem's title. This polyptoton does not repeat, however, what the poem really says, as it is as much Barnes's last journey as a signal: "the coffin of my friend [...]/ Turning to the road from his green,/ To take his last journey forth—[...]" (l. 11 to 13).

    A particular link between the poem and the real world is perceptible. The flash of light at the heart of the poem emerges from contrasts: from darkness ("dark" and "cloud" l. 4, "shadow" l. 5) to light ("livid" l. 5, "light" l. 6, "sun" l. 7, "shine" l. 10). "Something flashed the fire of the sun that was facing it,/ Like a brief blaze on that side" (l. 7 and 8) might appear as an image to suggest both the sudden loss of his friend and the end of Barnes's particular historical period. The obvious alliterative pattern, consecutively in /f/ and /b/, may help convey the swiftness of the light and the sense of a ricochet effect. The reflected light of the sun dazzles the poet, as if Barnes had received a flash of light that he in turn passes on to Hardy. This seems to correspond to what Dennis Taylor calls a "visual pattern":

> a constant image which symbolises the way a typical impression develops. [...] It embodies what Hardy sees as the tragic relation of mind and reality. This relation begins as a unity and ends in a shocking discord. The pattern symbol-

ises both the way we realise our world and what happens to that realisation: it grows in somewhat unconscious ways, it obsolesces in ways we do not immediately see, it is belatedly exposed. [...] In an unpublished notebook, Hardy copied: "We live forward, we understand backward."[13]

Applied to "The Last Signal," this "visual pattern" symbolizes the intellectual light Barnes gave out; one might say a philological, poetical, lingual legacy. This image is reinforced by a stylistic effect, as the poem goes from the indeterminate noun "something" (l. 7) to the determinate "coffin" (l. 11). There is first the phenomenon (the "visual pattern"), and then the partial signification (the "backward" "understand[ing]") of this phenomenon is given twice by "it meant" in lines 9 and 11.

It is clear that when Hardy wrote the poem "The Last Signal," he had long been conscious of the importance of his lingual inheritance in relation to Barnes. He therefore followed Barnes's path, both metaphorically in the form of linguistic inheritance, and literally as he was walking on the same road, looking out at his friend's coffin from uphill (l. 1; l. 12). Alan Chedzoy indeed records that "Thomas Hardy was too late to join the procession at the Rectory [Came Rectory is the parish where Barnes was living, Came Church is the place where he was buried]. [Hardy] had just left Max Gate for the funeral when Barnes's coffin was pushed onto the road. But as he looked out on that dark day, something seemed to flash before his eyes."[14] Philologically speaking, Hardy also followed some of Barnes's peculiarities, such as the use of creative compounds, the root-matching principle or the heavy alliterative style, which will be discussed further down. Hardy mingles "the present and past [linguistic] forms of rural life that England possessed"[15] and then goes a step forward to provide a poem mixing his own "visual pattern" and Barnes's linguistic and poetic legacy.

As has just been said, Barnes's linguistic influence may be visible first through creative compounds as, for Barnes, "[n]o language more than English had been and still remained capable of deft, luxuriant and advantageous growth out of its own character and quality. [...] He denoted the vast richness of affixes and the fertile compounds inherent in the native speech."[16] Compounds in particular offer infinite possibilities for the creative use of the English language , as one can compose and re-compose using existing roots and words, Anglo-Saxon and otherwise. In "The Last Signal," the compound adjective "yew-boughed" (l. 2) is literally the branch from a solid tree, a tree which is indeed often found in graveyards. Therefore, here, the "spot yew-boughed" is the graveyard where the funeral cortège is headed. It can symbolize immortality as it also does in the first stanza of "Transformations," a near neighbor to "The Last Signal" in the collection *Moments of Vision*:

> Portion of this yew
> Is a man my grandsire knew,
> Bosomed here at its foot:
> This branch may be his wife,
> A ruddy human life
> Now turned to a green shoot.[17]

Another "yew" reference appears in the last line of the poem "Lament" for, presumably, Hardy's late wife Emma, "In her yew-arched bed."[18] If we apply the "Transformations" metaphor to Barnes, it is as if Barnes the yew were transferring his linguistic knowledge, the ramifications of his philological background to the next generation: Hardy. The substantive "bough" in the compound adjective "yew-boughed" is turned into a past participle. It is slightly archaic and even Teutonic, a language Barnes cherished more than the Standard English more prevalent in Victorian literary texts. "Yew-boughed" also creates an interesting phonetic effect, as its homophone is "you-bowed," thus possibly evoking both Hardy's reverence for his elder and Barnes's farewell signal. It is therefore a compound combining both an archaic and creative form of language. "Yew-boughed" is a compound epithet; the very type of compounds Hardy prized most in his poetry. In his introduction to the selection of Barnes's poems,[19] Hardy quotes three compound epithets: "the blue-hill'd worold," "the wide-horn'd cow[s]" and "the grey-topp'd heights of Paladore," respectively from Barnes's poems "The New House A-gettèn Wold," "Milkèn Time," and "Shaftesbury Feäir."[20] Another compound appearing in Hardy's poem is the noun "grave-way" (l. 15), where a possible pun might be perceived. Hardy might signify both his path to the grave and his grave solemn tread, as it is a funeral. The younger poet somehow adds his personal touch to Barnes's linguistic legacy.

Such a sign of linguistic inheritance is also present in the rhymes. The "Celtic Poetry of the Bards"[21] one can find in Barnes's *Philological Grammar* relies on "a kind of under-rhyme or rhyme called *union*, which is the under-rhyming or rhyming of the last word or breath-sound in one line, with one in the middle of the following one."[22] One allusion to this under-rhyme is noticeable in "The Last Signal," precisely in the first two lines of each stanza: "road"/ "abode," "east"/ "least," "meant"/ "sent," and "prime"/ "time." This linguistic tribute is even reinforced at the end of the poem, as in the very last two lines one can find "grave-way" and "wave." This emphasis of the under-rhyme is an echo of Barnes's work and especially here of his research on Irish Celtic poetry, "constructed on [among other things] under-rhyme and full-rhyme."[23]

The tribute is also visible through other types of rhymes to be found in Barnes's work. Barnes attached great importance to the matching of sounds within the same line, an alliterative style which is indeed insistently used by Hardy in "The Last Signal": "Yellowly the s̲un s̲loped" (l. 3), "Where the l̲ight was l̲east," (l. 6), "Something f̲lashed the f̲ire" (l. 7), "Like a b̲rief b̲laze" (l. 8), "Looking h̲ard and h̲arder" (l. 9), "The s̲udden shine s̲ent" (l. 10), "T̲urning t̲o the road" (l. 12), "T̲o t̲ake his last journey" (l. 13), "T̲rudged so many a t̲ime" (l. 14), "As w̲ith a w̲ave of his hand" (l. 16). One can even find a "root-matching" principle in "hard and harder" (l. 9), which is perhaps reminiscent of Barnes's *Philological Grammar*: "Root-matching, called by the Persians Ishtikôk, or derivation, is the matching of words from the same root. Under root-matching we may class the Greek *polyptoton*; as in Latin."[24] Other than Irish or Persian verse, Barnes was also interested in Welsh poetry. In his *Grammar*, he made the distinction between those types of poetry: "Welsh clipping-rhyme (*cynghanedd*) is of its own kind, different from that of the Irish as well as that of the Teutonic languages."[25] In *Hardy's Metres and Victorian Prosody*, Dennis Taylor, without attempting to analyze "such sequences" and rhymes, goes along this idea: "["The Last Signal"] is a tribute to William Barnes which follows Barnes's instructions in his *Philological Grammar* concerning union (the rhyming of the end word of one line with the middle word of the next) and *cynghanedd* (consonant patterns within the line)."[26] Furthermore, echoing Barnes's love of Welsh rhymes, one can find in Hardy's "Last Signal" a mark of this poetry under "another kind of clipping-rhyme, called *cymmeriad* (taking), which is a taking of the same clipping or breath-sound for the beginning of two, four, or more lines."[27] In the examples Barnes gives, the rhymes are consecutive. In Hardy's poem, we have for instance: "T̲urning" (l. 12), "T̲o" (l. 13), "T̲rudged" (l. 14), where "Turning" does not belong to the same stanza and likewise for the pair "Like" (l. 8) and "Looking" (l. 9). The small changes from Hardy could be considered as a personal renewal. As Taylor concludes, "Hardy's most conscious artistic interest in sound symbolism was in his verse skeletons, and their symbolic or ironic possibilities. Here he was ahead of the Victorian prosodists."[28] The variation in the rhymes one can find in "The Last Signal" might prove that despite his reverence for his inheritance, Hardy did not wish to emulate Barnes too closely. Under the passing-on of the torch, a sign of evolution is conspicuous in the new generation, mingling both the old and the new.

The second poem under consideration, "Liddell and Scott,"[29] starts with the marker of orality "Well" (l. 1). It is an informal marker and an exclamation, expressing surprise or joy, or it might even be a sigh of relief, because Liddell and Scott have reached the end of their task. The poem can be seen as an elegy. Yet unusually for the latter genre, it is written in the form of an imaginary dialogue, and has a humorous tone, which might seem to jar with its elegiac inclination. Hardy uses the stylistic figure of prosopopeia to give Liddell and Scott a voice, each of them being heard in turn in the dialogue that constitutes the poem. The poem thus stands as the eulogy of the cooperation between the two lexicographers, one might say their synergy. Their dialogue seems natural and intimate in the way it reflects the easy working and personal relationship between the two men. "Liddell and Scott" is more informal and pays a more relaxed tribute, especially with the dialogue form and markers such as "Well" (l. 1 and 58), "Yea" (l. 49), or elisions ("'Twas," l. 38). In "The Last Signal," one might discern a kind of orality not in dialogue form but in the Hardyan style itself, sometimes bluntly monosyllabic, such as the second part of line 9, "I knew what it meant" or "As with a wave of his hand" (l. 16). However, one cannot be so adamant about the form of language Hardy uses in "Liddell and Scott." It would be fairer to say that the relaxed form is what the first general impression reveals, as a closer look shows that there is a mixture in the language registers used. "Liddell and Scott" does contain some poetic or formal words such as "nigh" (l. 16) or "quill" (l. 51). "Nigh"—"When the end loomed nigh"–might be both an effect of poetic diction and possibly a dialectal form of language. The *OED* has the following definition:

> = near adv. and a. (which in all senses has taken the place of *nigh* except in archaic or dialect use.) The original comparative of *néah* as an adv. is *near*, *néor*, NEAR adv., while the adj. from *néarra* finally became *ner*, *nar* a. The OE superlative *níehst* is latterly represented by NEXT a. and adv. After phonetic changes had obscured the relationship of these forms to the positive, a new compar. and superl., *nigher* and *nighest*, were formed, and have been in common use since the 16th cent.[30]

Incidentally, "nigh" is found in both the National English and Dorset Dialect versions of Barnes's poems such as "Jay A pass'd"[31] ("Zome other geäme wud still be nigh," l. 17), and its National English version "Joy Passing By"[32] ("With us, another joy was nigh," l. 9). Other examples of this adverb might be noticed in a National English poem called "Stillness or the wind" ("And words, where not a tongue is nigh," l. 18),[33] or in the Dorset Dialect poem "Seats" ("The while the waggon, wi" his lwoad,/ Do crawl the rwoad a-winden nigh," l. 23–24).[34] This word is indeed used by Barnes—and it appears, in the examples given, in final position in the line, as it does in "Liddell and Scott"–as both dialectal and part of the more standard poetic diction. In this sense, in his tribute to Liddell and Scott Hardy again echoes words used by Barnes.

In the same poem and same part of the dialogue, a couple of lines before, Hardy uses this surprising phrase: "I've often, I own,/ Belched many a moan" (l. 12). "Belch" is more commonly used as an intransitive verb, meaning "To void wind noisily from the stomach through the mouth, to eructate,"[35] or as a transitive verb, in the sense of "To ejaculate, to give vent to; to vent with vehemence or violence (words, feelings)"—the term had originally "no offensive meaning; but in later use confined, by association with other senses, to the utterance of things foul or offensive, or to furious vociferation compared to the action of a volcano or cannon."[36]

This word may sound unexpected coming from a Victorian academic and lexicographer, suggesting a use of language both vehement and colloquial, perhaps surprising for such a cerebral sort of character. The proximity of "Belched many a moan" and "When the end loomed nigh" (l. 16) creates a strange and contrastive image of Scott's speech. One might explain this intermingling of registers of language as a contrast between the private and the public forms of language one uses, as an adaptation to address different persons or contexts. It is indeed typically Hardyan to mix words from different forms of language, which makes the tribute more personal and creative.

More than merely expressing esteem for the two lexicographers, the poem "Liddell and Scott" goes beyond their erudition and academic achievement, as it also highlights the human aspect of their work. Hardy seems to feel empathy for the huge task they have accomplished, as even after "[t]he job's done" (l. 59) the question of publication still needs to be resolved:

> "And yet it's not [done],"
> Considered Scott,
> "For we've to get
> Subscribers yet
> We must remember;
> Yes; by September." [l. 60–65]

An authentic note of uninhibited relief is heard in the colloquial exchange between Liddell and Scott in the concluding lines of the poem:

> "O Lord, dismiss that. We'll succeed.
> Dinner is my immediate need.
> I feel as hollow as a fiddle,
> Working so many hours," said Liddell. [l. 66–69]

Hardy most likely invented the simile "as hollow as a fiddle" to describe Liddell's hunger (in a sense the opposite of the expression "as fit as a fiddle"). The "hollow" of "a fiddle" might also metaphorically refer to the production of a refined sound that this instrument can provide. The quality of the shape and making of the hollow will define the quality of the fiddle's sound. Hardy was a fiddle player himself and mentioned this instrument in other poems such as "The Fiddler,"[37] "To My Father's Violin,"[38] or "Old Furniture."[39] In "Music in a Snowy Street,"[40] the sound of this instrument appears as a relief from pressure for the speaker:

> One wakes from a harp,
> The next from a viol,
> A strain that I loved
> When life was no trial. [l. 3–6]

For the poet, the music of the fiddle might also conjure up the remembrance of dead souls, as in "The Dead Quire" which evokes the "The viols of the dead" (stanza XIV).[41] With their work over, Liddell and Scott may now rest in peace.

Liddell and Scott's work on their dictionary is a question of linguistic legacy in a more extended way than just in the implications it had for England or Europe. Even if Liddell has doubts, it is in a way his duty, as he says:

> And how I often, often wondered
> What could have led me to have blundered
> So far away from sound theology
> To dialects and etymology;
> Words, accents not to be breathed by men
> Of any country ever again! [l. 28–33]

The tribute itself goes further than Liddell and Scott's own generation. It crosses geographical frontiers as well as temporal ones—and crossing borders is one motif which unmistakably runs through Hardy's language. In "Liddell and Scott," as in several other pieces, the integration of ancient Greek words in the English poem is particularly striking: "To write *aaatos* and *aagês*" (l. 52); "Assured that we should reach *wwdês*" (l. 56). This presence of ancient words might be interpreted in two ways. First the poem might be a direct tribute to Liddell and Scott's Greek-English dictionary in relation to both languages. But one is also reminded of *The Waste Land* and its foreign-language words. In this sense, Hardy's Greek words could be seen as not entirely foreign to poetic Modernism. If one looks at the meaning of these words, it is possible for example to find "*aaatos*" in Liddell and Scott's dictionary. It means "not to be injured, inviolable." The word "inviolable" is significant: couldn't Hardy be saying that their work and reputation are themselves inviolable? The presence of Greek opens up the expressive possibilities of the poem or of poetic language, and there is meaningful creativity in Hardy's play with Greek words.

Thus, what Liddell and Scott did for the Greek-English studies, Hardy seems to be doing for poetic language through his own creation. Liddell and Scott wanted to go beyond Donnagan and Passow's works. Likewise, through "The Last Signal," Hardy is going a step beyond Barnes's work. In order to be their heir, their (philological) descendant, each had to integrate their predecessors' knowledge: Liddell and Scott had to integrate Donnagan's and Passow's lexicographic skills, and Hardy to assimilate Barnes's philological knowledge. The intellectual and linguistic inheritance is relevant to the creative process.

Thus, in these two very different tributes, Hardy foregrounds his love of language, the work of philology and lexicography. And as Ralph W.V. Elliott explains in *Thomas Hardy's English*:

> A particular, even peculiar, linguistic flair is necessary to produce rhymes [one finds in] Byronic doggerel (like "optim.: cupp'd him; stopp'd 'em"; and so on through *Don Juan*) as in Hardy's "Liddell and Scott" ("Donnegan: con again"; "*wwdês*: bodies") [...]. The doggerel emphasizes that Hardy was certainly not without a sense of humour, despite all the gloom and melancholy which readers encounter in his work.[42]

Robert Gittings likewise notices this touch of humor on Hardy's part:

> [I]n astonishing variety, Hardy's protean verse is comic too. *Liddell and Scott*, a tongue-in-cheek account of the great lexicon, is in Hardy's best style of learned humour. One of its most sprightly Browning-like couplets was actually added in the last few months of Hardy's life, rhyming the name of Donnegan, an earlier lexicographer, with "con again."[43]

Hardy conveys his passion in a humorous tone—although he can elsewhere be bitterly ironic—as he brings Liddell and Scott back to life. There is a possible parallel between Hardy's resuscitation of them and their attention to ancient Greek, in a sense a dead language.

Besides, in the philological context of the end of the Victorian area, Hardy's challenge to language seems both revealing and typically paradoxical of him—paradoxical since Hardy uses Barnes's, Liddell's and Scott's old language, but renews it as well. And indeed, "[t]here is no poetry," he wrote in a notebook entry, "but the new poet—if he carry the flame on further (and if not he is no poet)—comes with a new note. And that new note it is that troubles the critical waters."[44] Hardy shares with Liddell, Scott and Barnes the Victorian linguistic wealth. He shares with Barnes the ability to combine knowledge from different fields. As Taylor explains:

> Both literary writer and lexicographer are engaged in an assessment and clarification of the standard language if that is their focus. (Even dialect poets and dialect dictionaries define themselves in modern times by comparison with the received standard.) The writer, of course, is generally in advance of the lexicographer, but the lexicographer comes hastily behind, trying to define the current state of the language which writers have helped to establish. Writers look up words in the dictionary, and the dictionary quotes writers.[45]

Therefore, poets such as Barnes or Hardy are, according to Taylor's logic, more advanced than lexicographers. Both of them challenge the linguistics and the language of their period; Hardy does defy language, enjoying a very notable place in the *OED*[46] not only for his standard words, but also for his neologisms, nonce words or dialect words. He might also have been influenced by Barnes's visually narrative approach to poetry, as described by Douglas Ashdown in *An Introduction to William Barnes the Dorset Poet*: "[Barnes] simply told a tale, usually rural in character, sometimes humorous, sometimes sad, often with a moral and Christian content and usually in this odd Dorset dialect."[47] Hardy did not much use the Dorset dialect as Barnes did, but he shared the peculiarity Barnes had of seeing images and writing them down. One of Hardy's late comments from 2nd November 1913 confirms this similarity: "I saw all the dear scenes and well remembered events and beloved faces of youth all distinctly before me, and all I had to do was to write them down ... the thoughts and words came of themselves."[48] Hardy's past experiences and close relationship with Barnes helped him to integrate Barnes's techniques. And even if Hardy's comment was made later than "The Last Signal," one might assert that Hardy used his own experience—that of Barnes's funeral—to put into words such vivid images in that poem. The use of the slightly unfamiliar but eminently concrete verb "to foot" clinches the authenticity of the first lines of the poem: "Silently I footed by an uphill road/ That led from my abode to a spot yew-boughed" (l. 1–2). Likewise the first two lines of the second stanza—"Then, amid the shadow of that livid sad east,/ Where the light was least, and a gate stood wide" (l. 5–6)—mingle the apparently prosaic (the open gate) with the poetic ("livid sad east").

Yet unlike Barnes who received an education on the techniques of poetry writing from the Reverend J. H. Richman of Dorchester,[49] Hardy was inspired by different sources and did not get such scholarly training. Hardy had a stronger inclination for poetry and writing than philology in the sense of Barnes; that is to say Hardy cherished the language and its philological aspect in a more literary and poetic manner, compared to Barnes who was looking at the language in terms of philology, more as a linguist. This is a slightly different way of treasuring language and words: Barnes is more theoretical than Hardy.[50] Thus, in "The Last Signal," Hardy adds his own touch with the surprising adverb "Yellowly" (l. 3). The initial position of this word in the line might be interpreted as a sturdy image to represent his friend's soul or memory, as if Hardy wanted to strengthen the importance of such a brilliant poet-philologist, who marked the Victorian period. "Yellowly" reveals the literary and imaginative side of Hardy. Associated with the sun, this golden color brings Barnes metaphorically alive. In a similar way, in the second stanza, Hardy dramatizes his elegy with the almost Hopkinsian image of "Something flashed the fire" (l. 7), as stated above. The compound "Farewell" (l. 15) provides a certain sense of reverie and nostalgia. Consequently, in the poem, Hardy embraces Barnes's philological and poetic techniques and adds his own touch.

"Liddell and Scott" might echo, in another context, Barnes's "Eclogues," described by Arthur Quiller-Couch as "stray eclogues of rustic chat and challenge, between ploughmen, harvesters, old 'commoners,' while set in scholar's frame. [They] seem [...] more natural, racy, lusty, than anything in that form yet written in English."[51] "Liddell and Scott" is "racy" in the way that it is atypical, with the dialogue and humorous tone Hardy employs in the poem.

A parallel can also be drawn between Liddell and Scott's sense of precision in their dictionary, described by Liddell at the beginning of the poem as "Blotless and fair" (l. 7), and Hardy's precise use not only of English but of Greek words and also letters of the alphabet given in their rightful order, through Liddell's voice:

> Even now, if people only knew
> My sinkings, as we slowly drew
> Along through Kappa, Lambda, Mu,
> They'd be concerned at my misgiving,
> And how I mused on a College living
> Right down to Sigma,
> But feared a stigma [l. 19–25]

Hardy here not only plays with rhymes, but he also plays with language itself: "Sigma" is the Greek word for the English "stigma"; the pun comes to nail down the stigmatization which the speaker might suffer.

The connection to philology and lexicography in Hardy's poetry finally goes hand in hand with the use of the various resources of the language within the activity of poetry to reflect the void left by the deaths of Barnes, Liddell and Scott. In both poems, a core common to Barnes's, Liddell's and Scott's linguistic research, and to Hardy's poetic activity, takes shape. By composing the two poems "The Last Signal" and "Liddell and Scott," the inheritor Hardy is both paying tribute to his masters through his own art, and challenging their legacy—in a sense thus writing himself into the landscape, not only of the poetry, but also of the philology and lexicography, of his age.

Notes

1. Dennis Taylor, *Hardy's Literary Language and Victorian Philology* (Oxford: Clarendon Press, 1993), 90.

2. *Ibid.*, 6.

3. *Complete Oxford English Dictionary*, CDrom v4.0, Oxford University Press, word searched: "philology."

4. R. A. Scott-James, C. Day Lewis, *Thomas Hardy* (London: Writers and their Work 21, Longman Group, Ltd., 1965), 38–39.

5. Robert Gittings, *The Older Hardy* (Harmondsworth: Penguin Books, 1978), 181. The "selection" refers to Hardy's own edition of Barnes's poems from 1908: *Select Poems of William Barnes*, ed. Thomas Hardy (London: Henry Frowe, 1908).

6. Thomas Hardy, "The Reverend William Barnes B.D." in *Athenaeum* 16 Oct 1886 in *Thomas Hardy's Personal Writings: Prefaces, Literary Opinions, Reminiscences*, ed. Harold Orel (London: Macmillan, 1967), 101.

7. Alan Chedzoy, *The People's Poet: William Barnes of Dorset* (Stanbridge, Wimborne, Dorset: The Dovecote Press, 1985), 9.

8. The reference is to a flash of fire which appeared in front of Hardy's eyes, as mentioned in lines 7–8 of "The Last Signal": "Something flashed the fire of the sun that was facing it,/ Like a brief blaze on that side." Thomas Hardy, *The Complete Poems*, ed. James Gibson (Basingstoke: Palgrave, 2001), 473.

9. Florence Emily Hardy, *The Life of Thomas Hardy 1840–1928* (London: Macmillan, 1970), 183.

10. He was also the father of Alice Liddell, who inspired Lewis Carroll's *Alice's Adventures in Wonderland*.

11. *Complete Oxford English Dictionary*, op. cit., word searched: "landscape" 4.g.

12. *The Complete Poems*, op. cit., 473.

13. Dennis Taylor, *Hardy's Poetry, 1860–1928* (Basingstoke: Macmillan, 1989; first edition 1981), 40–41.

14. Chedzoy, *op. cit.*, 195.

15. *Thomas Hardy's Personal Writings*, op. cit., 101.

16. Willis D. Jacobs, *William Barnes Linguist* (Albuquerque: The University of New Mexico Press, 1952), 76.

17. *The Complete Poems*, op. cit., 472.

18. *Ibid.*, 344–345. Published in the "Poems of 1912–13" series from *Satires of Circumstance* (1914).

19. *Select Poems of William Barnes*, op. cit., xi.

20. William Barnes, *The Poems*, ed. Bernard Jones (London: Centaur Press, Vol. 1 and 2, 1962), 398, 291, 450.

21. William Barnes, *A Philological Grammar, Grounded Upon English, and Formed from a Comparison of More than Sixty Languages* (London: John Russell Smith, 1854), 291.

22. *Ibid.*, 292.

23. *Ibid.*, 291.

24. *Ibid.*, 295.

25. *Ibid.*, 293. This is similar to Hopkins, who "was one of Barnes's closest readers, and ranked his wordlore as highly as his poetry." "Words used by Hopkins that had seemed to come out of the blue were in fact in Barnes's *TIW* (1862) or others of his philological writings" (Bernard Jones, *William Barnes: The Philological Society and The English Dialect Society* [East Stour Gillingham: Meldon House, 2010], 48, 50) If one picks up the compound verb "Betweenpie" in "skies/ Betweenpie mountains" from Hopkins's poem "My Own Heart Let Me More Have Pity On" (*Poems of Gerard Manley Hopkins*, ed. Robert Bridges, [London: Humphrey Milford, 1918], 67), "this word might have delighted William Barnes, if the verb "to pie" existed" (Jones, *op. cit.*, 48).

26. Dennis Taylor, *Hardy's Metres and Victorian Prosody* (Oxford: Clarendon Press, 1988), 81–82.
27. Barnes, *A Philological Grammar, op. cit.*, 293.
28. Taylor, *Hardy's Metres and Victorian Prosody, op. cit.*, 81–82.
29. *The Complete Poems, op. cit.*, 844–846. The poem's length does not allow us to reproduce it here in its entirety.
30. *Complete Oxford English Dictionary, op. cit.*, word searched: "nigh."
31. William Barnes, *The Poems of William Barnes*, ed. Bernard Jones (London: Centaur Press, 1962), Vol. I, 513 -514.
32. *Ibid.*, Vol. II, 890–891.
33. *Ibid.*, 850–851.
34. *Ibid.*, Vol. I, 310–311.
35. *Complete Oxford English Dictionary, op. cit.*, word searched: "belch" vb_1.
36. *Ibid.*, word searched: "belch" vb_2.
37. *The Complete Poems, op. cit.*, 248. Published in *Time's Laughingstocks* (1909).
38. *Ibid.*, 451–452. Published in *Moments of Vision* (1917); probably written in 1916.
39. *Ibid.*, 485–486. Published in *Moments of Vision* (1917).
40. *Ibid.*, 735–736. Published in *Human Shows* (1925).
41. *Ibid.*, 255–259. Published in *Time's Laughingstocks* (1909); written in 1897.
42. Ralph W. V. Elliott, *Thomas Hardy's English* (New York: Basil Blackwell, 1984), 331.
43. Gittings, *The Older Hardy, op. cit.*, 277.
44. Hardy quoted in Samuel Hynes, *The Pattern of Hardy's Poetry* (Chapel Hill: University of North Carolina Press, 1961), 64.
45. Taylor, *Hardy's Literary Language and Victorian Philology, op. cit.*, 6–7.
46. "the number of different Hardy citations in the *OED*, its Supplements, and second edition is: 1,436 words illustrated by 1,472 quotations" (*ibid.*, 123).
47. Douglas Ashdown, *An Introduction to William Barnes: The Dorset Poet* (Tiverton: Dorset Books, 1996), 49.
48. Taylor, *Hardy's Poetry, op. cit.*, 163.
49. Ashdown, *op. cit.*, 18.
50. However, it does seem necessary to distinguish between Barnes's research as a pure passionate philologist and, for instance, the *Philological Society's* aims, which were more realistic and scientific than he was.
51. Giles Dugdale, *William Barnes of Dorset* (London: Cassell & Company, Ltd., 1953), 215.

Works Cited

Ashdown, Douglas. *An Introduction to William Barnes: The Dorset Poet.* Tiverton: Dorset Books, 1996.
Barnes, William. *A Philological Grammar, Grounded Upon English, and Formed from a Comparison of More than Sixty Languages.* London: John Russell Smith, 1854.
_____. *The Poems of William Barnes.* Ed. Bernard Jones. London: Centaur Press, 1962.
_____. *Select Poems of William Barnes.* Ed. Thomas Hardy. London: Henry Frowe, 1908.
Chedzoy, Alan. *The People's Poet: William Barnes of Dorset.* Stanbridge, Wimborne, Dorset: The Dovecote Press, 1985.

Complete Oxford English Dictionary. CDrom v4.0, Oxford University Press, 2009.
Dugdale, Giles. *William Barnes of Dorset*. London: Cassell & Company, Ltd., 1953.
Elliott, Ralph W.V. *Thomas Hardy's English*. New York: Basil Blackwell, 1984.
Gittings, Robert. *Young Thomas Hardy*. Harmondsworth: Penguin Books, 1975.
_____. *The Older Hardy*. Harmondsworth: Penguin Books, 1978.
Hardy, Florence Emily. *The Life of Thomas Hardy 1840–1928*. London: Macmillan, 1970.
Hardy, Thomas. *The Complete Poems*. Ed. James Gibson. Basingstoke: Palgrave, 2001.
_____. *Thomas Hardy's Personal Writings: Prefaces, Literary Opinions, Reminiscences*. Ed. Harold Orel. London: Macmillan, 1967.
Hopkins, Gerard Manley. *Poems of Gerard Manley Hopkins*. Ed. Robert Bridges. London: Humphrey Milford, 1918.
Hynes, Samuel. *The Pattern of Hardy's Poetry*. Chapel Hill: University of North Carolina Press, 1961.
Jacobs, Willis D.. *William Barnes Linguist*. Albuquerque: University of New Mexico Press, 1952.
Jones, Bernard. *William Barnes: The Philological Society and The English Dialect Society*. East Stour Gillingham: Meldon House, 2010.
Scott-James, R. A., Day Lewis, C. *Thomas Hardy*, London: Longman Group, Ltd. (Writers and their Work N°21), 1965.
Taylor, Dennis. *Hardy's Literary Language and Victorian Philology*. Oxford: Clarendon Press, 1993.
_____. *Hardy's Metres and Victorian Prosody*. Oxford: Clarendon Press, 1988.
_____. *Hardy's Poetry, 1860–1928*. Basingstoke: Macmillan, 1989; first edition 1981.

Hardy's Crafting of Barnes
Heather Hawkins

Thomas Hardy is well known as a poet and author of fiction and occasional literary critic.[1] Less well known is his role as editor of one volume of verse, namely William Barnes's posthumous collection, *The Select Poems of William Barnes* (1908). In this essay I discuss the relationship between Hardy's editing of Barnes's poetry and his own poetry, particularly in relation to dialect. First, I compare substantive variants between two versions of the same poem taken from the 1844 edition of *Poems of Rural Life in the Dorset Dialect with a Dissertation and Glossary*[2] and the 1908 version in *The Select Poems of William Barnes*, which was edited by Hardy.[3] Then, I examine Hardy's editorial practice in relation to some of his own poems in James Gibson's edition of *The Complete Poems of Thomas Hardy*.[4]

There were many similarities between the lives of both poets. Barnes was born in 1801 and lived all of his life in the Dorset-Wiltshire area. Barnes's paternal grandfather had previously owned a small farm at Manston, near Sturminster, which fell into decline due to mismanagement following his death. Barnes's father farmed a small patch of rented land at Bagber, near Sturminster Newton, Dorset, and lived a tentative lifestyle perilously close to that of a farm laborer. Barnes's mother, Grace, came from an impoverished background, but although illiterate herself, she encouraged Barnes in his education. Barnes was an able student and was articled as a solicitor's clerk when he left school, a position which enabled him to progress socially to becoming a school master. Eventually Barnes became headmaster of his own school and later in life was ordained as rector of Whitcombe church in Dorset.[5] Hardy was born in 1840 at Lower Bockhampton, Dorset. He was the son of a self-employed builder and stonemason, Thomas Hardy, senior. The business grew and by 1870, Hardy's father employed eight men and a boy. Although Hardy's mother Jemima came from an impoverished background she, like Grace

Barnes, had a great interest in the education of her four children, buying Hardy gifts of works such as Johnson's *Rasselas* and Dryden's *Virgil*.[6] Both families occupied an ambivalent class position—neither fully of the middle class, nor entirely of the working class, they were acquainted with members of both.

The main disparity between the upbringing of the two poets was in their parents' attitudes towards the use of dialect in the home. Barnes's parents were dialect speakers and permitted the use of dialect at home.[7] In contrast, Jemima Hardy forbade the use of dialect in the house, but Hardy frequently heard some when his father addressed his employees and also when speaking to working-class children at the village school he attended.[8] As the poets grew up they were thus both equally familiar with standard English and the Dorset dialect. This familiarity with two languages was reflected in their interests in language and philological study in adult life and their ability to code-switch between languages. Hardy frequently used dialect words in his poetry and prose. He contributed to contemporary debates about dialect and was also involved in the compilation of the *Oxford English Dictionary*.[9] Barnes was an accomplished philologist and member of the Philological Society. He wrote various philological works on the English language, particularly identifying the etymological origins of the Dorset dialect, which he traced to the Teutonic languages.[10] In his work *An Outline of English Speechcraft* (1878), Barnes asserts the equal validity of oral languages with standard English. He argues:

> Some have spoken of cultivated languages as differing from uncultivated ones, and of the reducing of a speech to grammatical form. What is the meaning of "cultivate" as a time word about speech? [...] a speech is cultivated by the speaking as well as the writing of it, and a speech which is sounding over a whole folkland every moment of the day cannot be uncultivated.[11]

Barnes argues that correct usage of language is not created by written language alone. Speech initiates written language and thus is an equally cultivated component of language. In asserting the value of oral culture, Barnes attempts to write his poetry in his native dialect. He asserts in the "Preface" to the 1862 edition of his *Poems of Rural Life in the Dorset Dialect* that: "To write in what some may deem a fast out-wearing speech-form may seem as idle as the writing of one's name in the snow of a spring day. I cannot help it. It is my mother tongue and it is to my mind the only true speech of the life that I draw."[12] Barnes clearly considers dialect to be the most suitable mode of expression for the rural society he portrays. In the "Dissertation" at the beginning of the 1844 volume, Barnes outlines the grammatical conventions and phonology of the Dorset dialect. The inclusion of the "Dissertation" indicates that Barnes hopes his poetry will reach a standard English-speaking audience, possibly with philological interests, who reside beyond the rural periphery in the urban center.

The combination of linguistic theory alongside dialect poetry suggests that dialect is a subject worthy of serious academic study and gives Barnes the opportunity to demonstrate the outcome of his own research into the grammatical functioning of the dialect. The poems in the 1844 volume follow the conventions of the Dorset dialect outlined in the "Dissertation," such as his poem "The Hwomestead a-vell into Hand."[13] In this poem Barnes substitutes one vowel with another. Thus storm becomes "starm" and corn becomes "carn." Consonants are often substituted for alternative ones such as "z" for "s" in "besides," "avore" (afore) and "vrom" (from). "Paddock" becomes "parrick" in the dialect, and the "d" in "child" is substituted with a final vowel "chile." Barnes also highlights the Dorset dialect use of nouns, to which the suffix "en" is added to denote the plural, such as "chicken" for chicks, and in an example from the poem under discussion, "housen" for houses. Nouns can also have the "en" suffix to describe the material an object is made from. The oak door in the poem becomes "woaken." There is also great attention paid by Barnes in his "Dissertation" to the regular inflection of verbs in the dialect which are irregular in standard English. Barnes asserts that those who consider dialect to be a corruption of written speech:

> may not be prepared to hear that it is not only a separate offspring from the Anglo-Saxon tongue, but purer and more regular than the dialect which is chosen as the national speech; purer inasmuch as it uses many words of Saxon origin for which the English substitutes others of Latin, Greek or French derivation; and more regular inasmuch as it inflects regularly many words which in the national language are irregular.[14]

To confirm his findings Barnes lists verbs which are inflected regularly in the Dorset dialect, but irregularly in standard English, such as blow—"blew" in standard English, "blowed" in the Dorset dialect. Catch is another example—"caught" in standard English, but "catched" in dialect. The imperfect participle also omits the "ing" suffix of standard English and substitutes for it "en" so that "singing" become "singen." Examples to be found in "The Hwomestead a-vell into Hand" include "a-noddén" and "a-swayén." Barnes also attempts a phonetic representation of dialect via the use of breathings and accents such as the circumflex, acute, grave and dieresis. The poems in the 1844 edition of *Poems of Rural Life* are also arranged in subsections according to the seasons, followed by a "miscellaneous" section at the end of the volume. Barnes's arrangement echoes that of John Clare's *The Shepherd's Calendar* (1827), and further links his volume with the English pastoral tradition.[15]

Poems of Rural Life was reprinted in various editions. The 1888 edition indicates an increased standardization of dialect in Barnes's verse. Although the 1888 edition was published posthumously, the volume includes the preface to Barnes's 1879 edition and is a reprint of the earlier edition, which was sanctioned by Barnes. A surviving letter from Alexander Macmillan to Barnes suggests Barnes was under pressure from leading literary figures of the day to standardize the dialect. The Scotsman Macmillan agreed with Barnes regarding the value of dialect: "I can always make a good shot at what words mean, having Scotch characters in them. But it does not fall to the lot of the whole British public to have the blessing of a Scotch birth. For the sake of the more unfortunate can't you do something?"[16] Macmillan's criticism indicates that Barnes's decision to write in dialect restricts his audience to dialect speakers in the rural periphery. Few standard-English readers would have had the time and patience to decipher dialect, even with the aid of Barnes's glossary. Earlier reviews of Barnes's poetry confirm his regionalist status. For example, the *Gentleman's Magazine* said of language in the 1844 volume that it is "not brought from a distance to decorate or adorn the native complexion of pastoral life; it is twin-born with the subject, and between the thought and expression is nothing discordant or unsuitable."[17] Despite the harmony between language and subject in Barnes's poetry it nevertheless remains regionalist. Barnes eventually succumbed to Macmillan's pressure and by 1868 had produced one volume of his poetry in standard English which Macmillan duly published, but with objections by Barnes. He complained in his "Preface" that his decision to write in standard English in the volume is not "without a misgiving that what I have done for a wider range of readers may win the opinion of fewer."[18] The volume was not a success, and in contrast to his collected edition of dialect poems, which was reprinted in seven editions until 1905, was never reprinted.[19]

Barnes's 1888 version of dialect poems offers a compromise. There is an increased instance of the standardization of dialect in "The Hwomestead a-vell into Hand" in this edition compared to that of the 1844 version.[20] For example, the spelling of "var" (far) in the 1844 version retains "v" for "f" but alters the Dorset "ar" sound for the standard English "or." Similarly, "git" becomes the standard English "get," "cood" becomes "could" and "archets" becomes "orch'ds." The long-vowel spelling "aight" becomes the standard "eight."

One of the main criticisms by Hardy of Barnes's work is his attempt to replicate the phonetic spelling of dialect. In his review of the 1879 edition of *Poems of Rural Life* Hardy asserts:

> The quaint archaic spelling of the original edition puzzled the stranger's eye to an extent with which his industry was unwilling to cope. But by the adop-

tion of a modified style of spelling in the next edition, which has ever since been adhered to, this difficulty was to a great extent removed, and acquaintance has been made far and wide with a writer whose exceptional knowledge of rustic life is as unquestionable as his power to cast memories of that life in beautiful and pleasing form.[21]

This quotation indicates that Hardy viewed dialect as an impediment to understanding, particularly for non-dialect speaking readers. Such an impediment restricts Barnes's readership to a largely dialect-speaking, peripheral audience. Hardy is still of the same opinion in 1918, when in a short piece about Barnes for Thomas Henry Ward's *The English Poets: Selections with Critical Interpretations*, he argues:

> The veil of dialect, through which in a few cases readers have to discern whatever of real poetry there may be in William Barnes, is disconcerting to many, and to some chiefly, one thinks for a superficial reason which has more to do with spelling than with the dialect itself. As long as the spelling of standard English is other than phonetic it is not obvious why the old Wessex language should be phonetic except in a pronouncing dictionary.[22]

Evidently, Hardy considers that the non-phonetic rules of spelling standard English should also be applied to dialect. This stance is justified, especially as Barnes extols the equal validity of dialect with standard English. Hardy uses Barnes's 1879 edition as the copy text for the 1908 *Selected Poems*. His position on the representation of dialect in the quotations cited is reflected in his editorial policy in the *Selected Poems*. Hardy chooses not to restore the text of the "Hwomestead a-vell into Hand" to its 1844 version and uses the 1879 version as his copy text. He also omits stanzas three and four of the original poem for his 1908 *Selected Poems*. This could be due to space constraints of the 1908 volume. However, the content of the omitted stanzas provides a fuller explanation of why Hardy omitted them. In the two stanzas Barnes emphasizes the sense of pride rural laborers have in their work, under the guardianship of a benevolent squire. The laborer contentedly farms his "little patch o' parrick" in all weathers so that "ev'ry stroke o' work we het/ did better over lan's." In omitting these stanzas, Hardy negates Barnes's presentation of an idealized rural past in which the workforce contentedly labors under the eye of a benevolent landlord. Although such a rural society is never likely to have existed, the omission of these stanzas undermines Barnes's concern with the effects of enclosure for "liefers" such as Barnes and Hardy's parents, who rented property and were self-sufficient. Hardy is more interested in raising the profile of Barnes's poetry as lyric poetry in the 1908 volume, shadowing any concern Barnes has with the conditions of the rural working class. This is especially evident in Hardy's renaming of the subdivisions of

Barnes's earlier volumes into "Lyric," "Elegiac," "Descriptive," "Meditative" and "Humorous" poems rather than following the seasonal subdivisions made by Barnes. In doing so, Hardy reduces any connections Barnes has previously made with the pastoral tradition. In his "Preface" to the volume, Hardy compares Barnes to other mainstream poets such as Tennyson, Gray and Collins. Hardy distances Barnes from the "old premeditating singers in dialect" and describes him in the following terms: "Primarily spontaneous he was academic closely after [...] a far remove from the impression of him as the naif and rude bard who sings only because he must."[23] In equating Barnes with these poets Hardy proposes that Barnes is a pastoral poet, but one who resides within the mainstream literary tradition.

Hardy reiterates his view of Barnes's poetry through his reduction of his elder's dialect glossaries in the 1908 text. A full-length glossary is included in the 1844 and 1888 editions, which Hardy reduces to a series of glossaries at the foot of the page in the 1908 edition. Hardy says of the use of such glossaries in his "Preface" to the volume that:

> They are but a sorry substitute for the full significance the original words bear to those who read them without translation and know their delicate ability to express the doings, joys and jests, troubles, sorrows, needs and sicknesses of life in the rural world as elsewhere. The Dorset dialect being—or having been—a tongue and not a corruption, it is the old question over again, that of the translation of poetry, which to the full is admittedly impossible.[24]

Here Hardy identifies the inherent difficulty in translating dialect—that of replicating the essence of the original in the translation without obscuring meaning. This difficulty is identical to that involved in translating between standard languages. Hardy considers dialect glossaries to be more of a hindrance than a help in the translation process since the subtleties of a particular language can easily be lost in translation. The physical act of consulting a glossary distances the reader from the text and disrupts the flow of the poem. Such a disjointed reading is likely to affect the reader's perception of the text and renders the act of reading more arduous. A text which requires greater effort in reading is also likely to bring less enjoyment to the reader, leading to negative judgments of the value of dialect in the work. As Hardy argues, the "veil of dialect" does indeed distort meaning for non-dialect speakers and readers.

In his "Preface," however, Hardy laments the loss of the dialect which he also criticizes. He blames the passing of the 1870 Education Acts which encouraged the education of primary aged school children. The imposition of standard English upon school children leads to the decline in dialect. Hardy asserts:

> Education in the West of England as elsewhere has gone on with its silent and inevitable effacements, reducing the speech of this country to uniformity and obliterating every year many a fine old local word. The process is always the same: the word is ridiculed by the newly taught; it gets into disgrace; it is heard in holes and corners only; it dies; and, worst of all it leaves no synonym.[25]

According to Hardy the subordination of dialect by standard English leads to an impoverishment of the English language, leaving gaps in the language where there is no standard English substitute to replace the dialect word adequately.

Despite his concerns with the demise of dialect, Hardy's editing of Barnes's verse and his stance in the "Preface" indicate that he occupies an ambivalent linguistic position. He recognizes the limitations which dialect poetry imposes upon an understanding of the poem and its associated negative effects such as reducing readership, prompting negative reviews regarding the aesthetic value of the poem and restricting the poem to the periphery. On the other hand, he laments the loss of a language which is most fitted to describe the rural society beloved of himself and Barnes. So how is Hardy's ambivalent linguistic position manifested in his own poetry?

In Hardy's poem "In a Eweleaze near Weatherbury,"[26] included in his first collection of verse *Wessex Poems* (1898), the poet-speaker recalls a past rural dance upon the "leaze" (meadow) where he met and once danced with his lover. The relationship has since failed and the poet-speaker acknowledges that if he approached her again she would "scorn [his] brave endeavour." The poem can also be read as an elegy for a declining rural culture. The poet-speaker's lover is a metaphor for rural culture, and the poet-speaker a returning migrant. He scrutinizes rural culture from a renewed perspective upon his return. "Time" and distance have alienated him from the rural community to which he now returns. However, he attempts to reclaim the culture he has left in a vain hope that time, and implicitly, progress, have stood still. He contends:

> But despite the term as teacher
> I remain as I was then
> In each essential feature
> Of the fantasies of men.

However, in the second stanza, the poet-speaker concedes:

> Yet I note the little chisel
> Of never-napping Time
> Defacing wan and grizzel
> The blazon of my prime.

Although the poet-speaker asserts that given the opportunity he would "still go the world with Beauty" he realizes that a return to earlier rural culture is unrealistic. Memory and migration have alienated him from it to the extent that he neither belongs fully to rural culture nor to the culture he migrated to, and has a ruptured self-identity.

It is interesting that Hardy uses the only two dialect words in the poem, "wan" and "grizzel," to express this cultural and personal alienation. Hardy slips both words virtually unnoticed into the poem amongst the standard-English words. The inclusion of "wan" and "grizzel" indicates that the poet-speaker is not fully divorced from his rural origins. The fusion of dialect and standard English in the poem provides just two examples of linguistic hybridity in Hardy's poetry which suggest a rural society in a state of flux and which endeavors to retain its own identity against increased urbanization. Rural society was undergoing a transitional phase during the nineteenth century, originating in the enclosure of land and increased rural poverty, which by the mid to late 1800s had evolved into an increased migration of rural laborers to towns and cities. Hardy laments this migration and its associated loss of culture in his essay "The Dorsetshire Labourer" (1883). The effects he notes are especially evident in the use of language amongst rural laborers, and in particular, their children. In accordance with his 1908 "Preface," Hardy blames education as a key cause of this loss of dialect: "Having attended the National School they would mix the printed tongue as taught therein with the unwritten, dying Wessex English that they had learnt of their parents, the result of this transitional state of theirs being a composite language without rule or harmony."[27] This subordination of one language to another indicates that an evolution of language occurs over time. Charles Darwin identified the subordination of one language to another to be part of the evolutionary process. He asserted:

> Dominant languages and dialects spread widely, and lead to the gradual extraction of other tongues. A language like a species, when once extinct, never as Sir C Lyell remarks, reappears. The same language never has two birth-places. Distinct languages may be crossed or blended together. We see variability in every tongue, and new words are continually cropping up; but as there is a limit to the powers of the memory, single words, like whole languages, gradually become extinct.[28]

Philologists of the time made similar connections between the evolutionary process and linguistic development. For example, Archibald Sayce asserted in *The Principles of Comparative Philology* (1874) that "language, like the rocks, is strewn with the fossilised wrecks of former conditions of society."[29] Max Müller similarly asserted: "Here, too, the clearly marked lines of different strata seemed almost to challenge attention, and the pulses of former life were still throbbing in the petrified forms imbedded in grammars and dictionaries."[30] There was undoubtedly a marked development of evolutionary theories of language during the nineteenth century; they have been extensively examined by Dennis Taylor in *Hardy's Literary Language and Victorian Philology* (1993).

However, an alternative understanding of linguistic hybridity in Hardy's editorial process and his own poetry is also possible, one in which the rural periphery attempts to reclaim dialect from an increasing colonization by standard English found in the urban center. Bill Ashcroft and others in *The Empire Writes Back* (1994) identify two processes involved in the seizure and replacement of the language of the center by the periphery, namely: (1) the denial of the presence of "English"; (2) the appropriation and reconstitution of the language of the center.[31] The first process involves the rejection of metropolitan power over the dominant language, whilst the second constitutes an appropriation and reconstruction of the language of the center which seizes and remolds the language for new uses. An overtly dialectal approach, such as that employed by Barnes in his poetry, denies the presence of the standard English of the dominant urban center. This position is not necessarily subversive. Barnes's decision to write entirely in dialect does not in itself reclaim peripheral language from the center. Rather, his limited audience, created by the use of dialect, restricts his readership and ensures his poetry remains within the periphery.

Linguistic hybridity in Hardy's poetry and also his standardization of dialect during the editorial process suggests the second stage of cultural reclamation identified by Ashcroft. The appropriation and reconstitution of the colonizer's language occurs where the subjugated people claim the language of the colonizer to bring about social change. The creative impulses which initiate and respond to this act of abrogation produce a linguistic continuum in which overlapping forms of language converge to produce a language and literature which is hybrid in nature. Hardy's poetry and his editorial practice demonstrate the second phase of the reclamative process. His refusal to include lengthy dialect glossaries when editing Barnes's poetry and the inclusion of dialect words amidst the predominantly standard English of his own poetry act as a code of the other which is only decipherable to those with knowledge of dialect. In doing so, Hardy attempts to override the negative effects of the regionalist label upon his own and Barnes's work, and ensures that dialect co-exists as an equally valid language to standard English.

Another way in which the appropriation of language occurs is evident in Barnes's and Hardy's presentations of individual rural characters. Barnes's poem "The Shepherd o' the Farm," first published in his 1844 volume, follows the same dialect conventions found in the poems previously discussed. The poem describes the work of a shepherd, who is contented with his lot and is proud of his work. The first stanza reads:

> I be the shepherd o' the farm:
> An be so proud a-rovèn round
> Wi' my long crook a-thirt my yarm,
> As ef I wer a king a-crownèd.[32]

The 1888 version is revised, and the first stanza reads:

> Oh! I be the shepherd o' the farm,
> Wi' tinklèn bells an' sheep-dogs bark,
> An' wi' my crook a-thirt my eärm,
> Here I do rove below the lark.[33]

The phonetic spelling in this version assumes the increased standardized spelling more than the 1844 version. For example, "yarm" becomes "eärm" and "a-rovèn" becomes "rove." Such standardization continues in stanza two, where "da" becomes "do" and "sheädes" become "shaides." The poem follows the seasonal pattern of the rural year in accordance with the arrangement of the volume as a whole, portraying activities such as lambing, sheep dipping and shearing. Hardy uses the 1888 version as his copy text in the 1908 *Select Poems*.[34]

The shepherd in Barnes's poem lives off the land in harmony with the changing seasons. There is no social rupture in the poem, which reinforces the theme of the continuous rolling of the seasons, suggesting a solid, unchangeable certainty to the shepherd's existence. The shepherd lives an almost sedentary life, the pace of which is reflected in Barnes's choice of language. The shepherd "bide[s] all day" among the sheep, and "Da zit upon the zunny down,/ While shaides o' zummer clouds da vlee/ Wi' silent flight along the groun" (stanza 4). The silent flight of the clouds indicates that even the weather does not disrupt the harmony and tranquility of the scene. The sheepdog also passes a "zultry hour" with his "nose a-stratch'd upon the grass." The busiest time of year for the shepherd, shearing, finds him "at the barn vrom dawn till dark." The shepherd and his farm hands make the most use of the natural light given to them, until the sheep are finally sheared and stamped "wi' maister's mark." The marking of the sheep with the farmer's mark reinforces the social hierarchy of the farm. Once the shearing has been completed, the benevolent master welcomes the shepherd and the rest of the workforce into the farmhouse kitchen for a communal celebration: "Then we da eat, an' drink, an' zing/In maisters's kitchen, til the tun/Wi' merry sounds da shaike an' ring." The social order of the farm, and implicitly of society as a whole, is reinforced and celebrated at the end of the poem. The rural laborer toils happily and subordinately with no apparent ambition to increase his own wealth or improve his own social position. In contrast, the placid pastoral landscape of Barnes's poem undergoes sudden violent change in Hardy's "The Sheep Boy," included in his volume *Human Shows* (1925).[35] "The Sheep Boy" is written in a rising/ falling rhythm of double and triple metrical feet to articulate the crashing waves and storm clouds as a storm heads inland from the sea. The rhythm of the poem is mirrored in Hardy's choice of language. Hardy employs formal standard English to describe the movement of the storm. Words such as "concave," "myriads," "consternation," "demesne" and "flexuous" sound weighty and threatening and have Greek and Latin etymological origins. In contrast are the local, dialect words Hardy chooses— "entroughed," "Draäts-Hollow," "Pokeswell Hills" and "Kite's Hill." In a departure from his usual stance of not including phonetic spelling, Hardy emphasizes the local through the phonetic spelling of "Draäts." The approaching storm is a metaphor for the linguistic colonization of rural dialect by standard English which, as already discussed, increased as the nineteenth century progressed. Such colonization is compounded by the references to Paganism and Christianity in the poem. The shepherd boy notices the sudden flight of the swarming bumblebees and wonders if it is an omen of something to come. The bees instinctively know of the impending storm and take flight. Although the shepherd's natural instincts are not as fine-tuned as those of the bees, he reads and attempts to understand the warning signs of nature. He responds too late as the storm clouds travel "up the vale like the moving pillar of cloud raised by the Israelite." This Biblical reference reinforces the subordination of rural language and folklore by mainstream literary culture and religious belief. The presence of two cultures articulated by two distinct languages or dialects in the poem again indicates the articulation of a linguistic continuum in Hardy's work. Ultimately, the storm subsumes the boy and the landscape he is part of.

In contrast to Barnes's shepherd who acts as an articulator of the status quo upon the pastoral landscape, Hardy's shepherd is an intrinsic part of the landscape. Hardy's shepherd has no more control over his destiny than the subservient shepherd in Barnes's poem. Barnes's shepherd is answerable to the will of his "maister"; Hardy's shepherd is answerable to the destructive forces of nature. Hardy's use of metaphor in the poem allows him to demonstrate graphically one culture's being subsumed by another. The storm leaves nothing uncovered as it rolls "inward," "up" and "over" the vale, engulfing the landscape with its "clammy vapour curls" as it goes, until the entire vale is "folded into those creeping scrolls of white." Hardy's sheep boy is no player with nature; rather nature, like dominant culture, plays upon him.

Neither Barnes nor Hardy's shepherd are given any individuality in the poems. They are both rural types. Barnes's shepherd reinforces the status quo and is apparently happy with his subordinate position. Hardy's shepherd is presented as neither pleased nor otherwise with his position: the reader is not informed. Although Hardy's shepherd has no more independence than Barnes's, he represents the subordination of all cultures to another. Thus the rural voice is not accidental to the Victorian intellectual and philosophical debates of the period, but an inherent part of it. As Darwin argues, all cultures are subject to the incessant forces of cultural selection. Darwin asserts:

> I look at the geological record as a history of the world imperfectly kept, and written in a changing dialect, of this history we possess the last volume alone, relating only to two or three countries. Of this volume, only here and there a short chapter has been preserved; and each word of the slowly-changing language, more or less different in the successive chapters, may represent the forms of life, which are entombed in our consecutive formations, and which falsely appear to have been abruptly introduced.[36]

Although Darwin uses the word dialect as a metaphor for the geological record, an evolution of language is inherent in society. Just as the geological record is "slowly-changing," so also language undergoes gradual change. The poetry of Hardy and Barnes reflects this process of reclamation and abrogation throughout the nineteenth century. The reinforced standardization of Barnes's dialect poetry between the 1844 and 1908 volumes indicates the need to temper his language to accommodate an increasingly urbanized readership as the nineteenth century progressed. In his 1908 edition of Barnes's poetry Hardy attempts to strike a balance between the need to retain the dialect of the original verse whilst ensuring that dialect can be understood by an urban readership. It is a balance which is difficult to strike and one in which some aspects of language will inevitably be lost. In his sensitive editing of Barnes's poetry and in his own work, Hardy achieves this balance, and in doing so pays a poignant tribute to the past while embracing the present.

Notes

1. See, for example, "The Profitable Reading of Fiction" and "Candour in English Fiction," in *Thomas Hardy's Public Voice: The Essays Speeches and Miscellaneous Prose*, ed. Michael Millgate (Oxford: Clarendon Press, 2001), 75–88, 95–102.

2. William Barnes, *Poems of Rural Life in the Dorset Dialect with a Dissertation and Glossary* (London: J. R. Smith, 1844).

3. William Barnes, *The Select Poems of William Barnes*, ed. Thomas Hardy (London: Henry Frowde, 1908).

4. Thomas Hardy, *The Complete Poems*, ed. James Gibson (Basingstoke: Palgrave, 2001).
5. Alan Chedzoy, *William Barnes: The People's Poet* (Stroud: History Press 2010), 16–17.
6. Michael Millgate, *Thomas Hardy: A Biography Revisited* (Oxford: OUP, 2004), 29–56.
7. Chedzoy, *op. cit.*, 17–20.
8. Millgate, *op. cit.*, 30–31.
9. Thomas Hardy, "Dialect in Words" and "Papers of the Manchester Literary Club," in *Thomas Hardy's Public Voice, op. cit.*, 14, 28–29; Dennis Taylor, *Hardy's Literary Language and Victorian Philology* (Oxford: Clarendon Press, 1993), 96–172.
10. See for example Barnes's *TIW, or a View of the Roots and Stems of the English as a Teutonic Tongue* (London: J. R. Smith, 1862).
11. William Barnes, "Foresay" in *An Outline of English Speechcraft* (London: C. Kegan Paul and Co., 1878) (3–6), 4–5.
12. William Barnes, "Preface" in *Poems of Rural Life in the Dorset Dialect* (London: John Russell Smith, 1862), 3–4.
13. *Poems of Rural Life in the Dorset Dialect* (1844), *op. cit.*, 258–260.
14. *Ibid.*, 12.
15. John Clare, *The Shepherd's Calendar: With Village Stories and Other Poems* (London: James Duncan, 1827).
16. Alexander Macmillan, letter to William Barnes (21 October 1864), cited in Chedzoy, *op. cit.*, 166.
17. "*Poems of Rural Life in the Dorset Dialect*—Review" in *The Gentleman's Magazine* (December 1844): 564, http://hdl.handle.net/2027/uc1.31158013256143?urlappend=%3Bseq=587, accessed 18 July 2014.
18. William Barnes, "Preface" in *Poems of Rural Life in Common English* (London: Macmillan and Co., 1868).
19. Chedzoy, *op. cit.*, 169.
20. *Poems of Rural Life in Common English* (1868), *op. cit.*, 164–165.
21. Thomas Hardy, "Review of William Barnes's *Poems of Rural Life in the Dorset Dialect*" in *New Quarterly Magazine* (October 1879), in *Thomas Hardy's Public Voice, op. cit.*, 16–17.
22. *Thomas Hardy's Public Voice, op. cit.*, 389.
23. *The Select Poems of William Barnes, op. cit.*, ix.
24. *Ibid.*, vii–viii.
25. *Ibid.*, iii.
26. *The Complete Poems, op. cit.*, 70–71.
27. *Thomas Hardy's Public Voice, op. cit.*, 40. "The Dorsetshire Labourer" was originally published in *Longman's Magazine* (2 July 1883).
28. Charles Darwin, *The Descent of Man and Selection in Relation to Sex* (London: John Murray, 1883), 90–91.
29. Archibald Sayce, *The Principles of Comparative Philology*, cited by Taylor in *Hardy's Literary Language, op. cit.*, 249.
30. Max Müller, *Chips from a German Workshop* (London: Longmans, 1867–75), vol. 4, 66.

31. Bill Ashcroft, Gareth Griffiths and Helen Tiffin, *The Empire Writes Back: Theory and Practice in Post Colonial Literatures* (London: Routledge, 1994), 38–39.
32. *Poems of Rural Life in the Dorset Dialect* (1844), *op. cit.*, 84–86.
33. William Barnes, *Poems of Rural Life in the Dorset Dialect* (London: Kegan Paul, Trench & Co, 1888), 35–36.
34. Both the 1888 and 1908 editions omit stanza 5 of the 1844 version of the poem.
35. *The Complete Poems, op. cit.*, 789–790.
36. Charles Darwin, *On the Origin of Species*, ed. Gillian Beer (Oxford: Oxford University Press, 2008), 229.

Works Cited

Ashcroft, Bill, Gareth Griffiths and Helen Tiffin. *The Empire Writes Back: Theory and Practice in Post Colonial Literatures.* London: Routledge, 1994.
Barnes, William. *An Outline of English Speechcraft.* London: C. Kegan Paul and Co., 1878.
_____. *Poems of Rural Life in Common English.* London: Macmillan and Co., 1868.
_____. *Poems of Rural Life in the Dorset Dialect.* London: John Russell Smith, 1862.
_____. *Poems of Rural Life in the Dorset Dialect.* London: Kegan Paul, Trench & Co., 1888.
_____. *Poems of Rural Life in the Dorset Dialect with a Dissertation and Glossary.* London: J. R. Smith, 1844.
_____. *The Select Poems of William Barnes.* Ed. Thomas Hardy. London: Henry Frowde, 1908.
_____. *TIW, or a View of the Roots and Stems of the English as a Teutonic Tongue.* London: J. R. Smith, 1862.
Clare, John. *The Shepherd's Calendar: With Village Stories and Other Poems.* London: James Duncan, 1827.
Chedzoy, Alan. *William Barnes: The People's Poet.* Stroud: History Press, 2010.
Darwin, Charles. *The Descent of Man and Selection in Relation to Sex.* London: John Murray, 1883.
_____. *On the Origin of Species.* Ed Gillian Beer. Oxford: Oxford University Press, 2008.
Hardy, Thomas. *The Complete Poems.* Ed. James Gibson. Basingstoke: Palgrave, 2001.
_____. *Thomas Hardy's Public Voice. The Essays, Speeches and Miscellaneous Prose.* Ed. Michael Millgate. Oxford: Clarendon Press, 2001.
Millgate, Michael. *Thomas Hardy: A Biography Revisited.* Oxford: Oxford University Press, 2004.
Müller, Max. *Chips from a German Workshop.* London: Longmans, 1867–75.
"*Poems of Rural Life in the Dorset Dialect*—Review." *The Gentleman's Magazine* (December 1844): 563–576. http://hdl.handle.net/2027/uc1.31158013256143?urlappend=%3Bseq=587. Accessed 18 July 2014.
Taylor, Dennis. *Hardy's Literary Language and Victorian Philology.* Oxford: Clarendon Press, 1993.

Punctuating Voice and Space
CHARLES LOCK

in memoriam Malcolm Beckwith Parkes (1930–2013)

Novelist or poet? To the very end of his life Hardy resented the reputation that his novels had acquired, a reputation that the poetry seemed unable to shake. As late as 4 August 1927, within six months of his death, Hardy responded to an admirer from South Carolina who was "so interested to know that you are now writing poetry": "Your interest in having discovered that I write verse is very gratifying. I have been writing it more than thirty years."[1] Part of the resentment may be due to the suspicion that it was owing to class prejudice: that novelists could engage in social mobility but that poets (with the exception of Keats) were expected to come from a good background, even to have a university degree. And it was his fiction that had enabled Hardy to withdraw from London at the age of 43, to build his home at Max Gate, and from the age of 55, resting on his novels, to devote himself exclusively to poetry.

Though he was appointed in 1921 as Vice-President of the Royal Society of Literature, it is not clear in which year Thomas Hardy was elected a Fellow.[2] There is no record of the occasion, and so—if the custom had even been started by then—no clue as to the implement he used to sign the register: Byron's pen or Dickens's quill. The difference between the two indicates a difference in genre; it also points to a difference in the legibility of the hand.[3] A novelist typically writes more clearly than a poet for a novelist will have learnt to write in the expectation that writing is a skill to be put to use, in the keeping of books, in the clear ordering of contracts and pledges, transactions and instructions. A poet scribbles, writing as it were from above, and from above any sense of professional duty, in large measure indifferent to the difficulties that readers might have: it must be the printer's business to figure it out. The typical poet's education will have put little emphasis on the clarity of the hand. Our assumption that literature is whatever's written elides the fundamental distinction between writing as a prosthesis for voice—the logocentrism of thought, and poetry—and writing as craft, technique, menial, servile, subject to dictation and copying: the very antithesis of thinking, let alone genius. Writer as author or writer as scrivener.

Hardy's is amongst the clearest handwriting of any major English poet. This is not to be wondered at in a writer who had been a novelist first, and who had started out as an architect's assistant. The argument of this essay is that the clarity of Hardy's hand enabled him to do things in poetry that were denied to other poets, innovative things to which, indeed, most of them would have been indifferent. Hardy took control of punctuation in ways that no other poet's hand would have allowed. We do not know exactly when poets started submitting their work in typescript; 1913 marks the year, so defined by Hugh Kenner, of the very first poem to preserve in print evidence that it had been composed on a typewriter: Ezra Pound's "In a Station of the Metro," first printed in *Poetry* in April 1913.[4] The evidence is in the double-spaces between certain words, with even a space between its last word "bough" and the full stop: "bough ." This could never have been effected as a hand-written instruction to the printer, for space in handwriting is arbitrary. That is, not even in proof could a poet insist on such spacing; only typescript measures space, and can make demands of it.

Though he never used a typewriter for the composition of verse, nor for its submission to the publisher, Hardy seems to have taken advantage of the degree of control that printers were, in the light of typescript, prepared to concede to poets, especially in regard to accidentals. Here we shall look at a few of Hardy's adjustments of commas, semi-colons, colons, full stops and hyphens. Marks of punctuation may determine voicing and stress. A hyphen clearly belongs to orthography rather than to punctuation, but we might wonder whether any mark of punctuation does not have more far-reaching effects. That is to say, or merely to leave read but unheard, that punctuation is not just a guide to voicing, as in the properly understood sense of the phrase on the title-page of the King James Bible: "Appointed to be read in churches": "Appointed" here means not "authorized" but "punctuated." Yet punctuation is not entirely in the service of the voice; it has its own visual properties and proprieties, like spelling, which may be apprehended best in silence. We will see (and hear, or not) how some of the greatest poems in English—some of the most passionately "voiced"—achieve their power by graphic signs of slight or even negligible vocal consequence.[5]

There are sound professional reasons why medical doctors should write illegibly. It is not that none of them is able to write well, but rather that they are trained to write in a code—appearing as a scrawl—to which only the pharmacist has the key. Because the prescription is carried by the lay-person from the doctor's surgery to the apothecary, it is important that the message not be intercepted by the one who is both its bearer and its topic. Other professions need not labor under such constraints as must inhibit any doctor with a hand potentially good. Lawyers have always left it to clerks and scriveners to draw up their documents in elegant and unambiguous script. Yet in other professions precision and clarity of writing may be of the utmost importance, for these use skills in excess of a knowledge of orthography and punctuation. A lawyer's clerk cannot be an architect's clerk; only the latter is skilled in geometry and the measurement of spaces and angles.

An architect or an engineer cannot afford to be interpreted erroneously or imprecisely. We need only to think of a draftsman's implements to infer the neatness of text and diagram and blueprint that they will yield.

It is a draftsman who is being described here:

> His hand, a little uncertain and even careless in the very earliest letters, had settled by the beginning of his literary career into a firm, clear, and beautiful script which is always a delight to contemplate and almost always perfectly legible throughout, and which showed scarcely any deterioration even in extreme old age. The spelling, too, in these letters is almost faultless, the punctuation ample and precise, and a full address and date are customarily supplied.[6]

One registers a certain contentment on the editors' part that this disciplined writing should be in their charge. When he had barely turned sixteen Hardy was articled to a local architect to receive instruction "in architectural drawing and surveying."[7] It may not be the decisive factor in choosing the writer to whom you might devote the labor of a lifetime, but after some decades the quality of the handwriting can become an irritation and a burden. Richard Little Purdy and Michael Millgate, introducing in 1978 the first volume of their magisterial edition of Hardy's letters, cannot but confess to their delight in having been dealt such a very good hand.

With such a hand editorial decisions—or rather, indecisions—are reduced to a minimum. There is no need to interpret ambiguous words, nor to record deletions, nor silently to amend misspellings, nor (as some editors do) to leave them tactlessly intact. Nor are there many abbreviations to be expanded or left as is. Can any editor of the letters of any other poet, say Ezra Pound, feel that the job has been accomplished without significant distortion and loss? The facsimiles that are provided in editions of Pound's letters are self-admonishing, self-confessing: this in facsimile is the raw material out of which has been made that, the edited text, which some might call a confection. By contrast, a letter of Thomas Hardy looks much the same in his hand or in print: it is hard to imagine the grounds of any complaint about distortion or loss. Which may be to say that if Purdy and Millgate's edition is justly celebrated as an outstanding editorial achievement, this is in some part due to Hardy himself. Not only to the clarity of his hand but also to the disciplined practice of dating every letter and always giving the full address. Yet it could not be said that Hardy wrote his letters as though he expected them to be published posthumously, even in a scholarly edition. Had he thought they might be printed, he would surely have aspired to the level of interest of the letters of Keats, or Pope, or Cowper, all of which were of course "classics" in Hardy's lifetime. These are letters written with care because they are written by one trained as a draftsman, for whom writing was an educational attainment and clarity a skill as well as a virtue; these letters are overwhelmingly taken up with matters of business and professional concern.

As an architect to a mason, or a draftsman to a contractor, this poet writes not so much for his reader as for his printer. Other poets would treat the printer as mere accidental mediator between them and their readers, or—conceiving print itself as accidental—between their voiced thoughts and their hearers. We may compare Hardy's poetry with that of his near-contemporary Gerard Manley Hopkins, who had good reason to suppose that his poetry might never be printed at all. Hopkins, being very well educated, does not have a clear hand, nor did he leave any final drafts or fair copy for publication. It was largely at the discretion of Robert Bridges that any of Hopkins's poetry was published, and its effect was almost immediately recognized as something extraordinary in the history of English poetry. Had Hopkins himself dealt with printers at the time that he was writing, the years around 1880, we can be fairly confident that none would have tolerated any of those eccentric markings that are now reckoned so characteristic of his work. Had his poetry been issued then it would have been in a corrected and standardized form. Bridges was finally able to publish an edition of Hopkins's verse only thirty years after the poet's death, in 1918: just at the time, that is, when printers and publishers were coming to terms with the exactions demanded by poetry submitted in typescript.

In contrast to Hopkins, Hardy's hand is so precise and careful in the writing of poetry, to the smallest detail, that very little work is called for from editors or printers, and hardly any intervention would be tolerated. And yet for a hundred years it is Hopkins who has been reckoned the major poet whose rhythmical experiments somehow make sense of the otherwise abrupt transition from Browning to Pound. Slowly we are beginning to appreciate

Hardy's part in that movement, not least through Pound's own declared devotion.

> 2 April 1921
>
> Dear Mother,
>   We go back to Paris, presumably next week—mail to go via London.
>   I have had another and longer letter from Thomas Hardy—who has on this evidence managed to read my Propertius" & "H.S.M"—without thinking too badly of them.
>   I continue to play tennis.[8]

This recently published letter by Pound comments on the letter he had just received from Hardy, dated 18 March 1921. Among the longest and surely the most interesting that Hardy ever wrote, this one was, unusually, dictated and typed by a secretary:

> But I am compelled to be brief, and am also compelled to dictate what I do send, as I have just now a weakness of the eyes [...].
>   As to criticising the poems you so kindly sent I am afraid I cannot attempt that without knowing more clearly what you are aiming at. It is to be read only by the select few, I imagine? As I am old-fashioned, and think lucidity a virtue in poetry, as in prose, I am at a disadvantage in criticising recent poets who apparently aim at obscurity. I do not mean that *you* do, but I gather that at least you do not care whether the many understand you or not.[9]

The emphasis in the clause "I do not mean that *you* do" is uncharacteristic: "you" is set in italics, presumably to represent editorially an underlining in the typescript. Hardy would seldom if ever allow himself such an underlining in manuscript. Was this his instruction, or the secretary's own contribution which he allowed to stand? In the light of Kenner's account of Pound it is a most happy coincidence that this letter is not only typewritten but that the medium should visibly modify the message, relaxing the style so that Hardy can indulge in phrasing that strikes us as casual. The letter continues:

> As to the other book "H.S.M.," I don't agree with you at all in thinking it "thin." There is so much packed away in it that it, its racy satire included, can be called very solid indeed by those who really read it. To say that it is not, any more than some other of your poetry, lucid, is as I have stated merely saying that it is not what you don't wish it to be, assuming that I don't misapprehend your aims.[10]

Lucidity is a virtue for Hardy, not only graphically but also in those other aspects of poetry in which readers may be interested: rhythm, for example, or theme. In other aspects however, notably in syntax, Hardy can fall short of lucidity. For some readers the graphic is the most important, and it could be argued that modernism in verse was brought about not by a new metrics, for the rejection of the iambic pentameter was neither convincing nor enduring, but by a new sense of layout. Taking Mallarmé's "Un Coup de Dés" as its starting-point, this is a familiar argument. The importance of the typewriter, noted by Kenner under the influence of Marshall McLuhan, led Faber to set Pound's verse in a font that resembled that of a type-writer, itself a startling editorial innovation, or rather a decision to pretend not to intervene with print but instead to give the illusion of a facsimile of the typescript. If Hardy and Pound had a surprising degree of mutual understanding and respect, it must be because they sensed, though technologically diverse in their means, that they were similarly concerned with the layout of poetry and the look of writing.

In their introduction to Hardy's *Collected Letters* Purdy and Millgate do acknowledge one problem with Hardy's hand, a source of some indecisiveness:

> The only substantial difficulty regularly encountered in transcribing Hardy's holograph is that presented by his habit of forming certain of his initial capitals (especially "c," "d," "m," and "s") in precisely the same manner as the lower-case forms of the same letters. Since it is often impossible to make firm distinctions solely on the basis of the height of the letters—Hardy had a tendency to write the first letter of all his words somewhat larger than the remainder—the editors have, in all doubtful instances, chosen the form most consistent with the context. Whenever Hardy's punctuation has seemed indeterminate (e.g., as between a comma and a period, or a period and a dash), the demands of the context have again weighed heavily in editorial decisions.[11]

These are limited problems: occasional uncertainty over upper-case vs. lower-case, comma or period, period or dash. Whose handwriting dreams of aspiring to such a level of legibility? The clarity of Hardy's hand had immense consequences for his practice as a poet. A poem was normally sent in manuscript to the publisher, to be sub-edited according to house-style, and then sent to a compositor who would set it in print according to the norms of the printing-house. That is how poetry had been printed for about three hundred years. The Poet addresses his readers, and the editors and printers mediate between poet and reader, constrained on the one side by whatever in the manuscript is legible, but licensed on the other side by the demands of the reading and purchasing public: no funny punctuation, or deviant spelling, lest the reader think the editor has failed in his job, or the purchaser reckon he's made a bad bargain. While Pound was fashioning those white spaces that serve as icons of the petals on the wet black printed line of the bough, Hardy was doing his own thing, in the "Poems of 1912–13," poems whose greatness is usually assigned to such causes as a deep emotional state, as though mourning were conducive to art. The greatness of these poems is to be found in their graphic inventiveness and freedoms, and in the constraints that they impose on printers.

Long before 1914, when "Poems of 1912–13" was published in *Satires of Circumstance*, and before the typewriter had applied pressure to the printing of verse, Hardy had been exploiting the authority of his hand and its ungainsayable clarities. When we find a crux in a poem, lexical or semantic, orthographic or syntactic, we are likely to turn elsewhere, to examine the manuscript if it is available or, if not, an earlier printing; we will either re-interpret the text in the light of what we find elsewhere, or in the absence of any other version, we must simply hypothesize a solution. But what if a poet chooses to be incorrect, or at least deviant, and then forecloses the possibility of revision?

Hardy's poetry is notorious for its idiosyncrasies both syntactic and lexical. Might it not be the case that in "Neutral Tones" the impossible syntax of "And some words played between us to and fro/On which lost the more by our love" is quite deliberate? Deliberate, that is, in its oddity, in its incorrectness, in its lack of syntactic focus. We can imagine the printer's eyes going back to the manuscript, hoping to find some other word or other mark of punctuation and in regret and perplexity finding the whole poem written impeccably and unambiguously. There are revisions at proof stage: a comma was added at the end of the first line, and "withered" was replaced by "starving." The last line in the manuscript had read:

> And a pond, edged with grayish leaves.

The removal of the comma effects a minor transformation:

> And a pond edged with grayish leaves.

Only when the comma is removed can we hear in the line a word sensed clearly enough though it cannot be seen: dead.[12]

The manuscript also shows that the phrase "lost the more" was inserted at proof, replacing "was more wrecked." It would be easy to suppose that "lost the more" ought to have replaced "was more wrecked by," leaving the line a syllable short but syntactically coherent: "on which was more wrecked/ lost the more/ our love." It is the "by" that is the problem, yet Hardy has done nothing about it. He leaves traces of his worries over each comma, but displays no concern for the word that to readers is an offending word. And Hardy leaves the printer, and all subsequent editors, without recourse to an earlier version. One has often heard critics lament that Hardy as poet never found a good editor; the trouble is that few poets have ever been so meticulous as Hardy in their revisions and proof-readings.

In "The Darkling Thrush," "outleant" is impossible as a past participle: "the Century's corpse outleant." Yet is it not quite purposefully impossible? There is another comma-removal at proof, of those which had twice interrupted the line: "Was shrunken, hard, and dry." Their deletion is exquisitely judged. The last comma remains, to enforce the line-ending before the conjunction: "dry,/ And every spirit upon earth." Another instance of graphic delicacy yielding aural subtlety is the insertion, at proof, of the hyphen in "goodnight": "His happy good-night air," where the hyphen invites a slightly longer stay on "good." And yet, with all this astonishing subtlety in the evidence of the manuscript, the word "outleant" has quite eluded the poet's notice.

Hardy thus seems to show acute sensitivity to accidentals while letting the substantives take care of themselves. Might these moments in Hardy's poetry, these awkwardnesses, like a snag in the river, be precisely what was ordered, and that could be ordered only by the most precise means? These should not be regarded as lapses in good taste, the rather embarrassing reachings for sophistication of one who was, after all, a mere autodidact; no, they are moments of defiance enacted in the name of poetry by a masterdraftsman. Such moments address themselves first to editors and compositors; and they defy them to alter anything at all. Hardy knows such phrases are incorrect, or at least subject to "improvement," but it is wrongness alone that can provoke the power of others to amend and heal. The poet here asserts an astonishing sovereignty over his text, and makes unprecedented claims about what a poet can do with the English language. In his quiet way, Hardy is just as untrammeled by the conventions as is Hopkins.

It has been remarked that the two most inventive of English poets, in diversity of stanza-forms, are George Herbert and Thomas Hardy. Both of them are of course inspired by the church as a built structure, and by church monuments as shaped and built inscriptions. There is a thematic coherence between Herbert's shaping of stanzas and the figure of the church; a similar thematic coherence can be supposed in the link between Hardy's interest in graveyards and those nine hundred poems, almost all of which can be set on a single page, or could be incised on a tombstone. Yet there's a further connection. Herbert was not writing for the press, and never saw his poems in print. He was working within a residual manuscript culture that was influenced by the emerging print culture. Once that print culture had become dominant, it insisted on certain practices, one of which appears to have been a limited repertory of stanza forms. Printers make their demands, and they like to stick to their own practices, that which will emerge as house-style, a term whose earliest occurrence according to the *OED* is as late as 1905. Given the massive influence and control exercised by printers, it should not be cause of wonder that from c.1700 to c.1900 the great English poets are characterized by an extreme uniformity of lay-out: blank verse, rhyming couplet, or the indefinite repetition of a single stanza form. Very few poems in those centuries display a variety of stanza forms within one poem.

In 1911, when Hardy's wife died, the most celebrated modern elegy was Tennyson's "In Memoriam":

> But, for the unquiet heart and brain,
> A use in measured language lies;
> The sad mechanic exercise,
> Like dull narcotics, numbing pain.
>
> In words, like weeds, I'll wrap me o'er,
> Like coarsest clothes against the cold;
> But that large grief which these enfold
> Is given outline and no more.[13]

And each stanza (of which "In Memoriam" contains more than seven hundred) provides the very same outline. Hardy's "Poems of 1912–13" are problematic because in terms of layout they are not coherent; should we speak of them as a sequence? No, because they can be read in any order, and if read in the order printed lead to no narrative, thematic, argumentative or "poetic" resolution. But had they all shared one stanza-form, there would inevitably be at least a visual and metrical sense of unity and sequence. Each of the "Poems of 1912–13" resists the printed constraint that would give to the poet's grief "outline and no more." Hardy's "set" is more like a collection of gravestones haphazardly arranged: diverse orders commissioned and executed by a number of stone-masons without regard for the look of the churchyard as a whole.

If one is to create within one poem a variety of stanzas the poet needs to deploy an authoritative instrument of measure. Exact proportions need to be conveyed to the compositor if the poet is to insist on the peculiar identity of each stanza, and to resist the assimilative and coercively homogenizing practices of the print-shop. Such is demanded of the printing of the alternated stanzas in "The Going"; of the utterly irregular indentation of "Rain on a Grave," where each stanza has nine lines, of which four or five or six are indented, and none according to a pattern; "Without Ceremony," two stanzas of six lines followed by one of five; "The Voice" with its short-measured coda. Those are the poems with unequal stanzas; of all twenty-one poems in the "sequence" no two follow the same stanzaic pattern. The contrast with "In Memoriam" is striking, and deliberate. Here each poem has its own outline, and some have more than one. Far from exhibiting "outline and no more" each of Hardy's poems works through and by its own outline, than which, we might add, nothing more could be wished for.

As with Donne or Herbert or Vaughan, who set the pattern of Hardy's love of stanzaic variation, there is an inevitable iconicity in the layout of each poem, from the spatteringly unpredictable indentations of "Rain on a Grave" to the blocked marmoreal solidity of "Without Ceremony," each of whose five-line stanzas forms a near-square. Hardy's readers would at once acknowledge the importance of punctuation to poetry; they should be attentive also to its absences, and to all the white spaces. Dennis Taylor draws our attention to Henry Newbolt's words, read by Hardy in 1925: "In reading poetry we are frequently aware that every stanza-form has a mood-creating or thought-compelling power of its own."[14] Within the stanza we might think of enjambment as a sort of invisible punctuation: marked by being unmarked. If it were entirely unmarked why would we need the term "enjambment" at all? Enjambment draws the ear to the next line, while it leads the eye into the white spaces that surround the poem, those spaces against which we figure the shape of a stanza and measure visually the length of a line. The white spaces around a poem could thus be conceived as punctuation: to be more explicit, as additional punctuational resources available only to a draftsman. Expressed conversely, the entire print-area of the page could be seen as a punctuation of whiteness: letters looming out of the mist, presumably in a graveyard.

"Whenever Hardy's punctuation has seemed indeterminate," so write Purdy and Millgate. Yet punctuation is in its very constitution and purpose ambiguous, not least in poetry. Does the depth of indentation, or the extent of the margin, have any bearing on poetry? Might this not also be treated as punctuation? Accidental by printing conventions, but to some, such as Hardy and Pound, of poetry's very substance. M. B. Parkes observes:

> The difference between the signification of punctuation in verse and in other kinds of written discourse is simply one of degree rather than one of kind. The poet and the novelist have been able to exploit punctuation successfully for local effect, because they could rely on their readers' experience of existing conventions in other less ambitious writings. But such exploitation could extend the range of usage too, since it also depended on a fundamental characteristic of punctuation in general: that, apart from registering a degree of disjunction, few punctuational symbols have a precise value or exclusive specifying function.[15]

It is because punctuational symbols are so uncertain of purpose that they can be treated with indifference, and regarded even by textual scholars as "accidentals." Many editors of old poets silently emend the punctuation, as though it were not part of the poetical work but more like the paper or the print that brings it to the reader. And of course it is, in the sense that editors and compositors were largely in control of punctuation, as they were also of spelling and the use of upper-case line-initials. Most readers today will have first encountered Emily Dickinson as the poet of dashes, thanks to the editorial scruples of Thomas H. Johnson whose edition of 1955 took as its premise that the dashes in her manuscript are significant and should be represented in print. Others have argued that those dashes are deliberately unspecified marks of punctuation, to be determined by the printer. This could have been normal scribal practice where the printer would ensure that all punctuation conformed to house-rules; the more we understand of the relationship between copy-text and print, the less conviction Johnson's editorial principles seem to carry. We may suppose, as with Hopkins, that had Dickinson herself had to deal with a publisher, her poetry would have been printed in a much less strikingly idiosyncratic form.

Most poets have had insufficiently clear hands to determine their own punctuation; Hardy's hand gives him the authority to shape his stanzas, to give shape to the space around. It is the poetry of a draftsman, and Pound with his typewriter recognized at once the importance of Hardy's example.

There are three commas of particular interest in "The Voice"; two of them were added at proof, one was deleted. The voice is of course entirely independent of punctuation, though the text is rendered legible only by what Parkes elegantly terms "degrees of disjunction":

The Voice

Woman much missed, how you call to me, call to me,
Saying that now you are not as you were
When you had changed from the one who was all to me,
But as at first, when our day was fair.

Can it be you that I hear? Let me view you, then,
Standing as when I drew near to the town
Where you would wait for me: yes, as I knew you then,
Even to the original air-blue gown!

Or is it only the breeze, in its listlessness
Travelling across the wet mead to me here,
You being ever dissolved to wan wistlessness,
Heard no more again far or near?

Thus I; faltering forward,
Leaves around me falling,
Wind oozing thin through the thorn from norward,
And the woman calling.[16]

The two added commas are in lines 5 and 15. The first subtly disrupts the line and forestalls a hudibrastic rhyme: "Let me view you, then" is sublimely noncoincident with "as I knew you then." Moreover, a comma cannot be added in the corresponding place in the other line: "Let me view you then" cannot be read: "as I knew you, then." That is because "then" is used in two senses, the one a demonstrative temporal adverb, the other (*OED* "then" 4A) a conditional correlative conjunction responding to an implied "if so." Would we notice those two quite distinct senses of "then" had it not been for the comma, inserted only at proof? The other inserted comma follows "norward," and delays or obstructs the work of conjunction: "norward, and the woman calling" makes distinct the three terms of his awareness which may also be his identity, or that of the voice, whether his or hers: the leaves, the wind, the woman.

The full force of this poem rests on a brilliantly executed punctuational modification, deleting a comma after "I" and inserting not what would seem obvious, a colon, but a semi-colon: "Thus I;". Geoffrey Hill finds a notable semi-colon in Hopkins, one that disjoins or even sunders the last two words of the sonnet that begins "I wake and feel the fell of dark":

> As I am mine, their sweating selves; but worse.

Hill comments: "The semi-colon, here, is at once recognition, fact, and value."[17] That is an exorbitant claim to make for a mere accidental, yet it would fit as well the case for the work done by the semi-colon that follows "I" in "The Voice":

> Thus I; faltering forward

For those who seldom notice the difference between a colon and a semi-colon the finer pleasures of Hardy's verse are still to be realized. Novelist or poet? Foremost, a draftsman. Let us return to that typewritten letter to Ezra Pound of 1921, in which Hardy elaborates on his apology for having to resort to dictation:

> a weakness of the eyes which I sometimes suffer from though perhaps not oftener than can be expected for one who has used his so cruelly as I have used mine during a long lifetime.[18]

Notes

1. Thomas Hardy, *Collected Letters of Thomas Hardy, Volume Eight: Further Letters 1861–1927*, ed. M. Millgate & K. Wilson (Oxford: Clarendon Press, 2012), 276 (letter to Mrs O. L. Keith).
2. That he "had long been a fellow" we learn in the note to Hardy's letter to W. H. Wagstaff, Secretary of the RSL, 14 June 1921, *Collected Letters: Volume Six 1920–25*, eds. Richard Little Purdy and Michael Millgate (Oxford: Clarendon Press, 1987), 91;

and Thomas Hardy, *Thomas Hardy's Public Voice. The Essays, Speeches, and Miscellaneous Prose*, ed. Michael Millgate (Oxford: Clarendon Press, 2001), 375 (1916.08).

3. The ramifications of choice of implement for signing the register of the Royal Society of Literature are traced by Philip Hensher in and throughout *The Missing Ink: The Lost Art of Handwriting* (London: Macmillan, 2012). Hensher notes the legibility of Dickens's hand; Robert Douglas-Fairhurst in *Becoming Dickens: The Invention of a Novelist* (Cambridge, MA: Harvard University Belknap Press, 2011) brings out Dickens's fascination with handwriting, and with clerks.

4. Hugh Kenner, *The Pound Era* (London: Faber and Faber, 1972), 197; Charles Lock, "Beside the Point: A Diligence of Accidentals" in *Geoffrey Hill and His Contexts*, eds. Piers Pennington and Matthew Sperling (Oxford: Peter Lang, 2011), 48.

5. This essay thus extends the argument put forward in Charles Lock, "Inhibiting the Voice: Thomas Hardy and Modern Poetics" in *A Companion to Thomas Hardy*, ed. Keith Wilson (Wiley-Blackwell, 2009), 450–464.

6. *Collected Letters: Volume One 1840–1892*, eds. Richard Little Purdy and Michael Millgate (Oxford: Clarendon Press, 1978), xv.

7. Michael Millgate, *Thomas Hardy: A Biography Revisited* (Oxford: Oxford University Press, 2004), 55.

8. Ezra Pound, *Ezra Pound to his Parents: Letters 1895–1929*, ed. Mary de Rachewiltz et al. (Oxford: Oxford University Press, 2010), 481–482.

9. *Collected Letters: Volume Six 1920–1925*, op. cit., 77 (letter to Ezra Pound, 18 March 1921); of all the thousands of Hardy's letters this may be unique in its then very unusual style of address: "Dear Ezra Pound."

10. Ibid.

11. *Collected Letters: Volume One 1840–1892*, op. cit., xv-xvi.

12. For manuscript readings see Thomas Hardy, *The Complete Poems: Variorum Edition*, ed. James Gibson (London: Macmillan, 1979).

13. Alfred Lord Tennyson, "In Memoriam A. H. H." (1849), section V. *Selected Poems*, ed. Christopher Ricks (London: Penguin Books, 2007), 100.

14. Dennis Taylor, *Hardy's Metres and Victorian Prosody* (Oxford: Clarendon Press, 1988), 189.

15. M. B. Parkes, *Pause and Effect: An Introduction to the History of Punctuation in the West* (Aldershot: Scolar, 1992), 114.

16. *The Complete Poems*, op. cit., 346.

17. Geoffrey Hill, *Collected Critical Writings*, ed. Kenneth Haynes (Oxford: Oxford University Press, 2008), 393.

18. *Collected Letters: Volume Six 1920–1925*, op. cit., 77. See above, note 9.

Works Cited

Douglas-Fairhurst, Robert. *Becoming Dickens: The Invention of a Novelist*. Cambridge, MA: Harvard University Belknap Press, 2011.

Hardy, Thomas. *Collected Letters, Volume One 1840–1892*. Eds. Richard Little Purdy and Michael Millgate. Oxford: Clarendon Press, 1978.

———. *Collected Letters, Volume Six 1920–1925*. Eds. Richard Little Purdy and Michael Millgate. Oxford: Clarendon Press, 1987.

_____. *Collected Letters, Volume Eight: Further Letters 1861–1927*. Eds. Michael Millgate and Keith Wilson. Oxford: Clarendon Press, 2012.

_____. *The Complete Poems: Variorum Edition*. Ed. James Gibson. London: Macmillan, 1979.

_____. *Thomas Hardy's Public Voice. The Essays, Speeches, and Miscellaneous Prose*. Ed. Michael Millgate. Oxford: Clarendon Press, 2001.

Hensher, Philip. *The Missing Ink: The Lost Art of Handwriting*. London: Macmillan, 2012.

Hill, Geoffrey. *Collected Critical Writings*. Ed. Kenneth Haynes. Oxford: Oxford University Press, 2008.

Kenner, Hugh. *The Pound Era*. London: Faber and Faber, 1972.

Lock, Charles. "Beside the Point: A Diligence of Accidentals," in *Geoffrey Hill and His Contexts*, eds. P. Pennington and M. Sperling. Oxford: Peter Lang, 2011, 43–60.

_____. "Inhibiting the Voice: Thomas Hardy and Modern Poetics," in *A Companion to Thomas Hardy*, ed. Keith Wilson. Chichester: Wiley-Blackwell, 2009, 450–64.

Millgate, Michael. *Thomas Hardy: A Biography Revisited*. Oxford: Oxford University Press, 2004.

Parkes, M. B.. *Pause and Effect: An Introduction to the History of Punctuation in the West*. Aldershot: Scolar, 1992.

Pound, Ezra. *Ezra Pound to His Parents: Letters 1895–1929*. Ed. Mary de Rachewiltz et al. Oxford: Oxford University Press, 2010.

Taylor, Dennis. *Hardy's Metres and Victorian Prosody*. Oxford: Clarendon Press, 1988.

Tennyson, Alfred, Baron. *Selected Poems*. Ed. Christopher Ricks. London: Penguin Books, 2007.

Epilogue
The Transcendence of Things Seen
Michael Edwards

1

What do we *see* when reading a Hardy poem? What do we see when looking at the world he looked at? These are the things I want to "talk quietly and inconclusively" about, given their great importance and the difficulty of deciding. The phrase is Randall Jarrell's in the final essay of his lastingly important *Poetry and the Age*[1]; I hope to bear it in mind in trying to learn something about Hardy's poetry, something about poetry, and something about living.

We inhabit a visible world in which our mind sees, continuously, an invisible, with components too numerous to name: recurrence, darkness, Spring, mockery or love in someone's eyes—palpable abstractions which seem most certainly to be there; "calm" hills, "lowering" clouds, which are the result either of our forcing ourselves on the world or of the world's real involvement with us. We unceasingly transcend the visible, or the visible opens unceasingly onto the invisible, and the problem, as we know—the fundamental problem, a matter, literally and without exaggeration, of life or death—, is to decide whether this transcendence is entirely human and, as we say, natural, or whether the real transcends, "climbs beyond," itself into the supernatural, the divine. In deciding that nothing transcends what is discovered by our chosen organs and methods of research, and that the sense of God, of an afterlife, of a larger world pervading the one we see, is an unhappy aberration of evolution, ours is the first civilization to sink below all the others in denying, often with polemical glee, the presence of what transcends us. Hardy, we know, though suffering basically the same pressures as ourselves, and without certainty, refused to go along with that particular sway of the world.

But what has this to do with poetry? Language is involved, from early on, in this searching of the visible. Whether considered as a poor substitute for the wordless intuitive knowing of the infant once lost, or as the reaching across to the world it meets of a consciousness properly and simultaneously aware of itself and of an otherness to which it must attend, words fathom the invisible. "Man," "form," "color," "whiteness," lead into a world of abstraction inseparable from the equally abstract yet at the same time individually present "men" and "forms" and "colors" among which we move. Words as names are doors to the invisible: "field" or "wall" not only add their arbitrary and therefore singularly suggestive sounds, they change, if we take note, what we are looking at, they introduce us not merely to the idea of field or wall applicable in Dorset or China, in Weymouth or New York, but to what is latent in *this* field over the hedge, in *this* wall one walks alongside. To say "tree," or "birch" (knowing perfectly that in any other language we'd say something else) allows us to *see* in such natural presences our relation to them and the invisible that illumines them. The word "landscape" gathers a multiplicity of things visible into a visible and invisible unity; the word "countryside" performs the same task while moving closer both to what is there and to our feeling for it.

Naming is an uncanny business. As soon as we learn the names of things—and children also invent names of their own for what affects them particularly—the world changes, everything stirs with sound and takes on, or reveals, a new depth. Language is an initiation, and a lifelong rite of passage. According to the author of the opening of *Genesis*, the word of God was (to use our distinctions) both verb: "And God said, Let there be light: and there was light," and noun: "And God called the light Day." Our names operate like verbs, in that they too bring something into being: in the thing named they place a human presence and they discern an intrinsic unknown. When Adam names in the same story, as well as adding a human perspective and relationship he presumably sees entirely the being of what is before him, and especially its inherent divinity. Our naming cannot achieve that, but it does conduct us into a further apprehension of the thing named, where we may explore the kind of transcendence that we think we find. It is not easy to see this in terms of individual words, since we are not used to saying them reflectively and pausing on them. Poetry, which invites us to pause and which names the world and our experience of the world by words in new combinations and associations, shows us reality changing and revealing its complexity. The words of poetry also are "doors of perception," and they too need to be cleansed.

2

I turn now to Hardy, not as someone to test a theory on or to quote in support but because a certain direction in these thoughts resulted from reading him, and because, when it comes to transcendence and to the sublimity implied, he has a persuasively low-keyed way of proceeding. The title of his fourth collection, *Moments of Vision and Miscellaneous Verses*, underlines the lack of cohesion which he points to in each of his prefaces, but above all highlights, as nowhere else, visions that came to him as undeniable experience. *Moments of Vision* affirms their importance; *Miscellaneous Verses* retains them on this side of pretentiousness and places their possible elevation in the ordinary disorderedness of living.

The many visions in the book are all, quite clearly, vulnerable, and they are mostly questioned. Is Hardy clutching at straws, or honestly following genuine hints? In "A Kiss,"[2] a particular kiss, presumably at the origin of a long relationship, while nowhere to be found at the place where it occurred is imagined pursuing its flight, "Travelling aethereal rounds/ Far from earth's bounds/ In the infinite." How odd, and yet how well this corresponds to an obscure sense that whatever truly matters cannot surely, or must not, disappear; that the *quality* of an event suggests in itself that it belongs already to a higher world and continues in something like "aethereal rounds," through an "infinite" which in the poem's close surpasses the mere immensity of space. And the poem is unusually affirmative: "It cannot have died; that know we well." "The Occultation"[3] surprises even more. A cloud darkening the sun reminds the speaker of a joy likewise quenched many years before; the fact that the sun continues to shine above the clouds prompts him to wonder if his feeling of joy also continued to exist, somewhere beyond the known. Paraphrased, the poem becomes barely plausible, for the suasion resides in the poetry:

> But day continued its lustrous roll
> In upper air;
> And did my late irradiate soul
> Live on somewhere?

Imagination links an upper world illuminated into joy by the sun and a soul irradiated by the joy of a spiritual light; poetic language enforces the realization—quite unmystical, and yet rarely occurring to us—that beyond the clouds is always perfect sunshine, by renewing the thought through an arresting combination of words. The hint of transcendence lies less in the final explicit question than in the sequence "day continued its lustrous roll/ In upper air," which transfigures the turning of the earth in sunlight to the point where the natural half-transcends itself.

As insinuations of otherness, a kiss and a former mood continuing in existence are peculiarly fragile—and not what anyone would much refer to in trying to help Hardy rediscover the Christian faith he had lost. The same can be said of "The Shadow on the Stone,"[4] where the speaker sees the shadow of a tree on a large stone resemble the head and shoulders of a woman who has died, and refuses to face about and verify that nobody is there. The strong feeling in the poem passes through his unwillingness to know, his more than half-certainty that no ghost is present: "to keep down grief/ I would not turn my head to discover/ That there was nothing in my belief," his lingering hope that he is mistaken: "I'll not unvision/ A shape which, somehow, there may be," and his sad ambiguous thought on moving away: "And left her behind me throwing her shade,/ As she were indeed an apparition— / My head unturned lest my dream should fade." I suppose it's the obstinate hesitation of the poem that makes it moving (as does the knowledge that the man and the woman are, also, Hardy and Emma), along with the reluctance to "unvision" a possible shape—a verb whose invention so appropriately defines Hardy's fear in this poem and in his whole life. And once again the actual glimpse of otherness is slightly off-center, not in the cast shadow but in the opening lines: "I went by the Druid stone/ That broods in the garden white and lone." The words take us elsewhere, or further in, not simply "Druid" with its obvious associations but "stone," which becomes a sudden presence, and not only "broods" and "lone" with their implication of personality but "white," which goes, in the context, so far beyond description.

The hope that troubles and hurts Hardy is not so much that Emma might appear as a ghost as that, in the manner of a kiss or a former joy, being dead she may "live on somewhere." What of other poems where Hardy feels for his old faith? The title poem, "Moments of Vision,"[5] asks who holds the mirror that reveals us to ourselves, that startles us with a self-knowledge to which we never attain when ordinarily awake. We see in it essentially our guilt, though the word doesn't occur: it "tests" us when unaware, its "magic penetrates like a dart." The phrase, as so many in Hardy, gives the impression of the poet stepping almost by chance into a weird and perfect articulacy on this side of eloquence: the "dart," the pain of seeing oneself, jars aptly with the usual associations of "magic," and "magic," a word as far from the *ayenbite of inwit* as from the searchings of psychoanalysis, expresses truthfully Hardy's questioning sense of the otherness that insists on reaching us. *Moments of Vision* is introduced by the disquieting strangeness of a poem ceaselessly interrogative, and which ends by reflecting that such a mirror could catch a person's last thoughts before death and so his whole life, and "glass" it in some transcendent elsewhere—but "where?"

That apprehension of another, time-free world recurs in poems where once again the real work of poetry lies in unexpected, unstressed places, where an apparent description discloses in the ordinary an inexplicable other dimension."Apostrophe to an Old Psalm Tune"[6] recounts the persistent returning over the years of a hymn met with first when a boy and "full of wonder." The conceit which presents the musician playing the tune as the "raiser" who "evoked" it prepares the moment when a new "stirrer of tones" calls up the tune,

> And wakes your speech, as she of Endor did
> (When sought by Saul who, in disguises hid,
>   Fell down on the earth to hear it)
>   Samuel's spirit.

The hyperbolic comparison and the delaying of the final words so as to make the sudden appearing of Samuel's spirit all the more awesome and real prepare the equally hyperbolic ending, where the hymn tune, which still lives on, might live "onward, maybe,/ Till Doom's great day be!" (In having the tune speak to him "as" Samuel spoke to Saul, Hardy seems drawn to a story he will disparage in the preface to *Late Lyrics and Earlier*, when mocking the belief, in a Darwinian age, "in witches of Endor."[7]) However, the passage between a haunting psalm tune and the possible existence of the divine world to which its words refer seems more clearly felt in a quite different passage where, hearing the tune as an adult, Hardy writes that it spread over him like a gauze, "And flapped from floor to rafters,/ Sweet as angels' laughters." "Flapped" is both an inelegant and unassuming word to suggest music moving rhythmically around one and a suggestion of wings rising. Above all, how fine of Hardy not to have written what any minor poet could have managed: "rafter" and "laughter" in the singular! By avoiding "rafter" as a synecdoche for "roof," he places the presentiment of another world in the actuality of this one, in the reality of individual rafters. By not writing of angels' laughter in general but of their particular and many "laughters," and by choosing a plural that surprises, he draws himself and his reader into an unknown world made possible by its likeness to ours, by its recurring profusion. If he only mentions his wonder when an "innocent" child, he allows it to return, here as elsewhere, in the age of experience.

"The Oxen"[8] can seem an "anthology piece" as defined by Donald Davie in *Thomas Hardy and British Poetry*: "a poem which, whether by luck or design, and whatever its other virtues, cannot give offence" (Davie thought of it as such a piece, along with "The Darkling Thrush").[9] It's true that, reading of his earlier belief that at midnight on Christmas Eve the oxen were on their knees and of his willingness even now to go "in the gloom,/ Hoping it might be so," one asks why he chose that sentimental image of the Nativity, that piece of para-Christian folklore that no one is required to believe. Perhaps as a rather desperate sign of transcendence proved, of another world visibly intervening. Yet, against all the odds, the poem is moving, no doubt because of Hardy's skill as a narrator, and because of the simple reality of the "meek mild creatures where/ They dwelt in their strawy pen." (The writing is far from naive: the oxen are both alien in their "strawy pen" and like us in their "dwelling" and in their recall of the Wesley hymn beginning "Gentle Jesus, meek and mild.") And doesn't mystery impress itself on the mind most forcibly to the side of what seems essential, in the words: "Come; see the oxen kneel// In the lonely barton by yonder coomb"? By naming in this way a farmyard and a hollow, by choosing an unfamiliar word (barton) which makes the countryside strange even without the miracle, by saying "yonder" as if we were at once present and aware of the farness, the unaccountable beyondness, of the place to which one might journey—, by all this Hardy renews the common countryside and opens the real to its own otherness. The sounds of the line and its four-stressed rhythm: "In the lonely barton by yonder coomb," quietly transfigure the imaginary seen.

3

All readers recognize these two features of Hardy's poetry: the exactitude with which he names facets, often quite small, of the world about him and a troubled reaching for transcendence. The relation between the two may be that the least uncertain sense of transcendence arises precisely from a response to these sharply focused particulars. The opening of "Afterwards,"[10] the final poem of *Moments of Vision*, surprises, once one listens to it: "When the Present has latched its postern behind my tremulous stay.""Latched its postern," so much closer to the details of the event and to the objects than, say, "closed its back door," also draws one near to the humble and familiar imagined reality by filling the mouth with consonants and focusing the voice. And why the Present, rather than the more logical Future? No doubt (one understands later on) so as to indicate the continually renewed present of the world still in being after Hardy's death, a world tirelessly contemplated while here and loved. Hardy also has the advantage of the English language where, in a temporal clause, one uses the present or perfect tense of the verb, projecting oneself into the future as into the present which it will have become. He deserves the gift by his self-effacement; the next line: "And the May month flaps its glad green leaves like wings," turns immediately from his death not to the indifferent or cruel nature found in other writings but to a non-human joy existing, beyond our response to Spring, in Spring itself. His comparisons—the leaves "like wings" and, in the following line, "Delicate-filmed as new-spun silk"—, rather than recognizing affinities in the search for a coherent whole, enable him to see more clearly and to say more accurately what he perceives. The intricate linking of vowels and consonants in "flaps its glad green leaves like..." has nothing to do with virtuosity and all to do with the gladness to which the words themselves respond while evoking it.

For the poem, as we know, is about noticing: "will the neighbours say,/ 'He was a man who used to notice such things'?" And "noticing" is an agreeably modest way of naming an intent and unwearied openness to the world about one, a poetic capacity to see far into the living otherness always present. What he then notices could well be taken, by readers ambitious for poetry, as trifling:

> If it be in the dusk when, like an eyelid's soundless blink,
>   The dewfall-hawk comes crossing the shades to alight
> Upon the wind-warped upland thorn [...]

Reading the lines carefully one hears how sensitive a musician Hardy is. And the details serve not to identify the species of the insect and of the bush and the latter's position but to plumb Hardy's response to the nice precision of the tiny event in the largeness of the evening. Think of what is gained by writing "upon" the thorn rather than "on," and "in the dusk" rather than "at dusk"; of the way the hawk-moth and its world become one in the Germanic compaction of "dewfall-hawk"; of the audible silence in "an eyelid's soundless blink." Thinking of his death, Hardy does not wish to become part of nature (like Edward King in Milton's "Lycidas" or Keats in Shelley's "Adonais"): he celebrates the autonomous life of nature and hopes to be present in the gift he will have left his readers, the gift of attention.

And what of his "noticing" a hedgehog? "If I pass during some nocturnal blackness, mothy and warm,/ When the hedgehog travels furtively over the lawn [...]." Can a poet simply describe a hedgehog walking across a garden? (In France one sometimes has to explain that Hardy's poems *are* poems.) Should we be embarrassed for him? Or for ourselves, going on about a hedgehog when we might be writing eloquently of another poet's tiger, or nightingale, or mountain, or "great-rooted blossomer"? If I try to recall that second line I may hear: "When the furtive hedgehog crosses the lawn," or "When the hedgehog furtively crosses the lawn." In writing: "When the hedgehog travels furtively over the lawn," Hardy gets closer, word by word, to the timid animal, he enters, by the subtlety of the rhythm, its movement as it ventures—"travels"—into a wide obscurity, and he makes of the insistent alliterations not a figure of style, an ornament added to the meaning, a mark of the poet's skill, but the progressive steps by which his mind meets the quiddity of the moving animal, and the means of discovering and perfecting an experience. (Will they say of readers of Hardy that we noticed such things?) If one catches the current of feeling running through the poem, one realizes that the more exactly the language of poetry (or of English poetry) names a visible world and renews it in sounds and rhythms, the more that world becomes unfamiliar. One is only, apparently, looking at a hedgehog, as just before at a moth, and yet.... In quite what world do they move? What presence, infinite, or transcendent, or divine, appears in their appearing?

And the poem gradually delves further, stanza by stanza. Hardy "notices," then finds certain sights "familiar," and then, when the neighbors consider the stars, is said to have had "an eye for such mysteries." He imagines his neighbors hearing of his death, standing at the door and "Watching the full-starred heavens that winter sees." Spring has given way to winter, the day has passed from morning or afternoon to dusk, to night in the garden and now to the night sky, where the light of the stars invites one to look up. Hardy has "an eye for" what doesn't meet the eye, for what he calls in a note on landscape painting the "half hidden," "the deeper reality underlying the scenic,"[11] and for the thought that winter itself "sees" the full-starred heavens, not through a poetic trick of personification but, as with the "glad" leaves of May, because Nature is felt as more than mere matter in time and space—as, somehow, a living creature.

Hence at once the climactic nature and the reticence of the closing stanza:

> And will any say when my bell of quittance is heard in the gloom,
>   And a crossing breeze cuts a pause in its outrollings,
> Till they rise again, as they were a new bell's boom,
>   "He hears it not now, but used to notice such things"?

In a final gloom recalling the gloom at the end of "The Oxen" as the place for hoping against hope, the "crossing" wind that interrupts his death-knell has already warped a thorn bush and belongs in part to the "harm" which counterpoints the gladness and warmth of a world open to the expanse of the stars. Yet it enables the "outrollings" to return even more vehement, and in reading the line: "Till they rise again, as they were a new bell's boom," with its three final stresses, it is difficult not to associate rising again, in a poem about death, with resurrection. The bell is only new by the "as if" of the imagination, yet one recalls that spring leaves were compared to "new-spun" silk, and as "wings" they again seem to foretell this final rising. (Hardy could even be remembering, consciously or unconsciously, the similar hints of resurrection in the closing lines of "Lycidas": "At last he *rose*, and twitched his mantle blue:/ Tomorrow to fresh woods, and pastures *new*."[12]) Does the poem also evoke—repeatedly, with hopeful uncertainty—, Psyche, the butterfly as symbol of the soul, in the silk-worm, the hawk-moth and the mothy blackness? The poem's undercurrent makes itself felt as Hardy sees the mystery increase, and senses, as an agnostic, just how far he can go too far. He earns the right, as it were, to speculate on death and afterwards by his unfailing attentiveness and his wonder at the observable real. And the very moment when a new bell sounds and the verse swells with enthusiasm, he returns to the quietness of the opening, to the neighbors saying to each other that he used to "notice" such things. The poem advances from a sense of the beauty and gravity of the smallest event to an awareness of the entire universe of the night sky, of "heavens" that might open at the door of death to another reality, yet it asks at the same time a series of anxious questions: "will the neighbours say...?," along with mere conjectures: "a gazer may think...."

4

Hardy says a great deal of what he has to say by a single word in the first line of "Afterwards," when describing his stay on earth as "tremulous." He trembles with uncertainty and doubtful hope, while representing himself, according to another definition in the *OED*, as "ready to vibrate in response to some influence." His sensibility responds to the least thing seen or heard. In "Apostrophe to an Old Psalm Tune," the "quired oracles" of the tune in question beat until they make him "tremble" at the intimacy and otherness of their almost eternal life. In "Afternoon Service at Mellstock,"[13] when he remembers the singing of psalms as a choirboy, the heart of the experience came from watching the elms and their rooks and clouds and "swaying like the trees." In an earlier collection, *Poems of the Past and the Present*, he imagines, at the famous and much glozed-at ending of "The Darkling Thrush,"[14] that through the bird's ecstatic song hope itself "trembled," as if trying to reach him.

His poetry is inconclusive, and determinedly so: think of the many poems containing regularly placed lines that abstain from rhyming, and the well known sentence from the preface to *Poems of the Past and the Present*: "Unadjusted impressions have their value, and the road to a true philosophy of life seems to lie in humbly recording diverse readings of its phenomena as they are forced upon us by chance and change."[15] In recording his diverse readings, those drawn from a tremulous response to often prosaic beings and events that become poetic as he observes them carefully and finds the language to name and to transfigure them, seem the most surely to discover an inviting invisible. With Hardy, the transcendence of things seen means not passing through and rising above the seen but discerning the unseen that already belongs to it. In "Afterwards" he crosses a series of thresholds, while never losing sight of chance and change and of "such things" as greet him. The whole world transforms under his gaze and in the warmth of his writing. The ideal would be that, thanks to the "moments of vision," one's whole life becomes vision, that the moments join and the vision remains.

Notes

1. Randall Jarrell, *Poetry and the Age* (New York: Knopf, 1953), 266.
2. Thomas Hardy, *The Complete Poems*, ed. James Gibson (Basingstoke: Palgrave), 467.
3. *Ibid.*, 463.
4. *Ibid.*, 530.
5. *Ibid.*, 427.
6. *Ibid.*, 431–432.
7. *Ibid.*, 561.
8. *Ibid.*, 468.
9. Donald Davie, *Thomas Hardy and British Poetry* (Oxford: Oxford University Press, 1972), 38.
10. *The Complete Poems, op. cit.*, 553.
11. Thomas Hardy, *The Life and Work of Thomas Hardy*, ed. Michael Millgate (London: Macmillan, 1984), 192.
12. John Milton, "Lycidas" in *The Major Works*, ed. Stephen Orgel and Jonathan Goldberg (Oxford: Oxford University Press, 2008), 44.
13. *The Complete Poems, op. cit.*, 429.
14. *Ibid.*, 150.
15. *Ibid.*, 84.

Works Cited

Davie, Donald. *Thomas Hardy and British Poetry*. Oxford: Oxford University Press, 1972.
Hardy, Thomas. *The Complete Poems*. Ed. James Gibson. Basingstoke: Palgrave, 2001.
_____. *The Life and Work of Thomas Hardy*. Ed. Michael Millgate. London: Macmillan, 1984.
Jarrell, Randall. *Poetry and the Age*. New York: Knopf, 1953.
Milton, John. *The Major Works*. Eds. Stephen Orgel and Jonathan Goldberg. Oxford: Oxford University Press, 2008.

About the Contributors

Richard D. **Beards** was an associate professor of English at Temple University and was twice a visiting professor in Europe (Lund, Sweden, and Odense, Denmark). He was a specialist in British Victorian literature. He died on December 20, 2013.

Stéphanie **Bernard** is an assistant professor at the University of Rouen. She wrote a thesis dealing with the treatment of the tragic in early modernism, especially through the later novels of Thomas Hardy. She is the secretary of FATHOM (French Association for Thomas Hardy Studies).

Melanie **East** is a Ph.D. candidate at the University of Toronto. Her work examines chance as an element of romance in late-Victorian and proto-modernist novels, and a large and significant section of her project focuses on Hardy; she has worked on various aspects of both his novels and poems.

Michael **Edwards** was professor of literary creation in English at the Collège de France, holding a chair that was created specially for him. He has published many books of literary criticism and philosophy, and is a practicing poet in his own right. His books include *Towards a Christian Poetic* (Macmillan Palgrave, 1984). He is a member of the Académie Française.

Laurence **Estanove** teaches at Université Paris–Descartes, France. She is a founding member of the French Association for Thomas Hardy Studies (FATHOM) and webmaster of the association's site (www.fathomhardy.fr). She is also co-editor of the association's e-journal (http://fathom.revues.org). In 2010 she edited the essays collected in *Thomas Hardy, Far from the Madding Crowd* (Paris, Atlande).

Adrian **Grafe** was educated at Oxford and Paris VII, and did post-doctoral research at the University of Caen. He taught at the Sorbonne for many years and is currently a professor of English literature at Université d'Artois, France. He is a Fellow of the English Association (GB). His previous publications include *Lines of Resistance: Essays on British Poetry from Thomas Hardy to Linton Kwesi Johnson*, co-edited with Jessica Stephens (McFarland, 2012).

About the Contributors

Heather **Hawkins** is a second-year English research degree student at Nottingham Trent University. She is the director of the Thomas Hardy Association's Course Syllabi Webpage, based at the University of St Andrews, and a regular contributor to their online bibliography of works on Hardy, also known as *Checklist*.

Charles **Lock** was educated at Oxford and taught for many years at the University of Toronto. Since 1996 he has been a professor of English literature at the University of Copenhagen. He is the editor of the *Powys Journal* and has co-edited the correspondence between John Cowper Powys and James Purdy (2013).

Emilie **Loriaux** teaches English at Lille Catholic University, France, and is a doctoral candidate at Artois University, working on the language of poetry in Hardy and Barnes. She is the author of articles and conference papers on Hardy's fiction and poetry.

Ilaria **Mallozzi** is a Dionisotti scholar in Anglo-Italian literature at Royal Holloway, University of London, researching the reception of Laurence Sterne in Ugo Foscolo's works. She is the author of essays on Hardy's poetry and Hardy in relation to Darwin, Bergson and Brodsky.

Emily Taylor **Merriman** is a research associate at Mount Holyoke College. She has degrees from Oxford and London Universities and earned a Ph.D. in religion and literature from Boston University. She is also a book review co-editor for the *Hopkins Quarterly*.

Fahri **Öz** is a lecturer at Faculty of Letters, Ankara University, Turkey. He has translated works by Bob Dylan, Jack London, William S. Burroughs, Saki and George Meno, as well as a selection of poems by Christina Rossetti soon to appear, and has published articles on lyric poetry, genre theory, narrative and translation.

Adrian **Tait** is a practicing eco-critic and member of the Association for the Study of Literature and the Environment. He recently published an article highlighting the eco-centric aspects of Hardy's poetic vision in *Green Letters*.

Stephen **Tardif** is a Ph.D. candidate in the English Department at Harvard University. His dissertation project explores the relationship between literary form and self-formation in Victorian poetry and British aestheticism. He holds an Hon. B.A. and an M.A. from the University of Toronto, and has also published on Gerard Manley Hopkins and James Joyce.

Index

Adorno, T.W. 13–15
"After a Journey" 57n24
"Afternoon Service at Mellstock" 215
"Afterwards" 2, 212, 215, 216
"ΑΓΝΩΣΤΩΙ ΘΕΩΙ" ("Agnosti Teoi") 111, 127
agnosticism 5, 61, 83, 87, 88, 100–115, 124, 139, 215
Ahrfeldt, Cecilia 44–45
Alain de Lille 63
Alpers, Paul 45
"Amabel" 109
"And There Was a Great Calm" 37, 39
Anderson, Benedict 38
animals 27, 84, 106, 213–214; birds 14, 27, 60, 69
"Apology" 4, 5, 60, 61, 70, 78, 84, 130, 134, 136, 141, 211
"Apostrophe to an Old Psalm Tune" 211, 215
Archer, William 84
architecture 14, 15, 29, 100, 109, 117, 156, 159, 194–196
Aristotle 63, 71n16
Armstrong, Tim 149
Arnold, Matthew 11, 92, 111
Ashcroft, Bill 187
Ashdown, Douglas 174
"At Castle Boterel" 44, 55, 109
"At the Dinner Table" 75, 80
"At the Entering of the New Year" 106
"At Waking" 86
Auden, W.H. 66, 111
Auerbach, Erich 65
"An August Midnight" 14
"Authors' Declaration" (*Times*) 34

Bailey, J.O. 109
Bakhtin, Mikhail 73n44
Bantz, Nathalie 125
Barnes, Grace 179
Barnes, William 163–175, 179–190
Bastow, Henry Robert 117
"The Bedridden Peasant" 120
"Beeny Cliff" 151
Beer, Gillian 100

"Before Marching and After" 34, 35
"La Belle Dame Sans Merci" 51, 151, 152
Benjamin, Walter 64
Benziman, Galia 2
Bergson, Henri 72n38, 109
Bible 83, 117; Corinthians 77, 141; Genesis 139, 208; Job 63; John 121, 139; King James Bible 194; Luke 121; Matthew 121; Psalms 129, 134, 135, 138–142, 211; Revelation 120, 137, 141
birds *see* animals
"Birds at Winter Nightfall" 14
Björk, Lennart A. 138
Blake, William 113n19
Blomfield, Arthur 29
Blomfield, Sir Reginald 39
Blyth, Caroline 3
Bockhampton *see* Dorset
body 27, 31, 32, 36, 76, 84, 101, 124, 137, 154
A Book of Remembrance (introduction by Hardy) 26
Borges, Jorge Luis 69, 71n20
Botting, Fred 136
Bradley, F.H. 96n32
Bridges, Robert 196
Bridgewater, Patrick 123
"A Broken Appointment" 117
Brooke, Rupert 32
Brooks, Cleanth 67
Browning, Robert 53, 56n12, 82, 173, 196
"By the Earth's Corpse" 129
Byron, George Gordon Lord 173, 193

"The Caged Thrush Freed and Home Again" 14
"A Call to National Service" 34, 36, 37
"Candour in English Fiction" 190n1
cemetery *see* death
"Channel Firing" 34
"The Cheval-Glass" 78–80
Christianity 11, 13, 20, 77, 84, 92, 117, 118, 120, 121, 123, 129, 130, 139, 142, 174, 189, 210; anti-Christian 116; para-Christian 212
"A Christmas Ghost Story" 32
"The Church-Builder" 123–124

219

Index

city 12, 44, 46, 50–51, 60, 155
Clare, John 181
Clark, Timothy 16, 18
Clough, A.H. 103, 104
Cockshut, A.O. 101
coffin *see* death
Coleridge, S.T. 85, 86, 92; "The Rime of the Ancient Mariner" 52
"The Colonel's Soliloquy" 117
"A Commonplace Day" 128
Compagnon, Antoine 13–138
"The Conformers" 127
Conrad, Joseph 94, 124, 125, 128
constellations *see* cosmos
"The Convergence of the Twain" 109, 110, 127
Corinthians *see* Bible
corpse *see* death
cosmos 12, 36, 39, 61, 63; constellations 16, 32, 35, 36; moon 15, 16, 79, 80, 152; stars 15, 16, 32, 36, 46, 107, 122, 154, 214; sun 16, 20, 52, 62, 111, 166, 174, 209
Cosslett, Tess 105
Cox, R.G. 61, 94n1, 96n29
Crang, Mike 45
Cresswell, T. 45
Cunningham Graham, R.B. 128
Currie, Felicity 96n40

Dante 78, 108
"The Darkling Thrush" 3, 14, 88, 142, 200, 211, 215
Darwin, Charles 13, 110, 186, 190; Darwinism 5, 12, 13, 109, 110, 111, 112, 211
Davie, Donald 149, 158, 211
Day Lewis, Cecil 148, 176n4
"The Dead Quire" 172
death 2, 5, 11, 15, 36, 46, 50, 51, 54, 65, 76, 89, 90, 105, 110, 118–120, 135, 136, 137, 148, 152–155, 157–159, 207, 210, 212, 213–215; cemetery 32, 39, 167, 200, 202; coffins 29, 166, 167; corpses 39, 86, 129, 200; of God 101, 120–123; graves 26–43, 50, 76, 78; mourning 4–5, 37, 38, 49, 52, 60, 69, 88, 123, 149, 156, 157, 198; suicide 123; tombs, tombstones 29–30, 32, 38, 200; *see also* elegy
Deleuze, Gilles 64, 72n38
DeMille, Barbara 123
Derrida, Jacques 72n38
dialect 100, 164, 165, 170, 172, 173, 174, 179–190
Dickens, Charles 193, 205n3
Dickinson, Emily 203
dimeter 54, 152
disillusionment 2, 56, 83, 86, 87, 89, 90, 92, 109, 117, 123, 127
Dobson, Andrew 24n67
Dockrill, C.W. 101, 102
"Domicilium" 44–57
Donne, John 67, 202
"Doom and She" 91, 126
Dorchester *see* Dorset

Dorset 26, 31, 36, 44, 117, 163, 164, 170, 174, 179, 180, 181, 182, 184, 186; Bockhampton 47, 179; Dorchester 26, 117, 174; Egdon Heath 29, 36, 136; Max Gate 29, 84, 153, 167, 193; Stinsford 117; Sturminster Newton 179; Wessex 28–29, 32, 36, 163, 183, 186; Whitcombe 179
"The Dorsetshire Labourer" 31, 186, 191n27
doubt 5, 15, 35, 87, 88, 92, 100, 101, 107, 108, 110, 111, 121, 123–125, 135, 215
drama 5, 90, 92, 143; dramatic form 10, 18, 127; dramatic monologue 53, 65; dramatization 33, 91, 124, 140, 159, 174
"The Dream-Follower" 119
"A Dream or No" 152
"Drinking Song" 13
"Drummer Hodge" 27, 31, 35, 36, 46, 79
Dryden, John 180
Dugdale, Giles 175
"During Wind and Rain" 156, 157, 158
The Dynasts 18, 19, 127, 128, 163

Ebbatson, Roger 7n23, 15
Eckhart, Meister 71n19
Education Acts (1870) 184
Egdon Heath *see* Dorset
ekphrasis 68
elegy 2, 5, 6, 27, 32, 36, 44–57, 117, 149, 154, 156, 157, 158, 160n38, 169, 170, 174, 184, 185, 201
Eliot, George 103
Eliot, T.S. 1, 2, 3, 5, 155–156; *The Waste Land* 172
Elliott, Ralph W.V. 173
"Embarcation" 26, 117
Empedocles 63
empiricism 101, 105, 111, 112
Empson, William 45
ethics 12, 13, 14, 20, 84, 85, 100, 112
evolutionism 12, 14, 28, 61, 78, 84, 101, 105, 169, 186, 187, 190, 207

Far from the Madding Crowd 102
Fichte, J.G. 70, 85
"The Fiddler" 171
folklore 164, 189, 212
Ford, Ford Madox 4
"Fragment" 106, 107, 108, 109
Freud, Sigmund 76–77
Frost, Robert 66, 77
Fuller, John 72n34
Fussell, Paul 27

"General Preface" (1912) 26
Genesis *see* Bible
George, 2nd Lt. F.W. 35
ghost 5, 32, 33, 38, 118, 119, 125, 126, 128, 129, 131n17, 153, 156, 159, 210
Gibson, James 47, 179
Gifford, Terry 46
Gilmour, Robin 12, 13

Index

Gittings, Robert 138, 163, 173
Glück, Louise 133, 137
"God-Forgotten" 111, 125, 128
"God's Funeral" 87, 89, 111, 121, 122
Goebel, Stephen 37
"The Going" 152, 201
Gothic 100, 134, 136
Gould, Stephen Jay 104
graves *see* death
guilt 46, 51, 150, 153, 156, 159, 210

Hall, Louisa 156
Hands, Timothy 116
"Hap" 109
Hardy, Barbara 55
Hardy, Emma 2, 29, 40*n*2, 46, 49, 52, 68, 129, 148–161, 168, 210; *Some Recollections* 2
Hardy, Florence Emily 143; *The Later Years of Thomas Hardy* 37, 77, 79, 80; *The Life of Thomas Hardy* 112, 128, 164
Hardy, Jemima 179, 180
Hardy, Thomas: "After a Journey" 57*n*24; "Afternoon Service at Mellstock" 215; "Afterwards" 2, 212, 215, 216; "ΑΓΝΩΣΤΩΙ ΘΕΩΙ" ("Agnosti Teoi") 111, 127; "Amabel" 109; "And There Was a Great Calm" 37, 39; "Apology" 4, 5, 60, 61, 70, 78, 84, 130, 134, 136, 141, 211; "Apostrophe to an Old Psalm Tune" 211, 215; "At Castle Boterel" 44, 55, 109; "At the Dinner Table" 75, 80; "At the Entering of the New Year" 106; "At Waking" 86; "An August Midnight" 24; "The Bedridden Peasant" 120; "Beeny Cliff" 151; "Before Marching and After" 34, 35; "Birds at Winter Nightfall" 14; *A Book of Remembrance* (introduction by Hardy) 26; "A Broken Appointment" 117; "By the Earth's Corpse" 129; "The Caged Thrush Freed and Home Again" 14; "A Call to National Service" 34, 36, 37; "Candour in English Fiction" 190*n*1; "Channel Firing" 34; "The Cheval-Glass" 78–80; "A Christmas Ghost Story" 32; "The Church-Builder" 123–124; "The Colonel's Soliloquy" 117; "A Commonplace Day" 128; "The Conformers" 127; "The Convergence of the Twain" 109, 110, 127; "The Darkling Thrush" 3, 14, 88, 142, 200, 211, 215; "The Dead Quire" 172; "Domicilium" 44–57; "Doom and She" 91, 126; "The Dorsetshire Labourer" 31, 186, 191*n*27; "The Dream-Follower" 119; "A Dream or No" 152; "Drinking Song" 13; "Drummer Hodge" 27, 31, 35, 36, 46, 79; "During Wind and Rain" 156, 157, 158; *The Dynasts* 18, 19, 127, 128, 163; "Embarcation" 26, 117; *Far from the Madding Crowd* 102; "The Fiddler" 171; "Fragment" 106, 107, 108, 109; "General Preface" (1912) 26; "God-Forgotten" 111, 125, 128; "God's Funeral" 87, 89, 111, 121, 122; "The Going" 152, 201; "Hap" 109; "The Haunter" 151, 158; He Follows Himself" 73*n*44; "He Wonders About Himself" 106; "Heiress and Architect" 14; "Heredity" 103; "His Immortality" 119; "I Found Her Out There" 46, 153, 154; "I Have Lived with Shades" 119; "I Look Into My Glass" 76, 77, 79; "I Said to Love" 91; "An Imaginative Woman" 95*n*11; "The Impercipient" 109; "In a Eweleaze near Weatherbury" 185; "In a Wood" 11–13, 51; "In Tenebris" 61, 84, 89, 129, 133–145; "In the Seventies" 2, 134; "In Time of 'The Breaking of Nations'" 30, 31, 106, 109; "The Ivy Wife" 12; *Jude the Obscure* 2, 28, 60–74, 100, 123, 131*n*17; "A Kiss" 209; "The Lacking Sense" 91, 109, 111, 130; "Lament" 157, 158, 168; "The Last Chrysanthemum" 14; "The Last Signal" 164–170, 172, 174, 175; *Late Lyrics and Earlier* 94; "Leipzig" 18; "Let Me Believe" 88; letter to Ezra Pound 197; "The Levelled Churchyard" 29; "Liddell and Scott: On the Completion of Their Lexicon" 163–178; *The Life and Work of Thomas Hardy* 12, 29, 47, 63, 83, 156, 214; *Literary Notebooks* 85, 96*n*32, 104; "The Lost Pyx" 130; *The Mayor of Casterbridge* 72*n*25; "The Melancholy Hussar" 18; "Memory and I" 119; "Men Who March Away" 34, 35, 36; "Middle Age Enthusiasms" 89; "Moments of Vision" 79, 80, 210; *Moments of Vision* 80, 106, 113*n*29, 113*n*31, 164; "The Mother Mourns" 15, 91, 111, 117; "Nature's Questioning" 10, 11, 104; "Neutral Tones" 52, 199; "The Obliterate Tomb" 29; "The Occultation" 209; "Old Furniture" 171; "On a Fine Morning" 90–92; "On the Departure Platform" 57*n*25; "On the Doorstep" 44; "Once at Swanage" 152; "The Oxen" 88, 130, 211, 212, 214; "The Pedigree" 79–80; *Personal Notebooks* 83, 96*n*38; "A Plaint to Man" 111; "Poems of 1912–1913" 5, 66, 129, 148–162, 198, 199, 201; *Poems of the Past and the Present* 13, 18, 20, 82, 129, 134; "Preface to Select Poems of Barnes" 4, 184; "The Profitable Reading of Fiction" 190*n*1; "The Puzzled Game-Birds" 14; "Rain on a Grave" 154, 201, 202; "The Respectable Burgher" 121; Review of William Barnes's *Poems of Rural Life in the Dorset Dialect* 183; "The Ruin'd Maid" 3; *Satires of Circumstance* 17, 27, 52, 82, 121, 148, 199; "The Schreckhorn (With Thoughts of Leslie Stephen)" 17; "The Self-Unseeing" 118–119; "The Shadow on the Stone" 210; "She, to Him" 3; "The Sheep Boy" 189–190; "The Sick Battle-God" 121–122; "The Sleep-Worker" 126; "The Son's Portrait" 79; "The Souls of the Slain" 33–34; "The Spell of the Rose" 153; "The Subalterns" 117; "The Supplanter" 117; *Tess of the D'Urbervilles* 112, 144*n*18; "Thoughts of Phena" 3; *Time's Laughingstocks* 83; "To a Motherless Child" 11; "To an Unborn Pauper Child" 117; "To Life" 91, 119; "To My Father's Violin" 171; "Transformations" 31, 39, 168;

The Trumpet-Major 18; *Under the Greenwood Tree* 11; "Under the Waterfall" 44–57, 60–74; "Valenciennes" 18; "The Voice" 151, 201, 203, 204; "The Walk" 155; "We Are Getting to the End" 93, 96n40; *The Well-Beloved* 65, 76; "The Well-Beloved" 117, 119; "Wessex Heights" 136; *Wessex Poems* 10, 14, 18, 134, 185; "Where the Picnic Was" 47, 49, 51, 55, 152; "Winter in Durnover Field" 14, 20, 21; "The Withered Arm" 119, 130; "Without Ceremony" 152, 201, 202; "A Young Man's Epigram on Existence" 3; "Your Last Drive" 154; "Zermatt—To the Matterhorn" 16
Harries, Karsten 63
Harrison, DeSales 116
Harrison, Frederick 101
Hartmann, Eduard von 19, 85, 95n13
Harvey, Geoffrey 23n50, 104
"The Haunter" 151, 158
"He Follows Himself" 73n44
"He Wonders About Himself" 106
Heidegger, Martin 7n23, 17, 21
"Heiress and Architect" 14
Henniker, Florence 149
Henry, Michel 73n47
Hensher, Philip 205n3
Herbert, George 200; "The Elixir" 77
"Heredity" 103
Hill, Geoffrey 135, 155, 204
"His Immortality" 119
Hölderlin, Friedrich 60, 70
Hopkins, Gerard Manley 71n16, 111, 143, 174, 176n25, 196, 200, 203, 204
Horkheimer, Max 13–15
Hughes, John 119
Huxley, T.H. 12, 110, 103, 110
Hynes, Samuel 19, 27, 33

"I Found Her Out There" 46, 153, 154
"I Have Lived with Shades" 119
"I Look Into My Glass" 76, 77, 79
"I Said to Love" 91
idealism 13, 82–97
"An Imaginative Woman" 95n11
Immanent Will 18, 19, 20, 127, 128
immortality 131n22, 167
"The Impercipient" 109
"In a Eweleaze near Weatherbury" 185
"In a Wood" 11–13, 51
"In Tenebris" 61, 84, 89, 129, 133–145
"In the Seventies" 2, 134
"In Time of 'The Breaking of Nations'" 30, 31, 106, 109
Insects at Home 110
irony 3, 30, 31, 35, 72n25, 79, 90, 107, 121–125, 129, 156, 169, 173; tragic irony 158
"The Ivy Wife" 12

Jarrell, Randall 207
Job *see* Bible
John *see* Bible

Johnson, Ben 180
Johnson, James Weldon 39
Johnson, Thomas H. 203
Johnson, Trevor 14
Jones, Bernard 176n25
Joyce, James 125
Jude the Obscure 2, 28, 60–74, 100, 123, 131n17
Jung, C.G. 142

Kafka, Franz 61
Kant, Emmanuel 85
Keats, John 133, 193, 196, 213; "La Belle Dame Sans Merci" 51, 151, 152
Keen, Suzanne 149
Kenner, Hugh 194, 197, 198
Kerridge, Richard 10
King, Edward 213
King James Bible *see* Bible
Kipling, Rudyard 28; "Recessional" 38
"A Kiss" 209
Knoepflmacher, U.C. 56n15
Kristeva, Julia 89, 92, 94
Kuhn, Joaquin 71n16

"The Lacking Sense" 91, 109, 111, 130
"Lament" 157, 158, 168
landscape 4, 5, 7n23, 29–43, 51, 158, 159, 165, 189, 208; painting 214; *see also* nature
Langbaum, Robert 45, 52, 56n12
Larkin, Philip 2–4, 111, 116, 134,
"The Last Chrysanthemum" 14
"The Last Signal" 164–170, 172, 174, 175
Late Lyrics and Earlier 94
The Later Years of Thomas Hardy 37, 77, 79, 80
Latour, Bruno 10, 21
Lawler, Leonard 72n38
Lawson, Tom 32
Leibniz 61
"Leipzig" 18
Leopold, Aldo 16
"Let Me Believe" 88
letter to Ezra Pound 197
"The Levelled Churchyard" 29
Levinas, Emmanuel 72n38
Liddell, Henry George 6, 163–178
"Liddell and Scott: On the Completion of Their Lexicon" 163–178
The Life and Work of Thomas Hardy 12, 29, 47, 63, 83, 156, 214
The Life of Thomas Hardy 112, 128, 164
Literary Notebooks 85, 96n32, 104
Locke, John 15
Longley, Edna 4
"The Lost Pyx" 130
Louis, Margot K. 113n19
Lovelock, James 19, 20
Lukács, Georg 62, 63
Luke *see* Bible

Macmillan, Alexander 182
Maitland, Frederic William 17

Index

Mallarmé, Stéphane 198
Mallett, Phillip 151, 154
marriage 2, 75, 127, 148, 150, 155
Matthew *see* Bible
Max Gate *see* Dorset
Maynard, Katherine Kearney 134
The Mayor of Casterbridge 72*n*25
McLuhan, Marshall 198
McTaggart, J.M.E. 96*n*32
"The Melancholy Hussar" 18
meliorism 28, 61, 78, 84, 89, 93
"Memory and I" 119
"Men Who March Away" 34, 35, 36
Merchant, Carolyn 14, 22*n*27
"Middle Age Enthusiasms" 89
Mill, John Stuart 104, 111
Miller, J. Hillis 64, 65, 72*n*25, 72*n*26,
Millgate, Michael 40*n*2, 44, 45, 195, 196, 198, 202
Milton, John 213, 214–215
mirror 5, 75–81, 210
modernism 44, 112, 197; poetic Modernism 172
"Moments of Vision" 79, 80, 210
Moments of Vision 80, 106, 113*n*29, 113*n*31, 164
moon *see* cosmos
morality 12, 84, 100, 101, 102, 104, 105, 174
Morgan, Rosemarie 101
Morgan, William W. 159*n*3
"The Mother Mourns" 15, 91, 111, 117
Motion, Andrew 4, 134
mourning *see* death
Müller, Max 186
Murfin, Ross C. 88, 92, 93, 108, 111, 160*n*38
music 63, 118, 157, 171, 172, 211, 213; song 93, 107; thrush's song 88, 215

nature 4, 5, 6, 10–25, 44–57, 62–63, 66, 68, 71*n*16, 71*n*21, 76, 80, 82, 87, 100, 104, 107, 110–111, 119, 135, 142, 153–154, 188–190, 208, 209, 212–214; *see also* landscape; tree; vegetation
"Nature's Questioning" 10, 11, 104
"Neutral Tones" 52, 199
Newbolt, Henry 28, 202
Newman, J.H. 138
Newton, Isaac 15
Nietzsche, Friedrich 64, 122–123,
nostalgia 5, 40*n*11, 87–88, 112, 117–118, 124, 129, 174–175
Noyes, Alfred 70*n*4, 96*n*41

"The Obliterate Tomb" 29
"The Occultation" 209
O'Donoghue, John 143*n*2, 144*n*26
"Old Furniture" 171
"On a Fine Morning" 90–92
"On the Departure Platform" 57*n*25
"On the Doorstep" 44
"Once at Swanage" 152

optimism 61, 82–84, 90, 105, 107, 136
"The Oxen" 88, 130, 211, 212, 214

paganism 109, 189
Parham, John 21
Parkes, Malcolm Beckwith 193, 202, 203
Parmenides 63
Pascal, Blaise 63, 71*n*21, 83
pastoral 5, 28, 40*n*11, 44–57, 66, 68, 181, 184, 189
Pater, Walter 69, 73*n*41
Paulin, Tom 134, 149
"The Pedigree" 79–80
Pendergrast, Mark 81*n*6
Perse, St John 133
Personal Notebooks 83, 96*n*38
pessimism 5, 35, 60–74, 78, 82–97, 105, 106, 122, 134
Pinion, F.B. 19
Pite, Ralph 101, 102
"A Plaint to Man" 111
Poe, Edgar Allan 151
"Poems of 1912–1913" 5, 66, 129, 148–162, 198, 199, 201
Poems of the Past and the Present 13, 18, 20, 82, 129, 134
Pound, Ezra 4, 194–198, 202–204,
"Preface to Select Poems of Barnes" 4, 184
"The Profitable Reading of Fiction" 190*n*1
Providence 64
Psalms *see* Bible
punctuation 6, 33, 88, 121, 193–206
Purdy, Richard Little 23*n*48, 41*n*23, 195–196, 198, 202
"The Puzzled Game-Birds" 14

Quiller-Couch, Arthur 3, 175

Rae, Simon 4
"Rain on a Grave" 154, 201, 202
Ramazani, Jahan 27, 32, 46, 51, 150, 151
"Recessional" 38
"The Respectable Burgher" 121
Revelation *see* Bible
Review of William Barnes's *Poems of Rural Life in the Dorset Dialect* 183
Ricks, Christopher 3, 4
Rilke, Rainer Maria 137
"The Rime of the Ancient Mariner" 52
Riquelme, John Paul 154, 158
Romanticism 4, 10, 11, 27, 46, 51, 52, 54–55, 85, 92–93, 96*n*33, 111–112, 148, 152
Roppen, Georg 22*n*14
"The Ruin'd Maid" 3
Rutland, W.R. 18

Sacks, Peter M. 51, 149, 156, 159*n*3
Saint Anselm 63
Saint Augustine 63, 71*n*19
Saint Thomas Aquinas 63
Samuel, Adrian 131*n*31

Sassoon, Siegfried 39, 111
Satires of Circumstance 17, 27, 52, 82, 121, 148, 199
Sayce, Archibald 186
Schelling, F.W. J von 85
Schopenhauer, Arthur 19, 95*n*13, 128
"The Schreckhorn (With Thoughts of Leslie Stephen)" 17
Schweik, Robert 23*n*58, 86
science 2, 10–25, 87, 100–115, 124, 128
Scott, Robert 6, 163–178
Scott-James, R.A. 176*n*4
"The Self-Unseeing" 118–119
Sexton, Melanie 159*n*3
"The Shadow on the Stone" 210
Shakespeare, William 134, 142, 150–151
"She, to Him" 3
"The Sheep Boy" 189–190
Shelley, P.B. 213
Sherman, Daniel J. 41*n*46
"The Sick Battle-God" 121–122
silence 11, 55, 68, 80, 88, 106, 120, 126, 129, 194, 213
"The Sleep-Worker" 126
Smith, Jonathan 101
Some Recollections 2
"The Son's Portrait" 79
Sophocles 70, 84
"The Souls of the Slain" 33–34
Southerington, F.R. 24*n*70
"The Spell of the Rose" 153
Spencer, Herbert 12, 102, 104, 110
stars *see* cosmos
Stephen, Leslie 5, 17, 100–115
Stinsford *see* Dorset
Sturminster Newton *see* Dorset
"The Subalterns" 117
subversion 39, 71*n*21, 72*n*26, 121, 129
suicide *see* death
sun *see* cosmos
"The Supplanter" 117
Swinburne, A.C. 92–93, 109, 111, 113*n*19

Taylor, Dennis 2, 72*n*35, 134, 148, 153, 157, 163, 166–167, 169, 173–174, 187, 202
Tennyson, Alfred, Lord 1, 184, 201
Tess of the D'Urbervilles 112, 144*n*18
"Thoughts of Phena" 3
Time's Laughingstocks 83
"To a Motherless Child" 11
"To an Unborn Pauper Child" 117
"To Life" 91, 119
"To My Father's Violin" 171
Tomalin, Claire 73*n*39, 117, 149–153
tombs, tombstones *see* death
tragedy 72*n*25, 76, 120–124, 127–129, 133–134, 158, 166–167
"Transformations" 31, 39, 168
tree 10–13, 29–30, 32, 36, 47–48, 51–52, 156–157, 208, 210, 215; *see also* nature

The Trumpet-Major 18
Turner, Paul 23*n*59, 144*n*24

Under the Greenwood Tree 11
"Under the Waterfall" 44–57, 60–74

"Valenciennes" 18
Vaughan, Henry 202
vegetation 30, 32, 48, 154; *see also* nature
Verdery, Katherine 37, 39
violence 17, 30, 54, 87, 111, 171
Virgil 152
voice 11–12, 14, 53, 67–68, 76, 124, 137, 141–143, 150–155, 193–206
"The Voice" 151, 201, 203, 204
Volsik, Paul 119
Voltaire 61, 121

"The Walk" 155
war 2, 4–5, 26–43, 46, 106, 113*n*30, 121–122, 127; of nature 12
Warren, T.H. 94*n*3
Warrior, Unknown 37–38
The Waste Land 172
"We Are Getting to the End" 93, 96*n*40
Weber, Carl J. 95*n*13
Weil, Simone 61
The Well-Beloved 65, 76
"The Well-Beloved" 117, 119
Wenborn, Neil 149
Wessex *see* Dorset
"Wessex Heights" 136
Wessex Poems 10, 14, 18, 134, 185
"Where the Picnic Was" 47, 49, 51, 55, 152
Whitcombe *see* Dorset
Whitehead, James 28–29, 31, 35, 39
Whymper, Edward 16–17
Widdowson, Peter 28
Wiener, Martin J. 40*n*11
Wilde, Oscar 69, 73*n*42, 75, 138
Wilson, E.O. 20
"Winter in Durnover Field" 14, 20, 21
"The Withered Arm" 119, 130
"Without Ceremony" 152, 201, 202
Wood, J.G.: *Insects at Home* 110
Wordsworth, William 11–12, 45, 47, 51, 70, 106
Wright, T.R. 87

Xenophanes 63

Yeats, W.B. 142
"A Young Man's Epigram on Existence" 3
"Your Last Drive" 154
youth 76, 79, 94, 118; Hardy's youth 48–49, 56*n*15, 117

"Zermatt—To the Matterhorn" 16
Zietlow, Paul 15, 89–90
Žižek, Slavoj 72*n*37

www.ingramcontent.com/pod-product-compliance
Lightning Source LLC
Chambersburg PA
CBHW032051300426
44116CB00007B/694